Picture: Colin Urquhart/*The Herald*.

MY FATHER
DIED
FOR THIS

by
**Lukhanyo &
Abigail Calata**

TAFELBERG

Tafelberg, an imprint of NB Publishers,
a division of Media24 Boeke Pty (Ltd),
40 Heerengracht, Cape Town, South Africa
www.tafelberg.com

Set in Photina
Cover by Fuel Design
Cover pictures by David Goldblatt/Africa Media Online
Book design by Nazli Jacobs
Edited by Claire Strombeck
Proof read by Russell Martin
Commissioning editor: Gill Moodie

Printed and bound by Creda Communications
First edition, first impression 2018

ISBN: 978-0-624-0-8164-7
Epub: 978-0-624-0-8165-4
Mobi: 978-0-624-0-8166-1

To our son, Kwezi,
and the next generation
of revolutionaries

The publisher and authors are grateful to the
Taco Kuiper Fund for Investigative Journalism, which gave
a research grant to the authors of this book.

Taco Kuiper

Contents

Foreword
by Father Paul Verryn

It was early in April 1984 when I received a phone call from Molly Blackburn. We had served together in the Port Elizabeth branch of the Detainees Parents Support Committee (DPSC). She told me that two comrades from Cradock had been detained under Section 28 of the Internal Security Act and were being held in what was known as Sun City in Johannesburg. They were Fort Calata and Mbulelo Goniwe, and they were leaders from the Cradock community.

When I was transferred to a Methodist congregation in Witpoortjie at the beginning of 1984, I had continued my association with both the DPSC and the South African Council of Churches (SACC).

The good news about Section 28 was that visits were allowed and one of the small mercies of this incarceration was that few who were held under this section were tortured.

I made my way to the prison in my clerical garb and, without much ado, I was granted access and met Fort and Mbulelo for the first time. Our first meeting was reasonably prosaic as we acquainted ourselves with our respective histories and, particularly in the case of Fort, with his immediate family – his wife and two children. I can distinctly remember his unambiguous pride in his most valued relationships. Just as a man in love, he did not seem to tire in remembering the finest detail of their uniqueness. I was left with a very clear picture of a family that carried an integrity in its relationships and commitment. The austerity of this unkind prison was a profound contrast to the tenderness and vulnerability of Fort's family. I left Sun City with a very clear picture of an indomitable dignity which could not be contradicted by the cruel machinery of a system seeking to break the essence of a person's humanity.

I was permitted to visit on a few more occasions, and in those visits gleaned considerable information of the nuances of the struggle in Cradock, a rural Eastern Cape town I had never visited before. The awakening of the community's conscience by a movement striving to give voice and rights to an oppressed people strangely became part of my own journey of awakening. The Machiavellian dispossession of people who were considered irrelevant by the powerful was not as successful as it was presumed. Paradoxically, the attempt to silence and intimidate people was a failure. As people, with very simple means, began to imagine an alternative narrative, a strange revolution was emerging.

Ultimately, our conversations progressed on one of my visits to a discussion of Marx and Communism. Of course, a major focus of our discussion was on the distribution of resources and the injustice that marginalised 80% of South Africans, economically. I was not permitted to visit Fort and Mbulelo again, and I realised that ears had been eavesdropping on our conversation. It was bizarre to imagine that a conversation of this nature could be any threat to the status quo at all – but it was.

Fort and Mbulelo were released from detention and returned to Cradock. Fort, however, was not allowed to return to his teaching position and was left unemployed. His main concern was the support of his family – Nomonde, his wife, and their two children, Dorothy and Lukhanyo. Fort then came to stay with me in the Methodist manse, which was in Wilro Park. He'd decided to procure a heavy-duty driver's licence, so that he could find employment to support his loved ones. I remember being amazed at his determination to pass the tests as efficiently as he could. Although he also spent time networking with people in the then-Transvaal, his impatience to return home was obvious. His separation from his wife was a stone in his shoe. He returned to Cradock and we kept in touch from time to time concerning developments in his family as well as the wider context.

As I read the book that Lukhanyo has written, there is a consistent theme which can be followed from the life of his great-grandfather, Canon James Arthur Calata, to Lukhanyo's own understanding of his commitments. The creation of a family that carries the integrity of faithfulness is as much a part of the discourse of their life as is the vigour of their political commitment to the freedom of all people in

South Africa. The willingness to hold ourselves accountable to those who are dear to us is as important as the rigorous accountability that secures the truth, which must be the hallmark of any political party of value. Of course, one cannot ignore the fact that Canon Calata's faith in Christ meant a radical engagement with the human rights and dignity of all people. One senses a restlessness in his ministry as he imagined an end to repression and the formidable insecurities of the apartheid ideology. There is something strangely reminiscent of the gospel when one considers Cradock as the springboard for this kind of revolutionary imagination. Who could ever imagine that hope for humanity could come from Nazareth? It is true, though, that the paradigms of the new creation somehow are repetitive. Just as it would be impossible to imagine the secretary-general of the ANC functioning in isolation, so it would be impossible to imagine Canon Calata achieving anything without his love for, and the determined support of his wife, Miltha. One hears her moral compass in the guidance and strength of the family in Lukhanyo's words. And so the book seems to weave a theme of honest personal relationships being congruent with the struggle for the freedom of a community and a country. The principles of truth with justice, of love with integrity, and of accountability with passion are threads that perpetuate themselves in all the lives described in this book. Our remembrance of them should not remain bland historical recollections, but should inspire our present interactions. For we are not yet free.

In 2008, Canon Calata was awarded the Order of Luthuli (gold). In 2017, Miltha Mary Calata was awarded the Order of Luthuli (silver).

It was again a phone call from Molly Blackburn that informed me of the disappearance of Fort Calata, Matthew Goniwe, Sparro Mkonto, and Sicelo Mhlawuli. Sicelo and Sparro's bodies were found near Bluewater Bay, and Fort and Matthew's bodies near St George's Strand. The pathologist's report on the state of their bodies indicated a perversity and darkness that explained the depravity and alienation of the system in power at that time. That we could live in a society which ostensibly betrayed not the slightest indication of deviation was itself sick. This kind of cruelty and abuse of power must force us to be vigilant about the violence and deceit which we cover up today. To insist that the public should not see the effects of the anger of service delivery protests – but should somehow be protected from what our reality is – is a denial of our fundamental right to know.

For me, the desecration of Fort's body remains a devastating demolition of the image of God in the life of a person I respected. If his extermination could have this effect on me, I cannot begin to describe the effect that this invasion had on the lives of Lukhanyo, Dorothy, and Nomonde, who was pregnant with Tumani at the time of Fort's death. I think that the perpetrators should meet this family face to face, make confession, and seek forgiveness now. No Truth Commission has the right to remove from them the dignity of seeing the eyes which saw their loved one last. Then forgiveness will carry integrity.

More than 60 000 people attended the funeral in Cradock. Nothing could have mobilised people more effectively. According to Tertullian's *Apologeticus*, the blood of the martyrs is the seed of the Church and indeed the blood of these martyrs inspired a consciousness in the nation that had not been evidenced in such intensity before. There was an interesting dialogue between politics and religion at the funeral. They could not be divorced. The headline in the *Sunday Times* on the next day was 'Priests March under the Red Flag'. There was also a deep sense of exhilaration coupled with the tragic sadness of loss. The community was robbed of four courageous, humble servants who had paid the ultimate price for their vision. What I do not think we could have anticipated was the resilience and hope that their deaths ignited in the minds of the masses. It was as if the evil deeds of the security apparatus of the then-government had actually unlocked an unprecedented solidarity among all people. The funeral epitomised a unity and connectedness that had been subverted until that day in July. Suddenly, the convergence of a huge diversity of people across the spectrum of South African society connected. There was a contrast, though, between the robust excitement of the crowd, which flowed like a river down all the streets of iLingelihle, and the sanctuary of the immediate families who had lost so profoundly. The presence of a pregnant mother as a chief mourner exposed a deep vulnerability in the face of the overt power in the march to freedom. I can still remember that as the bodies were lowered into their graves it was as if Nomonde's body was ripped apart by her grief as she was forced to bid farewell to her love.

A partial State of Emergency was declared after the funeral.

In 2006, Fort was awarded the Order of Luthuli (bronze).

Tumani, Lukhanyo, Dorothy, and Nomonde came to stay with me for quite some time in Wilro Park. At that time, activists from all over South Africa were living in my home. What was remarkable was that, while I was serving a traditionally conservative congregation on the edge of Krugersdorp, the predominantly white membership embraced my guests with respect and care. It was during this time that I interacted with Nomonde as a nursing mother and the extended Calata family in the PWV region. As one can imagine, the home reverberated with political debate and discussion. For many months, Nomonde was like a house mother to many young people on the run from authorities. She had a remarkable relationship with her children. They were wonderfully disciplined, but had plenty of space to express their own personalities. Somehow, the memories I had of Fort echoed in the tiny person of Lukhanyo. He cared for his mother like a young lion – protective, vigilant, and loving. Dorothy bristled with intelligence, was confident but not spoilt. Nomonde carried her grief with a dignity and truth that did not hide her pain, yet did not oppress those who were living with her. While she was in the home, there was an unspoken discipline of respect and also an ability for people to enjoy friendship and laugh late into the night. Paradoxically, one of the greatest sources of fun was people imitating their experiences with the Security Police. It was truly wonderful to see the powerful and important being reduced to commonplace, devoid of their terrifying power.

I have reconnected with the family frequently. The consistency of their value system and their intrinsic vigilance around human dignity remain intact. Nomonde has the characteristics of a mother who is not only concerned for her own family, but also for a wider community that in many respects remains diminished by poverty. She is spoken to as a confidante by those whom the world rejects as unimportant and irrelevant. Her own journey is not easy, and although she carries the scars of one who has given her life for her people, she bears the pain of being forgotten.

Recently, I was at a family celebration and interacted with a relatively young father, Lukhanyo. There was a point in the celebration when he mounted the stage, and like his great-grandfather and father, made music for the community. His ability to blend into the harmonies made me think that there must be something in the essence of this family that is quite regal in its ability to listen and give of themselves. I have a cameo sketched in my memory of his gentle care for his wife and child. I could remember his father, and as I looked from my memory to Lukhanyo before me, I could recall the voice of an old friend. He belongs to a community that seeks to tell the truth. Again, the echoes from the past can be heard to insist on exposing the new forces of darkness, especially as they relate to those in power. This will be dangerous and has already resulted in victimisation.

Will Cradock ever be free?

Will we ever be free?

Authors' Notes

The first two chapters of this book are told from our different points of view, which we indicate by putting our names – 'Abigail' and 'Lukhanyo' – before each narrator switch. From Chapter Three, whole chapters were written by one of us – and not the two of us together. We denote the change of point of view by putting the name of the writer at the start of the chapter.

Sometimes, the names of the Cradock Four are spelt differently in newspaper reports or government documents from how we have spelt their names. We have used the spelling given by their families, and believe this is the most accurate.

Documents without complete references in the footnotes and bibliography were supplied by filmmaker David Forbes.

Chapter One
Standoff with a Mad Hatter

ABIGAIL

I had been so busy at work that morning, it slipped my mind to check my cellphone after sending Lukhanyo a text message earlier. Although the students were on holiday, my workload as marketing and development manager at the law faculty of the University of Cape Town had not let up. 'Vac', at least for me, was a time to catch up and complete tasks I couldn't get to during term.

Around lunchtime I could finally catch my breath, so I sat down and attended to messages on my phone. One of them was from Lukhanyo. It read: *Hey Abs, take a look at this, and let me know what you think.*

'Today (27 June) marks 31 years since the murders of my father, Fort Calata, and his comrades Matthew Goniwe, Sparro Mkonto and Sicelo Mhlawuli.

Known as the 'Cradock Four', their killings and funeral on 20 July 1985 became a turning point in the struggle for liberation with apartheid president PW Botha invoking a State of Emergency that was to last for years.

I made the decision to become a journalist after years of watching journalists coming to our home as part of their drive to tell the story of my father and his comrades.

Thirty-one years later, I now work as a news reporter, with the sole purpose of telling stories of my people with dedication, truth, and freedom. A freedom that many like my father either died or were imprisoned for.

It is therefore with great sadness that I am confronted with the disturbing direction being taken by my employer. A direction I believe flies in the face of what many have sacrificed.

The decisions [one of which was to ban the broadcast of violent service delivery protest] taken recently by the SABC [South African Broadcasting Corporation] cannot be described in any other way but them curbing media freedom. A freedom to report ethically, truthfully, and without bias.

As I reflect on this day and remember the occasions when leaders of our liberation movements stood at my father's grave and waxed lyrical about the freedom he died for, I wonder where they are today.

How do they live with themselves? How do they watch as the rights and freedoms the 'Cradock Four' were brutally murdered for are systematically being undone?

Did I live without a father so that 31 years later, my own freedom and that of my colleagues are restricted within an institution that is meant to lead in media freedom?

What do I say to the son I have today about what his grandfather and my great-grandfather James Arthur Calata fought for?

I do not do this publicly to condemn my employers, but rather seek to remind some of them and all of us that we cannot forget that people like my father and many others died for us to have the right to speak truth to power when necessary.

They died so that we can in 2016 do what is expected of us, which is to lead where they left off: To serve this nation with pride, truth, dedication and ethics.

Aluta,

Lukhanyo Calata'

Gosh, Lukhanyo, this was heavy reading for a Monday. I immediately started thinking of the implications the release of such a statement would have for our young family. The week before, Lukhanyo had been interviewed for a vacant television assignments editor's post at the SABC's Sea Point office. It would be a step up for him, and by extension our family, were he to be the successful candidate. At the time of writing the statement, he was a television reporter for the SABC in its parliamentary office. He thought the interview the week before had gone well, but with interviews you can never be sure. I responded to his message, asking him not to go public with this statement, as he could kiss his chances of getting the assignments editor's job goodbye if he went public with it. Little did I know that by the time I'd read his statement, my husband had already released it and that it had gone viral.

LUKHANYO

I was on leave at the time. That Monday morning, Abigail was at work and our three-year-old son, Kwezi, at school. After my morning devotions, I picked up my phone to check for messages and scan Twitter for the latest news. I found that Abigail and my good friend Koketso Sachane had sent me text messages about Jimi Matthews's resignation. In June 2016, Jimi was acting group CEO of the SABC. I read his resignation letter, which he had posted on Twitter. To my horror, Jimi claimed to have compromised values he held dear 'under the mistaken belief that [he] could be more effective inside the SABC than outside'. He blamed the 'prevailing, corrosive atmosphere' at the SABC for negatively affecting his moral judgement and making him complicit in decisions he wasn't proud of. He ended the letter with, 'What is happening at the SABC is wrong and I can no longer be part of it.'

This was a complete surprise to me and I'm sure to many of us in the various SABC newsrooms. About a week prior to his resignation, Jimi had filed an affidavit at the Western Cape High Court in which he'd sung the praises of Hlaudi Motsoeneng, the SABC's chief destroyer, disguised as its Chief Operating Officer. In his affidavit Jimi had written, 'his presence at the SABC is vital to the public broadcaster and that the SABC would effectively suffer without Motsoeneng's leadership'.

The sentiment expressed in his resignation letter, however, was far removed from that in his affidavit. What could've happened in the space of a week that would so drastically change his opinion of Motsoeneng?

We (most SABC staffers) had known for a long time that something was amiss at the SABC, but to see Jimi finally stating it in black and white like this left me stunned. I read the resignation letter over and over, trying desperately to make sense of it all. I had always looked up to Jimi and had to some extent believed that as long as he was there, the SABC newsroom was a protected and sacred space. Now that he was gone, and having admitted so publicly that something was wrong at the SABC, I started to worry about those of us who would remain in the trenches, so to speak.

Just then, Koketso called. He was out of the country at the time, visiting his wife, Shanti, in Oslo, Norway. Usually our telephone calls start off with banter, jokes, and just plain nonsense. But this call was different. There was no banter, no jokes, none of the usual nonsense chit-chat. It was a very serious phone call, both in tone and content, right from the start. We had been good friends for around fourteen years at the time, and he was well aware of the significance of the date to me and my family. I was touched by his phone call, particularly as it was meant to commemorate this day with me. We then got to discussing Jimi's resignation letter and what it meant for the already embattled public broadcaster and its Mad Hatter COO. I told Koketso how disappointed I was by Jimi's decision, and that what perturbed me most was his frank admission 'that what is happening at the SABC is wrong'. I was angry that Jimi, at least in my opinion, had thrown in the towel and allowed Motsoeneng to get the better of him.

I just couldn't fathom how he and many others, including (at least) two non-executive boards of directors appointed by parliament, could allow this guy, a high-school dropout, to run roughshod over them like that. While I was in the middle of this rant, Koketso asked me what I was going to do about it. Something about his question struck a nerve in me. I mean, what could I do about it? It jolted me out of bed. I was now on my feet, pacing up and down the short passage in my home, the question hanging over me. About a minute passed and I still hadn't – or rather couldn't – answer the question. My emotions were in turmoil. I was angry; I was disappointed; I was fearful, yet I knew I had to do – or, at the very least, say – something publicly about what was going on at the SABC.

'Why don't you issue a statement?' Koketso asked. I liked this idea, particularly as I could link it to my family's commemoration of the 31st anniversary of my father's disappearance and murder. It was rather fortuitous – at least for me – that Jimi had chosen this day to resign. I agreed we should draft a statement.

I wanted the statement to be strong, critical of the current state of and issues affecting the broadcaster, but I did not want it to get me fired. Suspended maybe, but not fired. Once I was happy with the statement after a few drafts back and forth between us, I had to decide what to do with it. I asked Koketso to send a copy to our friend and former colleague Gasant Abarder, who at the time was editor of the *Cape Argus*, one of the most widely read daily newspapers in Cape Town.

I sent a copy of the statement to Andisiwe Makinana, the parliamentary correspondent of *City Press*, a national newspaper. At the time, Andisiwe boasted just over 33 000 Twitter followers. I knew that with just one tweet from her, the statement would reach a critical mass of people in an instant. Barely a few minutes after I sent Andisiwe the statement, she called. Her voice was cracking, as if she had been crying. She told me the statement had brought her to tears. I've known Andisiwe for several years. We started working as journalists at around the same time and I had grown quite fond of her over the years. I never really thought a statement – particularly one I had written – could bring her to tears. She was even kind enough to warn me that the SABC, and Hlaudi Motsoeneng in particular, would not take kindly to my statement and that I should prepare myself. 'They will surely come for you,' she said. I was touched by her genuine concern for me and my family. The only problem, though, was that by then I had already taken the decision to go public with the statement. I honestly couldn't care any more who or what would come at me in response. I had done what I needed to. Now it was up to them to do what they needed to do.

ABIGAIL

I expected Lukhanyo to be at home that Monday afternoon. So, after reading the statement, I called him hoping to chat to him about it. To my surprise, I found out that not only had he released the statement without my input, but he and our son, Kwezi, were by then on their way to the Cape Town offices of Independent Media. Upon reading the statement, Gasant (the editor of the *Cape Argus*), immediately asked Lukhanyo to come in for an interview. While I was speaking to Lukhanyo on the phone, the repercussions of what was happening slowly dawned on me. How could he go public with something like this without discussing it with me, his wife, first? How could he make a potentially life-changing decision without my input? I was getting worked up – an untenable state for me to be in at that point since I was still at work. In order to

21

calm myself down, I asked after Kwezi and his well-being. But before ending our telephone conversation, I let my husband know in no uncertain terms that I was terribly upset by his decision to issue the statement without my knowledge or input and that we would discuss this when I got home later that day.

After hanging up, I went onto social media. I wasn't surprised by what I found. The interest in and reactions to the statement on Twitter, Facebook, and news websites told me that what Lukhanyo had done resonated with people. I realised I could do nothing to stop it and that I, like the rest of the country, could only sit back and watch as things unfolded.

Unable to focus on work any more, I spent the rest of the afternoon staying on top of everything that had to do with the statement on Twitter and Facebook. The *Cape Argus* posted video excerpts of its interview with Lukhanyo on its platforms to whet readers' appetites for the story that would become their front page lead the next day, 28 June 2016.

As I watched the short video clips and listened to my husband speak, I felt a sense of peace envelop me. It replaced my anxiety about what could or would follow the statement, yet somehow I just couldn't reconcile myself to the fact that my husband had excluded me from the decision-making process when the consequences would directly affect the three of us – him, Kwezi, and me.

They were not home yet when I arrived there. The minute Lukhanyo walked through the door, with our excited son in tow, we started the promised discussion about the release of the statement. With Kwezi safely out of earshot in the bath, I told Lukhanyo that I did not appreciate his decision to issue the statement without my knowledge. I stressed that my problem was not with the content of the statement, but with the fact that I was completely excluded from the decision to release it when I, together with Kwezi, would be directly affected by its release. A heated discussion ensued. But Lukhanyo eventually realised his mistake and we agreed that going forward any and all decisions – particularly ones with such massive implications for our family – had to be discussed with me beforehand.

It was at this point that Lukhanyo informed me he had already accepted an invitation for an in-studio interview with eNCA, the SABC's rival news broadcaster, for later that evening. I did not object to his doing the interview and, having had my say – impressing upon him the fact that he no longer had the luxury of making decisions on his own – I took up my rightful place as my husband's main supporter (and cheerleader) in what in hindsight was *the* most pivotal moment of our lives together so far.

The next day, Lukhanyo and Kwezi graced the front page of the *Cape Argus*. Admittedly, I was extremely proud of my two boys.

LUKHANYO

Jimi Matthews was a veteran broadcast journalist, who had cut his teeth as a news cameraman and reporter, and was particularly active in the turbulent Eighties – probably the worst of the apartheid years. He was a role model to me – at least until the point of his resignation from the SABC. I felt Jimi should have expressed what he wrote in his resignation letter while he was still employed by the SABC. In my interview with Gasant and his deputy editor, Lance Witten, I recall saying, 'Jimi's resignation had hurt me personally because my father died for the freedom enjoyed by so many in South Africa today.' I felt he had made a mockery of the sacrifices of my family, of his own family, and those of countless other families who had fought and lost their loved ones for us to get to this point as a nation. I told them, 'I had to speak up while I was still at the SABC.' I could and would not wait until my resignation before I spoke out about the dastardly decisions the SABC management were busy taking.

My statement had voiced a deep sense of frustration and despair, which, I realised later, was shared by many South Africans with regard to the prevailing situation in the country. What was happening at the SABC reflected what was happening at many – if not all – state-owned entities. Almost everyone my family and I met and spoke to in the days and weeks following the publishing of the statement was relieved, with many celebrating the fact that someone had finally had the guts to speak out against the daft decisions of the SABC's management. I had fired the first salvo, they said.

Abigail also made me realise that, despite my being just 34 years old at the time, the public had responded to what she called 'an inherent moral authority' I possessed. She believed it stemmed not only from the legacy of activism left by my father but also that of my great-grandfather, Canon James Arthur Calata, a prominent black leader in the Anglican Church in the Eastern Cape. More significantly, though, my great-grandfather had served both as president of the Cape ANC as well as the movement's national secretary-general from 1936–1949. His years in that office remain among the longest for any secretary-general in the 106-year history of this liberation movement.

ABIGAIL

South Africans had responded with overwhelming positivity to Lukhanyo's statement, and soon my husband was no longer mine. Kwezi and I now had to share him with the rest of the country. Everyone wanted a piece of him in those first few days following the release of the statement. Practically every news outlet called, requesting interviews. We were happy to share him, though – particularly as I now believed with every fibre of my being that he was doing the right thing and that, whatever the outcome, we, as a family, would be all right.

We didn't have to wait long for the SABC to respond. Just four days after the release of the statement, Lukhanyo was charged with breaching the SABC's code of conduct. His charge sheet read:

> 'Re: DISCIPLINARY HEARING
> You are herewith notified to attend a disciplinary hearing to be held of Friday, 1 July 2016 at 09:00 in ASD Boardroom, Room 2442 of the Radio Park Building of the SABC Offices in Johannesburg, in order to investigate the following alleged offenses brought against you:
> CHARGE 1
> NON-COMPLIANCE WITH THE DUTIES OF YOUR CONTRACT OF EMPLOYMENT
> alternatively
> CONTRAVENTION OF SABC RULES & REGULATIONS
> In that
> You in your capacity as a Reporter, for Parliament Television News in Cape Town, allegedly liaised with the media i.e *Cape Argus* (28 June 2016), Star (28 June 2016), *Sowetan* (28 June 2016), eNCA (Interviews conducted on 27 & 28 June 2016) and *Radio 702* (interviews conducted on 27 & 28 June 2016) without having had permission to do so.

In doing so it is alleged that you contravened Regulation 2 (d) of the SABC's Personnel Regulations i.e.

"An employee:

(d) Shall not without prior written consent of the Group Chief Executive, make any comments in the media . . ."

Should these facts be proven it will constitute an act of non-compliance with the duties of your contract of employment on your part alternatively contravening SABC rules and regulations.'

This was the official charge. The unofficial charge, as we all knew, was that Lukhanyo had dared to speak out against the despotic rule of the SABC's COO, Hlaudi Motsoeneng. This is the same man whom the Western Cape High Court would later find to be 'unqualified to hold any position at the public broadcaster'.

Lukhanyo's charge sheet was sent to his work email address, which he could not access from home. He only became aware of the charges against him the following week when he returned from leave.

So, instead of appearing before a disciplinary panel on Friday, 1 July 2016, Lukhanyo, Kwezi, and I spent the morning protesting outside the SABC's offices in Sea Point. We were asked to be part of a picket organised by the Cape Town advocacy group, Right2Know Campaign. We wanted to voice our dissatisfaction with the SABC's decision to ban the broadcast of violent service delivery protests. In criticising this directive, Lukhanyo – inadvertently and unbeknown to him at the time – had joined six of his Johannesburg colleagues who had also opposed this directive.

Three of them, Thandeka Gqubule, Foeta Krige, and Suna Venter, were by then already suspended. They had raised their objections in a line-talk discussion about the directive not to cover a protest by the Right2Know Campaign right on the SABC's doorstep in Auckland Park, Johannesburg. Line-talk meetings are for editors and producers to discuss how to cover the top stories of the day. Three other SABC employees, Jacques Steenkamp, Krivani Pillay, and Busisiwe Ntuli, would under normal circumstances not have done anything wrong when they sent a letter to news managers requesting a meeting with them to clarify some of Motsoeneng's pronouncements. Under the abnormal circumstances prevailing at the SABC at the time, however, this innocent letter had become an offence punishable by dismissal. Another SABC employee, Vuyo Mvoko, took a page from Lukhanyo's script and went on to write a scathing letter, titled 'My Hell at SABC', which *The Star* and its sister publications carried on their front pages on 6 July 2016. Thandeka, Suna, Busisiwe, Krivani, Jacques, Vuyo, Foeta, and Lukhanyo – or 'the rebels', as Lukhanyo often refers to them – became known as the SABC 8.

On 8 July 2016, Lukhanyo and his colleagues were informed of more charges levelled against them by their employer. This time, notices in terms of Schedule 8 of the Labour Relations Act were issued.

Sections of their charge sheets read as follows:

> 'You are hereby notified in terms of Schedule 8 of the Labour Relations Act no 66 of 1995 that allegations have been received that you are continuing to commit further acts of misconduct after receiving your letter informing you of your disciplinary hearing in the following respects:
>
> On Sunday, 3 July 2016 you caused an article to be published in the *Sunday World* newspaper thereby criticising and displaying disrespect and persistence in your refusal to comply with an instruction pertaining to the editorial policy of the SABC as well as the directive not to broadcast visuals/audio of the destruction of property during protest actions.'

The letters end with:

> 'It undermines the editorial responsibility and authority of the SABC as vested upon its Chief Operating Officer in terms of paragraph 2 of the SABC Revised Editorial Policies, 2016.'

Outside of the SABC, the eight enjoyed great support from the public and their peers. On 9 July 2016, they were recognised by the South African National Editors' Forum (SANEF), which awarded all eight of them the 2016 Nat Nakasa[1] Award for 'media practitioner[s] who [have] shown integrity, commitment, and courage' in the course of

---

1 Nat Nakasa was a South African journalist who died in exile in 1965 at the age of 28, after a brief but dynamic career characterised by his journalistic courage and integrity.

their work. The public support would increase seven-fold a few weeks later when the SABC decided to summarily dismiss all eight of them.

LUKHANYO

18 July 2016 was a Monday. I'd been back from leave for two weeks and, besides an updated charge sheet, things were quite normal for me at the office until around six that evening. Krivani Pillay sent a message to our WhatsApp group urging us to check our emails urgently. She seemed in a bit of a panic. She had just received an email from management informing her of her dismissal. Within minutes of one another, Suna Venter, Jacques Steenkamp, and Foeta Krige all confirmed the worst possible news – they too had been dismissed.

I checked, double-checked, and then triple-checked my emails. Nothing, no email. I was safe for now, I thought, at least until my disciplinary hearing which was arranged for 29 July 2016. Surely the SABC wouldn't touch me until then.

Shortly after I got to the office the next morning the parliamentary editor, Vuyani Green, came into the newsroom to inform me that I should stay in the office, as there were managers from the SABC's Sea Point offices coming to see me. I knew then that I too would be dismissed.

The feeling of impending doom is one I would not wish on my worst enemy. For the first time during this entire ordeal, I was afraid. I couldn't stop thinking about my wife and son, and how I had let them down. The fear of losing all I had worked for in the five years while I had been at the SABC left me stunned for a few minutes. I tried to keep busy and not think about the meeting, but my eye kept catching the clock. Two hours of waiting eventually passed. The moment finally arrived when Vuyani returned to call me into his office. There, I found Western Cape human resources manager, Shouneez Moosajee, and a gentleman who introduced himself as James Shikwambana, then acting provincial general manager.

Shikwambana curtly informed me that he had been sent to deliver a letter to me, and to inform me officially that the SABC was terminating my contract. I looked at the big brown envelope he slid casually across the table and asked him how the SABC could dismiss me without having heard my side of the story. My question caught the HR manager off-guard. Obviously startled by this revelation, Shouneez asked if there had been no hearing at all, to which I replied no.

With nothing left to be said, I picked up the envelope, thanked Shikwambana and Shouneez, and excused myself. Vuyani walked me out of his office and kindly offered me his apology for the manner in which the SABC had handled my dismissal. By this time, my emotions were all over the place. In the corridor, just outside his office, I opened the envelope and read the one-page letter:

'Dear Mr Calata,

NOTICE OF TERMINATION OF EMPLOYMENT

I refer to the notice in terms of Schedule 8 of Labour Relations Act served on you on 8 July 2016. Further, I confirm receipt of a letter from your union, Bemawu, dated 11 July 2016. It is [the] SABC's considered view that the said letter from your union does not amount to [an] adequate response to the issues/concerns raised by the SABC against you.

It is common cause that you have made it known to the SABC that you will continue to disrespect the SABC, your employer. It has now become clear to the SABC that you have no intention to refrain from your conduct of undermining the SABC and the authority of its management. In the premise [*sic*] your continued acts of misconduct have become intolerable. Your employment with the SABC is thus terminated with immediate effect, being 18 July 2016. You have a right to refer a dispute at the CCMA in the event that you are not satisfied with this decision.'

I was scared, angry, disillusioned – and now officially fired. At that moment, the safest place I could think of was the office of my assignments editor, Isabelle de Taillefer. I had always enjoyed a good working relationship with her. There was a strong Cradock connection between us. She, a priest's daughter, had spent part of her childhood there, before her family relocated to Bedford, a town around 90 km from Cradock. Isabelle was also the same age as my mother, so even though she was an immediate line manager, she was also very much a maternal figure to me in the office. And as mothers so often do, she must've seen what I felt on my face because she jumped up from behind her desk, arms wide open, the moment I walked into her office with my brown envelope in hand. I could barely finish telling her that the SABC had fired me before she wrapped her arms around me and allowed me to cry on her shoulders, right there in her office.

After a few minutes, I was ready to face the rest of my colleagues again, who by now were aware that something had happened. So, with brown envelope in hand, I braved the newsroom as I made my way towards my desk. Once there, I took a picture of my letter of dismissal and posted it to our WhatsApp group. One of the guys in the group must have tweeted it. I had barely sent it when my phone began to ring incessantly and messages of support began streaming in. I was the last of the eight to be fired that Tuesday morning.

ABIGAIL

Ironically, 19 July is a day before yet another important date in my husband's life. On 20 July 1985, his father, Fort Calata, was buried in one of the biggest funerals in apartheid South Africa, alongside his friends and comrades Matthew Goniwe, Sparro Mkonto, and Sicelo Mhlawuli.

On that cold Saturday afternoon in Cradock, an estimated 60 000 mourners not only defied a government ban to travel there, but they made the funeral one of the biggest political rallies of the time. It was a true turning point in black South Africans' struggle against oppression and injustice. The funeral of the Cradock Four was a powerful political statement, one which the government of PW Botha could not just ignore.

With Lukhanyo now dismissed and my fears for our family realised, I felt we had to regroup. Our lives had been turned upside down in a matter of days and we hardly had a chance to catch our collective breath. My birthday was coming up in just a few days, on 22 July, which I thought would be the perfect opportunity to unwind, spend some quality time together as a family, and forget about our ordeals of the preceding weeks – if only for that day. In the few days leading up to and following his dismissal, Lukhanyo was busier than ever. There were meetings with his union, with lawyers, with former colleagues, and meetings with sympathisers from both civil and faith-based organisations. And the media requests for interviews had not let up. I suspect Lukhanyo's personal relationships with most of the journalists who approached him for interviews made it difficult for him to say no to them.

In one of those interviews, Carla Bernardo from the African News Agency wanted to know whether Lukhanyo would fight his dismissal. His nonchalant response was, 'Yes, of course, I come from a family of fighters.' This simple statement would again make the front pages of a number of newspapers the next day. By now, Lukhanyo and his seven colleagues had received various offers from lawyers prepared to argue their cases in the Labour Court as they sought their immediate reinstatement.

During this dizzying time, I got to witness a different side to my husband – a side I had not known existed until then. I saw how he was buoyed by and relished the battle with the SABC. Most importantly, though, I witnessed how effortlessly he had taken to activism. In one meeting, he managed to convince a group of pastors representing some 24 churches to issue a statement calling on then Minister of Communications, Faith Muthambi, to intervene immediately in the SABC matter and reinstate the SABC 8. He later casually told me that it had taken him less than an hour to get them to agree to this.

My birthday, however, would not work out as I had planned or wanted. Just two days before, Lukhanyo received a call from the office of the ANC's deputy secretary-general (DSG), Jessie Duarte. She requested a meeting, which meant he would have to travel to Luthuli House, the ANC head office in Johannesburg. So instead of a nice, quiet day at home with my husband and son, I ended up taking Lukhanyo to the airport early that Friday morning for his flight to Johannesburg.

Lukhanyo was now the latest Calata called up to ANC headquarters to brief its office bearers on a matter of national importance – much like his father once did and his great-grandfather before him. The historical significance of this fact was not lost on me and neither, it seems, was it lost on his mother, Nomonde. Although based in Cradock, she met him at the airport in Johannesburg and accompanied him to the meeting with Duarte.

LUKHANYO

I am always a ball of nervous energy just before boarding a flight. Strange thing is I don't really know why. These nerves are there every time, despite my job as a journalist, which requires that I travel by airplane quite regularly. This flight to Johannesburg would prove no different. Added to this, I felt terrible for leaving Abigail, who had taken ill with the flu, with Kwezi on her birthday to attend a meeting with Jessie Duarte. I had decided earlier that week that I wouldn't rack my brain trying to figure out why the ANC's DSG had called me to a meeting. This, however, was easier said than done. Until this point, my association with the DSG had been limited to purely professional engagements, mostly at press conferences either in Cape Town or Johannesburg. From those few encounters, I knew she was a no-nonsense kind of lady.

Fortunately, the flight to Johannesburg that Friday morning went by quite smoothly. We landed at OR Tambo International Airport ahead of schedule. It was a crisp mid-winter's morning in the city, which felt a lot colder than Cape Town. Despite the nip in the air, I chose to wait for my mother and elder sister, Dorothy, outside the terminal buildings at the airport. It had been a while since I had last seen them. My mother still lived in Cradock, although lately she seemed to be spending most of her time travelling between Cape Town, where I live with my family, and Limpopo, where Dorothy lived with her family. It was her desire to see and be with her grandchildren that had her traversing the country almost every other week. Anyway, after a brief wait at the airport, the two arrived to pick me up. The hugs and hellos were longer than usual from both of them. It made me realise then that they hadn't seen me since the statement had hit the headlines and, although they'd called almost every day, this was the first time I was physically in their presence. No amount of phone calls could ever make up for that. We set off for Luthuli House, with me in the back seat. In those few moments, as we drove from the airport, I felt completely unburdened. For the first time in weeks, I could just breathe, relax, and take it easy. I felt so reassured being with them, and I knew that despite all the drama of the last few weeks, my family and I would survive this.

I could gather my thoughts and listen to Dorothy regale me with messages of love from my niece – also called Lukhanyo – and two nephews,

Phumudzo and Junior. These two women in the car with me had taken care of me most of my life and here they were once again making sure that I was okay. I felt safe and deeply loved.

As we approached the Johannesburg CBD, inching ever closer to 54 Pixley Seme Street, I could sense the mood in the car change. We all grew quiet, until my mom snapped us back to the reality of why the three of us were reunited in Johannesburg. She mentioned how my ordeal had stirred in her a deep-rooted fear for my safety and well-being. In the same breath, she was outraged by the situation I found myself in. It was a very difficult time for her, more so than anyone in the family could have suspected. You see, my mother had over the years done almost everything she could to keep me as far removed from active politics as possible. She feared my involvement in politics or activism of any sort would more than likely result in my being killed just like my father. Yet, despite her desperate attempts, particularly as I got older, here I was, her only son, summoned to Luthuli House and her worst fears seemed realised. She had been on this emotional rollercoaster with my father before. She didn't like it then and she despised it even more now.

My mother was particularly scathing of the circumstances around my dismissal. According to her, the manner in which the SABC had fired me was far too similar to the circumstances surrounding my father's dismissal from his post as a secondary-school teacher, in the months leading up to his assassination. This SABC saga had been a terrible case of déjà vu for her. I could only apologise to her for my part and – although I think unconvincingly – tried to assure her that it had not been my intention at all for things to turn out the way they did.

Upon our arrival at Luthuli House, the security guard at the entrance to the parking lot said he had been informed to expect us, and directed us to where we should park. I'd been to Luthuli House once before for a press conference ahead of the 2009 national elections; this visit, however, was very different. Both my mother and sister were familiar with the building. My mom had visited Luthuli House several times before too, particularly during the period when Kgalema Motlanthe served as the movement's secretary-general. She had sought assistance from his office for the education of Dorothy, Tumani, my younger sister, and me.

We entered the building through the glass door nearest the parking lot. I informed the courteous lady at reception that we were there to see Jessie Duarte. 'The DSG?' she asked. I nodded. 'Sixth floor,' she said.

A gentleman named Lungi Mtshali was waiting for us on the sixth floor. He was the one I had liaised with to make arrangements for this meeting. As we walked towards his office from the elevator, I remember looking around, trying to take it all in. I was after all walking the corridors of the headquarters of the ANC, the liberation movement to which my family had such a deep-rooted connection. My family's history is inextricably interwoven with that of this movement. I had never given much thought to what the offices at Luthuli House looked like, but once I saw them, I was pleasantly surprised. I wasn't sure what to make of the gold-flaked wallpaper, but I thought the offices themselves were quite modern. They were well lit with spacious corridors, and rather busy despite it being a Friday afternoon.

Lungi was waiting for us outside his office about halfway down the corridor. He was a softly spoken guy with a beautiful smile. After the formal introductions, he informed us – much to my mother and sister's chagrin – that I would meet with the DSG alone at first before the two of them could join us. I was fine with this. It was after all the reason why I had come, but my mother wasn't pleased with this arrangement. Lungi tried desperately to assure her that she and Dorothy would join us in the meeting, but only after I had met one-on-one with Duarte. My mom's vehement protestations against this arrangement, unfortunately, came to nothing.

Up to that point, I had not allowed myself to think about this moment – what it all represented for me on a personal level, for my family, or indeed my father. Lungi then asked me to follow him. I glanced at my mom, who was close to tears. I told her I'd be fine, but I don't think she heard me and, if she did, she definitely didn't believe me. Lungi and I made our way through his neatly kept office. As I walked just a few paces behind him, I had a revelation of the significance of this meeting and my presence at Luthuli House. Despite the magnitude of the moment, I tried desperately to keep calm. I needed to be composed when I met Jessie Duarte.

I loved the amount of natural light shining into her office. The large windows seemed to make the office bigger than it actually is. It was warm too, spaciously laid out with very little pretence in the decor. It's a political office, I suppose. Duarte sat behind her desk, about to finish reading a document which I imagined to be a report of some kind. I'd seen her many times before in press conferences, and I'd always found her very stern and strict. Yet, as she took off her glasses and walked across her office to greet me, she had such a warm and friendly smile, which I, of course and very naturally, reciprocated. I remember being amazed by the fact that she wore takkies to work. I liked that about her. She immediately put me at ease. *She's harmless*, I remember thinking – a thought I took back almost immediately when she gave me quite a firm handshake, before inviting me to sit down at a meeting table. There was a genuine exchange of pleasantries and the obligatory question about the flight to Johannesburg. With that out of the way, we got down to the business that necessitated our meeting.

She began by apologising for the situation that my colleagues and I found ourselves in, and explained that she had wanted to meet with me to get my side of the sorry SABC saga. Telling me she found newspaper reports about what was unfolding at the public broadcaster quite contradictory, she said she needed a first-hand account of what was actually going on at the SABC. She added that our chat would help her put together a report to the officials for a meeting taking place the following Monday. My plan, or what little of it I had, was to make the most of the opportunity this meeting provided. I didn't know if I would ever get the chance to speak to an actual decision-maker again, so I began to tell her my story from the very beginning.

For me, it had all started on the evening of 13 February 2014, the night of the State of the Nation Address. This was the last State of the Nation Address before the general elections in May that year. By then, I had been in the SABC's employ for three years. Prior to that night, I had not come across anything out of the ordinary for a journalist working in any other newsroom. But around ten o'clock that evening, an encounter I had with Jimi Matthews, who was then head of news, changed everything. It was just outside the entrance to the Marks Building in the parliamentary precinct where I had my first-ever instruction to censor the news at the SABC. I demonstrated to Duarte how Jimi had grabbed me by the scruff of my jacket and instructed me not to get him into shit and that I had to go and cut him positive soundbites of reactions from opposition parties following the president's address.

My dilemma with this instruction was two-fold. Firstly, there were the obvious censorship issues; and, secondly, there were no positive soundbites to cut. 2014 was an election year. Politicians, particularly those from opposition parties, are shrewd enough to understand the value of those few minutes that we interview them live on air. They know that what they say is broadcast live to the nation, therefore none of them – particularly in an election year – would use those precious minutes to sing the then president Jacob Zuma's praises. So, without fail, not one of them had anything remotely positive to say about the president's address.

I told Duarte how my interaction with Jimi that night had troubled me, not only as a journalist working in a free and democratic South Africa, but also as the son of Fort Calata. It had upset me deeply that I had been asked to do something that had such strong ties to apartheid South Africa. In the apartheid years, particularly in the turbulent Eighties, the SABC was truly 'his master's voice', a tool used to great effect by the brutal and murderous regime of PW Botha. How could Jimi of all people dare to ask me to do to my people the exact same things successive apartheid governments had done to them before? It was something I was not prepared to do.

Today, I look back at that moment with Jimi and feel so proud of my defiance, particularly for not betraying the dreams and aspirations of all South Africans. I should add that I never did cut those soundbites or any soundbites for that matter. Instead, I relayed Jimi's instructions to the parliamentary editor, Vuyani Green. He too must have felt uneasy at these instructions, because he asked me to pass the message on to my colleague Bulelani Phillip, who was working on the reactions piece for the next morning. I refused to do that too.

I then grabbed my jacket, bag, car keys, and bid everyone a good night. I recounted other subsequent incidents to Duarte – such as the time I received the instruction that we (TV reporters in parliament) were no longer allowed to use an iconic and historically significant reel of footage, where members of parliament representing the Economic Freedom Fighters (EFF) disrupted a sitting of the National Assembly. Chanting

'Pay back the money!', they would not allow Zuma to address the National Assembly, saying he first needed to pay back several millions of rand, as per the findings and recommendations of then-Public Protector Thuli Madonsela.

In her report, titled 'Secure in Comfort', Madonsela had found that public money indeed was used illegally to build non-security-related structures, including a kraal, chicken-run, amphitheatre, and swimming pool at Zuma's private home in Nkandla, KwaZulu-Natal.

To this day, I have no idea who in the SABC had issued the directive that the EFF footage be banned. I remember, though, that I flatly ignored the instruction and continued using the footage to overlay my piece, which looked back at the key moments of the 2014 parliamentary year.

A few minutes after sending the package through to Johannesburg for broadcast that December afternoon, I received a call from Nyana Molete, TV news editor. His first words to me were, 'Calata, why do you want me to lose my job?' – a question that greatly puzzled me because I did not wield such or any other power for that matter at the SABC. He then asked me to re-edit my piece and drop the footage of the EFF MPs chanting 'Pay back the money!' I declined. In the ensuing debate about journalistic principles and ethics, he asked me, 'Calata, will you feed my children when they have to go to bed hungry?' My response was that, although I would not like his children to go to bed hungry, I was not prepared to re-edit the piece. I claimed to have already left the office by then anyway. He said, in that case, the re-edit would be done in Johannesburg. I had no response to that, so I ended our telephone conversation.

A colleague, who was in the office with me at the time, overheard my conversation with Nyana. I suspect it was she who may have leaked my conversation with him to Andisiwe Makinana from *City Press*. Andisiwe called me barely half an hour later, asking me to confirm whether it was true that the SABC had banned the footage of EFF MPs chanting 'Pay back the money!' in the National Assembly. I confirmed to her that this was indeed the case.

The article appeared in the newspaper the following Sunday. Suffice to say, it didn't go down well with the managers at the SABC. In the days that followed, both Isabelle and I were asked to explain in writing how this information got to the media.

About two weeks later, in January 2015, news management, in the person of parliamentary editor Vuyani Green, threatened us with immediate dismissal if we spoke out about internal SABC matters. This to me did not make sense at all, and I couldn't for the life of me understand this logic. Our livelihoods were being threatened because high-ranking individuals in the SABC newsroom had taken unethical and, in some cases, unlawful decisions. Although they were meant to protect us journalists on the ground, they were the very ones selling us out.

These two incidents led to several more instances where some of my colleagues and I had to object to other unethical and unlawful instructions. Sometimes these were issued to us in the name of the ANC. I told Duarte that, as someone who was raised to believe that the ANC – the movement of my great-grandfather and father – could do no wrong, I had become terribly disillusioned by instructions from some editors to act in a manner that I knew was contrary to what I was raised to believe about the ANC.

Duarte on several occasions assured me that such instructions were never issued by the ANC and that those behind such actions were doing so of their own volition. She said media freedom and the independence of newsrooms, particularly those of the national broadcaster, were guaranteed not only by ANC policy but were in fact enshrined in our Constitution. Censorship was not.

Duarte then asked about our dismissals. Although there was nothing funny about this question, we managed to smile about it because we both knew what or whom we were about to talk about.

I proceeded to describe to her the disciplinary process or lack thereof in detail. I specifically highlighted to her how the SABC had in its haste to fire us flouted its own rules and regulations. Worse still was that the SABC had not only violated the country's labour laws in the process, it had in essence violated our constitutional rights. I asked her how this had been allowed to happen in a democratic South Africa under the ANC's watch. At this point, I could feel my anger and frustrations of the last few weeks bubbling to the surface. I was getting emotional. I hadn't realised just how much the events of the recent past had affected me and the toll they had taken. But here I was, with a person of significant influence, who could potentially help me and my colleagues in our legal battle with the SABC. So I spoke from the heart and miraculously I didn't cry. I still have no idea how I had managed to keep it together.

All the while, Duarte was desperately trying to keep up as she took notes of our conversation. At some point, she looked up from her notepad and asked what she and the organisation could do to assist me. I hesitated for a second or two, and responded that we needed help getting our jobs back. She immediately agreed to help. But there was a problem. She said she would probably only be able to assist Busisiwe Ntuli, Thandeka Gqubule, and me. The three of us were represented by our union, Bemawu (Broadcasting, Electronic, Media, and Allied Workers Union), in our labour dispute with the SABC.

Duarte said there was little she could do to help my other colleagues Suna Venter, Foeta Krige, Krivani Pillay, and Jacques Steenkamp, as they were represented by Solidariteit, an organisation which represents Afrikaner interests. She said it held ideologically different views to the ANC. I didn't understand. And quite frankly, I didn't want to understand and neither did it matter to me which organisation was representing whom. This had nothing to do with Solidariteit or any other organisation for that matter. I respectfully pointed out to her that I didn't think it would reflect kindly on the ANC if it emerged that it had helped the three black journalists (two of whom, Thandeka and myself, had strong historical ties to the ANC) and not those from other races in the fight against the SABC. I impressed upon her the fact that eight of us were dismissed and that if she or the ANC was offering us help, they would have to help all eight of us, not just some of us. I was very pleased when she eventually agreed with me.

With this now settled and out of the way, we invited my mom and sister into the meeting. I've always known that my mother is a mighty soldier of a woman. I thank God every day that He chose her to give birth to me, raise, and guide me on this earth. In the meeting with Duarte, my mother once again proved just what a powerful force she is. She began by telling the DSG how she had read my letter in the newspapers and how she couldn't understand why I had been dismissed based on what I had written in that letter.

For her, the parallels between my ordeal and that of my father were too much to bear. She then compared the circumstances between my father's dismissal and mine, pointing out some uncanny similarities. She said that, at the time of my father's murder, he had been waiting to be reinstated after being fired from his job as a school teacher in Cradock. Like him, I too had been charged, allocated a date upon which I would appear before a disciplinary hearing, and – once again like my father – I had been dismissed without my employer ever hearing my side of the story. To make matters worse, she said, on the day my father left our home never to return from a meeting in Port Elizabeth, I was just three years old and sick with the mumps. My three-year-old son, Kwezi, was sick with tonsillitis on the day I was dismissed. 'Where is this all going to end?' she asked, adding that she was praying not to have to relive the searing pain of death and loss again as she had done with my father.

After an emotionally charged two hours for all four of us around that table, the meeting ended with Duarte promising to do all she could to assist the eight of us fired by the SABC.

While in Johannesburg, I also wanted to meet with the lawyers who would represent Thandeka, Busi, and me in our Labour Court challenge. I had been a little annoyed with my union, Bemawu. In the hours and days after our dismissal, I had spoken to Advocate Dumisa Ntsebeza, whom I wanted to represent me in the case. Bra D, as he was commonly known, had had a long-standing relationship with my family and the other families of the Cradock Four. He and his brother, Lungisile, were arrested alongside Matthew Goniwe in 1976 for having been part of a 'terrorist' cell group. Bra D also later worked with my mother and the other widows when he served as a commissioner of the Truth and Reconciliation Commission (TRC). I had specifically requested my union's president, Hannes du Buisson, to brief Bra D for my defence. The union, in its infinite wisdom, had never done so, and this had pissed me right off. Instead, Busi, Thandeka, and I would be represented by a gravelly voiced attorney called Nick Robb from Webber Wentzel. I wanted to at least meet the man who would help determine whether or not I could return to my job at the SABC.

Nick turned out to be a really cool guy, excellent lawyer, and was best friends with Judge Clive Plasket, who had represented my mother and the other widows at the second inquest into the murders of the Cradock Four in the early Nineties. Nick opted to brief Advocate Steven Budlender, who was already representing Suna, Jacques, Krivani, and Foeta. After my meeting with him, I called Bra D to inform him of everything that had happened, and to express my sincere apologies to him as the union in this case hadn't assented to my request. Bra D was very understanding and supportive, particularly when I told him that my case would be argued by Budlender. 'You're in very good hands with Steven,' I recall him saying.

The case of the first four rebels, Suna, Jacques, Krivani, and Foeta, would be heard the following Tuesday with our case – Busi, Thandeka, and myself – scheduled for two days later. Vuyo Mvoko's case was slightly different to ours – he would challenge his dismissal in the High Court, as he was on a fixed freelance contract at the time of his dismissal.

On Tuesday, 26 July 2016, four days after my meeting with Duarte, the Labour Court ruled that four of the SABC 8, Foeta Krige, Suna Venter, Krivani Pillay, and Jacques Steenkamp, be reinstated. This was obviously good news for all of us. The court ruling meant Busi, Thandeka, and I could also return to our posts at the SABC. Our case was due in court that Thursday, but our lawyers assured us that the ruling meant we probably wouldn't appear in court, and that they would seek to have the first judgment made an order of the court. I was very happy not to have to go to court, particularly as this would've involved another flight from Cape Town to Johannesburg and back.

The SABC management, however, cut our celebrations and congratulatory messages short. Barely an hour after the court ruling, management announced they would appeal the Labour Court's decision that we be reinstated.

Just like that, our jubilation turned to despair. We asked ourselves how the SABC with its depleting cash reserves could waste taxpayers' money on a trivial matter like this. Did most of those 'crazy baldheads' on the 27th floor of the SABC offices in Auckland Park not know they were merely delaying the inevitable? Did they not know that we were on the right side of the law and history, and that it was just a matter of time before we would get our jobs back despite their obstinacy? Did they not know – or did they just not care? Well, I was ready to fight. Thandeka,

Busi, and I were due in court for our case on Thursday, 28 July. We instructed Nick, our lawyer, to prepare to give the SABC a bloody nose. I was baying for it. On Wednesday, 27 July, the SABC suddenly backed down from its threats, announced it would not appeal the Labour Court ruling, and that we were free to return to our posts the very next day. This was such welcome news for all of us.

I suspected that this sudden about-turn may have had something to do with my meeting with Duarte, but I wasn't sure how much of it did, and I never called to confirm if Duarte or the ANC had anything to do with the SABC's decision to let us return to work. I was just so happy to return to my job. It had been an awfully tough few weeks. I wanted to put it all behind me. So on Thursday, 28 July 2016, I woke up, got ready, and went to the office instead of the Labour Court. Seven of us – Suna Venter, Krivani Pillay, Thandeka Gqubule, Busisiwe Ntuli, Jacques Steenkamp, Foeta Krige and I – went back to work that day. Sadly, Vuyo Mvoko did not. The SABC had found a loophole in his contract as a freelancer, which they could exploit to block his reinstatement at the broadcaster. Vuyo would eventually be vindicated when, over a year later, on 29 September 2017, the Supreme Court of Appeal ruled that the SABC was wrong in terminating his contract, which was valid until 2019, and ordered the public broadcaster to pay his legal costs.

Our first day back at work was just five or so days before the local government elections on 3 August. I remember being quite happy to walk back into the Marks Building in the parliamentary precinct, where the SABC's offices are located. A few colleagues, Zalene Merrington, Pam Zokufa, Joseph Mosia and Abongwe Kobokana, were there when I walked in. The reception and their genuine happiness to see me back in the office made me feel so welcome. I spent most of the day catching up with colleagues and combing through hundreds of emails. I don't recall doing much else that day. On the bus home later that evening, I thought back on everything that had happened over the past few weeks, what I had managed to pull off and how – to my own astonishment – I had actually accomplished some of the things I had done. I wondered if my father had been watching, guiding, and helping me along the way. I wondered too if he would've been proud of me.

Chapter Two

'He Was the Gentlest of Them All'

– Sarie Smith, childhood friend

LUKHANYO

This question is something I have often wondered about at great length. What kind of relationship would my father and I have, if he were alive today? My mother has told me about how happy he was when I was born, and that he always referred to me as his best friend. Would we still be best friends? Would we be almost like brothers? Would we get along at all? Or would we have a more conventional father-and-son relationship built upon well-defined boundaries of communication, personal interactions, and relating to each other?

Pondering these questions inevitably leads me to ask a number of other questions, such as: What course would our lives, specifically mine, have taken were my father still alive? Would I be the man I have turned out to be today? Would my dreams, aspirations, fears, beliefs, successes, failures be what they are? Would I have become a journalist? Would I have met Abigail? So many questions, which I will never have the answers to – at least not on this side of eternity.

I usually console myself by telling myself that I am the man God intended me to be. And just like any other person on this earth, I am shaped by my lived experiences to be the unique, beautiful soul that I am. Those lived experiences are what led me to Abigail, the second daughter born to Brian and Mary Isaacs. A beautiful young woman from Stellenbosch whom I fell in love with the very instant I laid my eyes on her in late January 2008. We were both younger journalists then, she a parliamentary reporter for the Afrikaans newspaper *Beeld*, and I a general news and sports reporter with eNews, as eNCA was still called then. We were sent to cover an ANC meeting in Philippi, a township just outside Cape Town. Mathews Phosa, who was elected treasurer general at the ANC's 52nd National Conference in Polokwane in December 2007, was in Cape Town to deliver the movement's birthday or its January 8th statement, as it's more commonly referred to.

I remember that Sunday morning like it was yesterday. Abigail first caught my eye as she walked towards the area where a group of us reporters were chatting, while idly waiting for Phosa to arrive. At the time, both of us had been working as journalists in Cape Town for around five years, but that morning was the first time we'd met. I remember asking my colleague, Nawaal Deane, the cameraperson I was assigned with that day, who that beautiful woman was. I couldn't keep my eyes off her. I knew I had to speak to her, so I waited for an opportunity when I could go over and at least introduce myself to her when she was alone. That opportunity never came, so I went over while she stood talking to Chantall Presence, a fellow journalist. I'm sure Chantall must've thought me very rude for interrupting them. Abigail later shared with me that she thought I was quite forward to intrude on their conversation like that. I introduced myself to Abigail and made sure that I complimented her beauty. She was then, and remains to this day, one of the most beautiful women I have ever seen.

Back in 2008, I was sharing a flat with my friend Koketso Sachane. He still teases me about that day when I returned home from work and couldn't stop talking about this woman I'd met and whom I was convinced I would marry. Mind you, I knew very little about her. I had no idea if she was married, in a relationship, or gay – all I knew was that if there was any chance at all, she would become my wife. How this would happen was inconsequential. I had it bad. After our first meeting, I saw Abigail again a few weeks later. This time it was during the melee that followed the 2008 State of the Nation Address. The second encounter confirmed just how completely enchanted I was by her. A few days later, she gave me her business card. I don't think I waited a day before I called to ask her out for dinner. I was more relieved than happy when she agreed. I remember telling anyone who cared to listen that I had scored myself a date with the prettiest girl. Abigail and I eventually married three years later on 24 September 2011. Over a year later, on 21 December 2012 she gave me arguably the greatest gift a woman can give a man, when she gave birth to our son, Kwezi Mikah Calata.

Our son's birth that Friday afternoon brought me full circle. I, now, was the father to a little boy with all the responsibility that fatherhood and parenting carry with it. Although Kwezi's birth in our flat in Mowbray remains the singular highlight of my life, I was then, and continue to be, daunted by the prospect of fathering him. How do I become the best father I can be when my father was not there to model what fatherhood is for me. My frame of reference for what fatherhood is, is largely pieced together from the odds and ends my mother has relayed to me over the years about the kind of man my father was.

Unfortunately, I don't have any memories of the brief three years I spent with my father before he was murdered. Instead, my first and only memory of him is of his funeral.

I've since come to find out that the date of his funeral was 20 July 1985. On that Saturday, I was just three years, eight months, and two days old. I remember it being bitterly cold. I remember the many, many buses and the thousands of people, some of whom had spent several days camped outside my great-grandfather's home. My mother, elder sister, and I moved there at my father's family's insistence after his and Matthew Goniwe's bodies were found five days after their disappearance in thick bushes just outside Bluewater Bay, a suburb of Port Elizabeth. I remember a moment when I clutched my mother's dress so tightly as she sat sobbing in the back of a slow-moving, blue Mitsubishi kombi. Its rear sliding door was open and it was surrounded by thousands of people. I also remember being terrified at the gravesite that the ground underneath me would cave in and that I would fall through it as it shook from the force of toyi-toyiing comrades. I remember the choking dust. The red coffins.

Despite many desperate attempts over the years to conjure up memories of my father alive, I just don't seem to have any. My most fervent wish is that I will remember something about him – irrespective of what that memory is, just as long as it is of him alive. I know it would be a memory I'd treasure forever.

An estimated 60 000 people from all around South Africa, and including diplomats from France, Norway, Denmark, Canada, Australia and Sweden, defied a government ban and travelled to Cradock to pay their last respects to my father and his comrades. The funeral is said to have been one of the biggest political funerals in the Eastern Cape, at least since that of the leader of the Black Consciousness Movement, Bantu Stephen Biko, in 1977.

Mourners had made their way to Cradock in trains, at least 160 buses, even more minibus taxis, and private cars. Newspaper reports and personal accounts claimed that many more people were stopped at roadblocks as far afield as Worcester in the Western Cape and ordered to return home.

ANC president Oliver Tambo called all the way from Lusaka, Zambia, to pass on his and the movement's condolences to the people of Cradock. Zuko Vabaza was the one tasked to deliver the message from the ANC president to those attending the funeral. My sister Dorothy recalls how uBhut' Zuko always joked he would never again wash his left ear because that was the ear he had pressed against the telephone when he spoke to OR Tambo.

On that afternoon, the mourners who had gathered in my hometown of Cradock in the Karoo – which was already such a thorn in the side of the apartheid government – sent PW Botha and his cabinet a message, louder and clearer than anything they had ever heard before. In a supreme act of defiance, those present at the funeral hoisted two massive liberation movement flags. One displayed the black, green, and gold of the ANC, while the other, almost one and a half times bigger, was red with a yellow hammer and sickle neatly painted onto it. In 1985, both the ANC and the South African Communist Party had been banned for well over 20 years. It was inconceivable at the time that these two flags would be hoisted inside the republic, never mind that they would be hoisted in a relative backwater like Cradock.

I guess it was inevitable that, just a few hours after my father's coffin and those of Matthew Goniwe, Sparro Mkonto, and Sicelo Mhlawuli were lowered into their final resting places, 'Die Groot Krokodil', President PW Botha, would go on SABC radio and television to declare the country's first (partial) State of Emergency in 25 years. The last State of Emergency had been declared after the Sharpeville massacre on 21 March 1960, a day that would prove one of the darkest in the country's history. Sixty-nine black people were shot and killed during a protest march against apartheid-era pass laws. An estimated 180 others were injured in the senseless and wanton violence meted out by the police.

The 1985 State of Emergency started in 36 of the country's 260 magisterial districts. The vast majority of the districts were in the Eastern Cape and included Cradock and its surrounding towns, Cookhouse, Somerset East, Graaff-Reinet, Steytlerville, Hofmeyr, Grahamstown, Port Alfred, Tarkastad, Bedford, and Adelaide. It included districts in the Witwatersrand and the Vaal Triangle (these areas are now part of Gauteng).

So, who was Fort Calata? What was it about his death alongside that of Matthew Goniwe, Sparro Mkonto, and Sicelo Mhlawuli that led to such anger, militancy, and large-scale defiance of the brutal apartheid government from South Africa's oppressed people?

ABIGAIL

As much as this book is an attempt to tell Fort Calata's story, it's also an attempt to get to know the man. In my quest to uncover my father-in-law's history, I listened intently to all the stories that would give insight into what kind of person he was. The longing Lukhanyo and I share to know the sound of his voice, how his singing voice differed from his speaking voice, what he smelled like, how firm his handshake was, or what he would have look like aged 60, will never be satisfied in this life. This realisation weighs heavy on my soul, and I can't begin to know what this truth over three decades does to the people who loved Fort and then lost him in such a brutal way.

At four years old, Kwezi is at an age when he's starting to grapple with the concept of death. He and Lukhanyo went to the grave on a recent visit to Cradock. He asked Lukhanyo, 'Do you know what killed Fort?' And proceeded to answer this question with, 'The apartheid killed Fort.' Lukhanyo and I were both surprised by this answer, and both of us assumed the other had given him an answer similar to this when Kwezi asked that question. But he'd come up with it himself. Neither of us had ever heard that question from him before, nor provided an answer resembling anything like that.

Kwezi also wanted to know from me whether Fort was with God in heaven. I told him yes, he was. He wanted to know whether heaven was a place where one 'saw God for real'. I told him, yes, that is what you can expect, and this seemed to really please him.

By all accounts, Fort Daniel Nqaba Calata was a remarkable person. As a child he was introverted, but not unfriendly, and a bit of a clown. His late sister Peggy described him as, 'talkative. He liked to joke around. He was nice to us, but he also liked to spend time by himself.'

Fort, his two sisters, Sisana and Peggy, as well as his brothers, Patutu (Patrick) and Roy, grew up with their cousins Mandisa, Gangumzi, Bangilizwe (Bangi), Nonthuthuzelo (Ntutu), and Nomzi. Their grandparents, James and Miltha Calata, raised all of them as their own children, while their mothers, Nontsikelelo, Vuyelwa, and Noluthando, were working outside of Cradock.

His cousin Bangi Solo remembered him as a 'somewhat sickly baby' who comforted the family after they lost baby Joy, Peggy's twin sister. For Peggy, Fort filled the void left by the passing on of her twin: 'Fort was very important in my life because he was my *imfusi* [the child born after twins]. In Xhosa culture, if one of the twins dies, the child who's born after that must take the place of the late twin. That is how close I felt to him. You must also bear in mind how close we were in age. I was born in July 1955. Fort was born in 1956. We were, however, very different. I am an extrovert, while he was an introvert,' she said.

LUKHANYO

The little boy who would one day become my father was born on the morning of 5 November 1956 to Nontsikelelo Gertrude Calata and Macdonald Maphike. He was their third child, born just over one year after twins, Peggy and Joy. Joy died while only a few months old. Nontsikelelo – or Sis' Ntsiki as she was known – and Macdonald were not married, but lived together in Sophiatown, a vibrant black suburb just outside Johannesburg's city centre. Both the little boy's parents were musicians. Sis' Ntsiki was a classically trained pianist, while my grandfather, Mac, was a gifted tenor saxophonist. Both, I am told, also sang quite well and played for several bands and groups in the area at the time. But under apartheid (and I guess even today), very few black couples could raise a family on musicians' wages. So, my grandmother kept her day job as a primary school teacher, which provided the family with a steady income.

A few weeks after his birth, Sis' Ntsiki took her newborn along when she visited her father, Canon James Arthur Calata, in detention. He had

47

been arrested and was held at the Old Fort Prison on charges of high treason alongside 155 other anti-apartheid leaders. Among them were the likes of Yusuf Dadoo, Ruth First, Archibald Gumede, iNkosi Albert Luthuli, Nelson Mandela, Professor ZK Matthews, Vuyisile Mini, Lilian Ngoyi, Reginald September, Walter Sisulu, Joe Slovo, and Oliver Tambo.

It was during this visit when her father, or Tatou, as he was known by the family and the community of Cradock, named his new grandson Fort – adding that, like a fort, the young boy would become the strength of the family.

During this visit, Tatou also expressed his unhappiness regarding the family's situation in Sophiatown. Just a year before, Sophiatown had been declared a white area under the Group Areas Act. By November 1956, when my father was born, the government had started its forced removals programme. Its bulldozers had moved into the suburb and had already begun demolishing families' lives, dreams, and aspirations alongside their homes, schools, clinics, and other community structures and amenities.

This was not the life Tatou had wanted for his daughter and, more particularly, his latest grandson. I suspect the fact that Sis' Ntsiki wasn't married to Macdonald also weighed heavily on him; he was after all an Anglican priest. So, just days after their visit, he arranged for a group of Anglican clergymen to transport his daughter and her newborn son to the relative safety and peace of their home in Cradock. Here, Sis' Ntsiki was eagerly awaited by her mother, Miltha Mary Calata, or Mamou as she was affectionately called. It's unclear how many times the young Fort would see his father again, if at all, after this hastily arranged relocation to Cradock.

Tatou remained in prison for at least another year as the apartheid state prepared to prosecute him and his fellow detainees on charges of high treason. He was eventually released alongside OR Tambo, iNkosi Luthuli, and about 70 others in December 1957, due to a lack of evidence against them. Shortly after this release, OR Tambo went into exile. My great-grandfather returned home to his family, church, and community in Cradock. Fort's cousins and siblings, my aunts and uncles, had over the years told me how energised Tatou was by having a baby in the house. By the late Fifties, Tatou was serving as senior chaplain on the

ANC's National Executive Committee. Walter Sisulu had succeeded him as secretary-general of the movement at the Bloemfontein National Conference in December 1949.

Despite his on-going health issues, family and community members in Cradock recalled that all Tatou ever seemed to do was work. Almost everybody we spoke to talked about the formidable organiser he was. One of these people was Mbulelo Goniwe, a childhood friend of my father's and Matthew Goniwe's nephew. I asked him what his impressions were of Tatou as he and Fort were growing up in Cradock's old location. After a long pause, he said to me, 'Tatou was the true embodiment of humanity. He was someone who loved children, who, despite being this well-respected person, often spent time talking to the youth, particularly about our education.'

Mbulelo recalled that at some stage Tatou owned a blue Ford Anglia, and that he and Fort had on more than one occasion had the privilege to accompany Tatou when he visited schools on several farms around Cradock. He said, 'Tatou did not distinguish between his ministry and political work. Tatou also had a deep faith in future generations.' Bhut' Mbu, as I call him, then cited an example of the kind of attention Tatou would give to youngsters in Cradock: 'Tatou would often stop to speak to us youngsters, and in the course of that conversation he would ask one of us whether we had eaten. I found him to be someone who had a genuine love for humanity and righteousness.'

This description of Tatou is corroborated by author Stanley Manong. In his book, *If We Must Die*, Manong writes of Tatou, 'He was revered by everybody and became a people's priest in the literal sense.'[2]

To the Anglican Church, however, Tatou's duality – as a priest and politician – was a major concern. Bishop Archibald Cullen, based in Grahamstown, wrote to him on several occasions in a bid to have him scale down his political activities. Tatou, it's said, would politely disagree and decline each time. Despite his busy schedule, Tatou took a keen interest in the upbringing of the young Fort. Mamou was very encouraging of this, as it meant her husband was spending more time at home than usual.

---

2   Manong, S. 2015. *If We Must Die*. Nkululeko Publishers: Johannesburg.

According to Fort's cousin Bangi, they (the children) had to get used to seeing Tatou at home more often. Although Tatou was still working as hard as ever, he began to take meetings, mostly political, at home. Bangi added, 'This meant a change in routine for everybody, especially us, the children. With Tatou at home, Mamou was stricter than usual. She demanded silence above all, so we didn't disturb Tatou while he worked.'

ABIGAIL

Fort was perhaps the first of what I've come to term the Calata sons of favour, a status he shared with his son, Lukhanyo, and grandson, Kwezi. I became aware of this phenomenon after Kwezi's birth in 2012. Our research revealed that from very early on Fort established himself as Tatou's favourite – a fact confirmed by both Peggy and Bangi.

'Fort was Tatou's favourite because of that calmness. Parents will always have their favourite,' explained Peggy. Fort was also the lucky recipient of any food that was left over on Tatou's plate after dinner. And Bangi's sister, Mandisa, surreptitiously passed her meat to Fort at meal-times. She didn't like meat and had an agreement with Fort that he would eat her meat. Mamou expected the children to eat all the food on their plates and therefore the cousins had to pass the meat secretly under the table.

Peggy remembered that Fort was the only one of the grandchildren who was allowed, to some extent, to interrogate Tatou's decisions and teachings. Peggy cited several incidents of Fort's pushing the envelope at times and posing rather difficult questions directed at his grandfather regarding the Scriptures they read at evening devotions or in church. Tatou always engaged Fort earnestly in debate, much to the annoyance of the older children, who were forced to sit at the table until Fort had asked the last of his 'many, many questions'.

One such debate started when Fort questioned Tatou about a statement he'd attributed to Jesus in his Easter Sunday sermon. Peggy recalled, 'Fort said to Tatou, "I do not understand when you say, when they crucified Jesus Christ, it is written, *Father, forgive them for they know not what they do.* Because that [the crucifixion] was planned."

'We were part of these arguments. Tatou would try to convince Fort of the way things were. Fort would say, "The bottom line here, Tatou, is that they planned and it was well planned, so it was not accidental. And for you to stand in front of the congregation and say, *Because they know not what they do*, I think there is something amiss there."

'That drew him closer to Tatou. We wouldn't talk to Tatou like that. We'd tell Fort, "You can't talk to Tatou like that," but Fort said, "I want to get to the bottom of this because Tatou stood there and said, *They know not what they were doing.*"'

Of course, Fort was emboldened to question his grandfather like that because of the close relationship they had. This story also illustrates his bright, questioning mind. He didn't take things at face value, even that which he heard from the pulpit, despite the reverence he had for the church and priest, who was both his spiritual and earthly father.

Sitting with Tatou while he worked or played the piano was a privilege none of the other children was afforded. Bangi explained, 'Fort would just vanish, only for us to find him quite close to Tatou. He was a very quiet child and that's what he used to do. Whenever Tatou was around, Fort vanished.' At these times, Fort would be right there next to Tatou. He would just sit there listening, watching attentively, and trying to sing along as Tatou's hands moved up and down the piano keys. Tatou would play and sing his original compositions or traditional church hymns. I can only imagine how the young Fort must have been musically educated and inspired by watching his grandfather during those moments.

Bangi added, 'You know my grandmother was very strict. She didn't want us to disturb Tatou because he was doing so many things, but Fort would find space [in close proximity to Tatou] and she eventually grew to accept that.'

The favour Fort enjoyed extended beyond the walls of his (grand)-parental home. Fort's arrival in Cradock as a baby coincided with a growing hope in the community that Tatou would be released from prison and everything would turn out fine. 'When Fort first arrived from Johannesburg, community members came around [regularly] to hear the latest news regarding Tatou. That is why almost everyone had this attention for Fort all the time. Everyone, we all, had a very soft spot for Fort,' said Bangi.

He went on to explain that their (the grandchildren's) love for music was a direct result of Tatou's love for music. 'Every day Tatou came home for lunch and before he left he always played either the organ or the piano. That was how music came into our home. Because of Tatou, Fort started playing too. He went deeper and deeper into music, and by virtue of his being close to Tatou, I think he was like, "I must do everything this old man is doing," to the extent that we all thought that one day he would also become a priest. Our nickname for him was Archdeacon.'

A childhood neighbour and family friend Sarie Miles (née Smith) remembered how Fort, shortly after starting at primary school, began to play piano. 'He'd say, "Sarie, *kom speel* [come and play]."' These play dates would happen mostly on Sunday afternoons once Tatou and Mamou had gone on home visits. She said Fort would sit at the piano and imitate Tatou, playing and trying to sing the very songs his grandfather did. She vividly remembered how the young Fort displayed musical talent back then already.

Sarie recalled it was Fort's gentleness that drew her to him. They used to play a game where boys and girls would pair off. She always chose Fort as her partner. 'He was such a gentle person. He was the gentlest of them all. He understood me,' she said, smiling to herself.

Like his father, Lukhanyo is also a son of favour. I make this statement because of the obvious respect he commands in the family despite being among its younger members. Dorothy, who attended Peggy's memorial service with Lukhanyo in September 2017, told me, 'Afterwards, we got together with all the cousins, who came to Cradock for the memorial. Everyone wanted to greet and be acknowledged by Lukhanyo – or *ubhuti* as he is affectionately referred to in the family. It had nothing to do with his being on television or even the SABC 8 saga, and everything to do with the esteem in which he is held in the family.'

He hardly notices it – and if he does, he pays it no heed. Yet even older people outside of the family harbour a deep respect for him. He approaches people, both young and old, with great deference, and most times they reciprocate this respect even when they have never met him before and don't know anything about him. It is quite something for me to behold, as the only people I've experienced being treated this way are clergymen.

Lukhanyo is Nomonde's favourite, and his sisters, like Fort's cousins before them, accept this fact with grace. I asked her once whether it was more a joy or pain to have a son who resembles his father in so many ways. She answered that having Lukhanyo has brought her more comfort, but that there are some moments when the pain of her loss is felt more acutely because of him. One of those times was the day of his graduation. 'On that day he looked more like his father than he normally does. Also, when he got to the stage, he walked to the microphone to correct the pronunciation of his surname. I thought Fort would have done exactly the same,' she said, recalling the pride and pain that pierced her heart at that moment.

As Lukhanyo's wife, I too find myself on the receiving end of much favour from the Calatas. My mother-in-law completely embraces and loves me like her own. I am humbled by the high regard with which she and her daughters hold me and can only hope I don't ever disappoint them, and, in doing so, lose that regard.

With all this favour surrounding us as a couple, favour upon Kwezi is inevitable. This favour is evident in the delight he elicits from my mother-in-law, her daughters, and their children. I expected Lukhanyo and me to delight in our son, but nothing prepared me for the pure delight Nomonde and her daughters find in him.

Tumani (my younger sister-in-law) would use the fact that she witnessed his birth to justify this reaction to her much-loved and cherished nephew. I once caught Dorothy casting a long, adoring look at Kwezi, who was busy with one of his favourite pastimes, drawing and watching television at the same time. Later, when I mentioned my observations concerning the Calata sons of favour, she drew my attention to that very look earlier. When I asked what had caused it, she answered, 'Kwezi is a Calata in all the ways that really matter. Not only because he is Lukhanyo's son, but also because he embodies the best of the Calata qualities. He is extraordinarily bright. I love how he reasons and questions things even at this young age. He's talkative, like me. Why should I not delight in him? He is my brother's son in every way – physically and in character.'

If Kwezi and his father are alike, Lukhanyo and his father are even more so. In the process of writing this book, I've come to greatly respect the Calata intellect. When speaking of the years at the Mission House in iLingelihle, and Tatou and Mamou's persecution by the apartheid state, Peggy mentioned that as the children of so-called troublemakers, they did not have it easy at school: 'The only thing that served us was that we were clever – we did our school work well,' she explained.

Lukhanyo and his sisters are indeed very clever, but I believe they got it from both parents. Peggy remembered the time Tatou promised he would slaughter a sheep for each child who came first in their class. By then, the older cousins had left the house and there were only four of them staying with Tatou and Mamou. They were Peggy, Fort, their youngest brother, Roy, and cousin Ntutu. 'We all knew that Fort would be the one [for whom the sheep would be slaughtered]. He was at the same time very calculating and plotted against Tatou.

'He told us, "What if all of us came first? What would Tatou do if we all [obtained] first place? Would those sheep come? So, let's try it." That year, myself, Fort, and Ntutu came first in our respective classes and three sheep were slaughtered. We knew then we could take Tatou at his word.'

Peggy also mentioned that Mamou's strict rules did not bother Fort too much. Being an introvert, he didn't care to socialise outside of the house. This lack of interest in the outside world and people was not something he shared with his cousins and siblings, who very much longed to be part of the world beyond the four walls of their home. 'There used to be what was called an afternoon spend [a dance for young people] in the [church] hall. We wanted to go there to show off our beautiful dresses, but we were not allowed to. Fort would be in the [bed]room reading. If he was not reading the Bible, he was reading his school books. We would try to convince Mamou [to let us go] because now we have finished our housework, but Mamou would hand us the Bible, saying we would never be finished with it. Fort would then laugh at us and say, "Come join me." We were not impressed with him. If he wanted to be alone and close himself off in a room, let him be. We wanted to mingle with other children.'

Over the years, Tatou acquired several musical instruments and encouraged his grandchildren not only to learn to play them, but also to form a family band. Fort of course took this wish – and his interest in music – quite seriously.

'Fort would never get out of the garage, where the instruments were,' said Bangi. 'If he was not on the keyboard, he was playing the guitar. When he was not playing the guitar, he was on the bass or the drums. He was teaching himself [to play]. There were some guys who at a later stage were helping him, but for most parts he taught himself.'

'We mostly taught ourselves to play the instruments,' added Peggy. 'Fort was solitary. He liked spending time by himself. Sometimes Mamou would just decide, "Let us bring him food right there," because it was useless to try and get him out of the garage.'

Bangi remembered that, though Fort was proficient on all the instruments, the keyboard remained his favourite. 'Fort and Bhut' Gangumzi were gifted singers. Sometimes they would fight about who would sing. Peggy also sang. Patutu and myself used to buy LPs on an almost weekly basis. American soul was popular back then – the kind of music you'll hear these days on Saturdays and Sundays on [Radio] 702.'

Michael Allens, better known as Oom Kallie, was among those who played with Fort in the late Seventies and early Eighties. The band was called The Survivors. Oom Kallie was the lead vocalist with Fort on the piano. He recalled, 'Fort, in most cases, was a better singer and player than other band members. He didn't lord that over us, though, and was content to play whatever instrument he was required to play.'

The band that preceded The Survivors was The Heartbreakers, which was made up of musicians from the black township, whom Fort auditioned before they could join. According to a former band member Zolile Kota, also known as Zorro, the band practised quite religiously every afternoon after school.

Fort ended up becoming Tatou's right-hand man. All the boys in the family were expected to serve as altar boys in the church, with Fort being the only one who stuck with it even after all his cousins and brother, Roy, had bowed out. Bangi elaborated, 'He knew at which farm Tatou was going to preach this Sunday and the next. He was like Tatou's PA. That was his focus and his music. He was a very orderly person.'

Fort even exhibited a tolerance for the white archdeacon who served with them, which his fellow altar boys did not share. 'We had this attitude toward whites, and the archdeacon was a white person, [called] Heath. Now Fort was the only one who understood Heath, and sometimes we would just rebel and say, "No, we are not going to perform our service as choir boys. We are not going to dress up and help him in the altar." It would be only Fort who was always willing to be there with Heath,' said Bangi.

LUKHANYO

The relationship between grandfather and grandson grew stronger as Fort got older. He was a willing and receptive student, learning everything he could from the old man – be it music, politics, religion, or Xhosa culture and tradition. It didn't matter; he soaked up everything. Everyone I spoke to agreed that Tatou was more a father than grandfather to Fort.

Bhut' Mbu confirmed that Tatou and Fort were close. He said by the time he and Fort were teenagers, they had some sense of Tatou's prominence in the ANC and that he was under constant surveillance from the police. So they, the young men of iLingelihle – and Fort in particular – were constantly at Tatou's side. They believed nobody would harm Tatou in their presence. He chuckled softly when he recalled that they would have been unable to offer any physical resistance were there to have been an attempt on Tatou's life in their presence. He added that as Fort grew up he became Tatou's bodyguard.

Bhut' Mbu was also convinced that these years at Tatou's side served as my father's political education, when he was groomed by Tatou to take over the political leadership in the community. He described Fort as being very secretive about politics. He believed this stemmed from my father's understanding that the ANC was a banned organisation and therefore conversations about the movement or politics were only allowed under specific conditions.

Fort's close relationship with his grandfather also had a rather undesirable consequence. On numerous occasions, he witnessed the brutality of the South African Police. As a former secretary-general of the ANC, Tatou, as you can imagine, was a rather high-profile target, particularly for the conservative or *verkrampte* whites in a small Karoo town like Cradock. Tatou had run-ins with the police on an almost daily basis and Fort was, more often than not, the only witness to this constant harassment over a long period.

Despite this, I think, it must have been wonderful for the young Fort to receive his political education and moorings from his grandfather, a man who would later be described as 'one of the greatest sons of Africa'[3]. I often wonder if it was a conscious decision by both my father and his grandfather, or if it was fate that led to Fort's being the one who would be handed the baton by his grandfather.

I've come to learn so much more about my father in the last few months. For instance, that he liked to suck his thumb as a young boy. That as a teenager he preferred to spend time with his grandfather than his friends. I've learnt that, much like me, he too never really had a relationship with his own father, but unlike me, he at least had a tremendous father figure in his grandfather.

As I learn and discover more about my father, I realise that in order for me to understand his character (his motivations, his ambitions, his fears, and shortcomings), in order to tell his story completely, I have to take a step back and tell the story of his grandparents James Arthur and Miltha Mary Calata.

Tatou and Mamou were the foundations upon which the family – not just Fort – built their political activism. This is their story.

---

3   Duka, Dr MM. 2011. *Canon James Arthur Calata: A Biography of One of the Greatest Sons of Africa*. Khoi Publishers: Queenstown.

Chapter Three
Moorings of a Leader

LUKHANYO

James Arthur Calata (Tatou) was born on 22 June 1895 to James and Eliza Calata. His parents were simple rural folk, descendants of the Ngqika tribe, and lived in the village of Emoyeni, near Debe Nek, southeast of Ntaba kaNdoda in the district of King William's Town, in what is now known as the Eastern Cape. His father was a peasant farmer, while his mother practised as a midwife. James Snr was Presbyterian and Eliza Anglican. James Snr is said to have displayed exceptional intellect, despite having had no formal education, while Eliza had reached standard four[4].

Shortly after James Jr's birth, the family – who already had an elder son, Alfred – moved to the nearby village of Rabhula, where his paternal grandfather was an evangelist of the Independent Presbyterian Church. It's here where James Jr was baptised around October 1895 by the Reverend Bryce Ross at Pirie Church.

James Jr began his schooling at Rabhula's Ngudle Primary School, where he attended up to and including standard two. From there, he moved to St Barnabas Primary School, where he attended up to and including standard five. Around this time, the young James Calata is said to have already displayed a heart and yearning for the ministry, particularly in the Anglican Church.

His elder brother, Alfred, had helped blaze the trail for his secondary education. He had previously won a scholarship to attend St Matthew's High School. James Jr would follow in Alfred's footsteps, winning the same scholarship to be educated at St Matthew's. The scholarship was

---

4   Verwey, EJ (ed.). 1995. *New Dictionary of South African Biography*, Volume 1. HSRC Publishers: Pretoria.

awarded by the Society for the Propagation of the Gospel in Foreign Parts (SPG), an overseas missionary organisation of the Church of England.

St Matthew's, which boasted a renowned teacher training college, was at the time under the leadership of Rev William Palmer. Rev Francis Binyon was the warden of the college. In 1911, James Jr was awarded the Reverend Maneli prize for the highest marks that year in arithmetic. That same year, he was confirmed, admitted into the church choir, and began to serve in the church. In 1912, he wrote and passed 'the prescribed Examination in Musical Memory, in time, in tune, and in Sight Singing' and was awarded the elementary award by the Tonic Sol-fa College[5]. At the age of nineteen, in 1914, he graduated top of his class when he obtained a first-class pass in the third-year pupil teachers' examination.

During this time, James had shown a particular fondness for playing sports, with cricket and football his sports of choice. As a cricketer, he was an all-rounder: he could bowl reasonably well and batted sixth in his team line-up. It's a pity I couldn't get hold of any bowling or batting statistics, though; it would be fun for me to compare figures from back then with today.

In January 1915, a now 20-year-old James Arthur Calata began his teaching career when he was appointed as an assistant teacher at the St Matthew's Practising School for the standard four class. He taught this class for two years until December 1916. In January 1917, he received a slight promotion – if you could call it that – when he began to teach the standard five class, again spending two years with this class. In this period, under the supervision of Mr Farrington, the music inspector, he arranged the boys in the standard five class into an all-boys' choir which, within a matter of months, went on to win several choral music competitions in and around the region. Later that year, following the departure of Father AW Norton from the school, James was appointed the school's choir master. This was the first time a black person was entrusted with this responsibility[6].

---

5   Rev James Arthur CALATA Papers 1909–1974. University of the Witwatersrand.
6   Calata Papers. Cory Library, Rhodes University.

The years 1917–18 marked two significant events in James's life. The first was his courting of a beautiful young woman named Miltha Mary Koboka, who had previously been one of his pupils. The other significant event was his taking up studies as a private student in theology. He had earlier passed his section G in 1916[7].

On 26 December 1918, at just 23 years old, James and Miltha married. Earlier that year he had passed the Third Class Senior Teachers' Course under the guidance of Mrs Dowthwaite and Mr WP Corry, who had helped him in mathematics and physics. Another promotion followed in January 1919, when he began teaching the standard six class. On 8 October that same year, the young couple welcomed their first child, a little girl they christened Nontsikelelo Gertrude Calata. Shortly after the birth of their first child, James, while representing St Matthew's in a cricket game played at Fort Hare University, was struck in the face by a ball that he was fielding. Fortunately for him, a Dr Mcvicar was at that game and quickly attended to his injury. Although he avoided any serious damage, the incident left a deep cut just above his left eye. Also in 1919, James joined the Cape Native Voters' Convention, an organisation comprising middle-class Africans who wanted to extend the voting rights of Africans to other areas beyond the Cape Province. This is the first evidence I could find that points to his political outlook and views. It seems to have been an issue which he deeply cared about.

Halfway through 1920, James enrolled at the theological school alongside Arthur Magabela and David Nxele, and by June 1921, he was ordained as deacon at St Andrew's in Queenstown. A month later, in July 1921, James was back in class. But things were a bit different the second time around. Not only was he now teaching both standard five and six classes, he had also been promoted to school principal and was transferred to St Cyprian's Higher Mission School in Korsten, Port Elizabeth. The city and a new adventure beckoned, so he and his young family set off towards its bright lights.

St Cyprian's, however, proved to be a work in progress. There were

---

7   Section G: foundational teaching on some basic theological categories in scripture, including the doctrine of God, God in Christ, the Holy Ghost, the church, and the end times from an Apostolic perspective.

just three teachers at the school when my great-grandfather arrived and no mention of any kind of extra-curricular activities. James and his family took a few weeks to settle down in the new environment. As soon as he had done so, he began to put a school choir together, followed by the St Cyprian's Cricket Club. The choir was ready to perform within a few short weeks. And almost as soon as it was ready, James began to organise concerts and arrange for the choir to perform at other events to raise funds first to build St Cyprian's Church and then its mission house.

Throughout this time, though, James's heart yearned for the ministry. It had been a boyhood dream ever since he began duties as a server in the church. In her study of my great-grandfather, Professor Mary Goedhals writes, 'As a young boy James would dress up in his mother's dresses and with Bible in hand preach to the family goats'[8]. He would begin the journey to realise that dream at the age of 27, when he began his ministry in 1922 as an assistant missionary at the St Stephen's Mission in Korsten. This complemented his term as principal at St Cyprian's. In the same year, he also celebrated the birth of his second daughter, Vuyelwa Mary Calata.

In time, and with the assistance of Canon Matoyo, the rector at St Mary's, James obtained permission from the city council for concerts to be hosted at the city hall, which would be attended by both black and white audiences. It was at one such concert, this time held at the Feather Market Hall, which was attended by over 40 different schools under the inspectorate of a Mr Bennie, that the St Cyprian's choir distinguished itself. It performed an original composition by a Ms Exley from Port Elizabeth. Mr Bennie, the Chief Inspector of African Schools at the time, was so impressed with my great-grandfather's St Cyprian's choir that he later visited the school for a private audience[9].

Throughout this time, James continued to write music, both his own as well as reproducing some of the hymns already sung in church. In 1923, he sent Canon Wyche of the Diocese of Grahamstown manu-

---

8   Rev James Arthur CALATA Papers 1909–1974. University of the Witwatersrand.
9   Calata Papers. Cory Library, Rhodes University.

scripts of some of the music he had been writing. In the accompanying letter, he wrote:

'Dear Sir

I am sending you the manuscripts which I desire to be published with the few hymn-tunes.

I enclose two other pieces which we used to sing at St Matthew's, one at the end of the Holy Communion Service and the other at the end of Matins. The aim of the manuscripts is to encourage tune-making with a view to improvising our hymn-tunes in future. It is not to make a new hymn-tune book of my own. I believe you will, after reading my manuscripts, find that, although my compositions are not worthy of any praise yet for the sake of the aims stated above, they are worth seeing.

It is such a pity that Revd Bokwe is dead for he is the man I was dealing with in this matter. I enclose an old copy by his own handwriting where he shows the absurdity of singing hymns with unfitting tunes.

I know that Father Norton, although a strong supporter of mine as far as theory is concerned, may not agree with my tunes, as he does not understand modern music in tonic sol-fa, nor does he care for harmonics music. He is for Gregorian music and plain song. Mr James Rodger, I believe may support me, though I never consulted him. Father Willis would strongly support me if he were here. I need not mention Canon Binyon, for he so strongly encouraged me at St Matthew's that he allowed me to run the whole of the Church Xosa Music entirely on my own lines. Archdeacon Mather and Canon Wyche are my backbone and I fear nothing.

I know the Lordship has very deep sympathy with the matter and if occasion arose he would support me and, as Mr Matoyo says in his letter that I am enclosing (not for publication), many other natives who cannot express themselves. I am, dear Canon,

Yours in Music
James A Calata

PS. If the church after counting the cost finds that it will not benefit by these manuscripts, I shan't mind having them returned to me, as what I am doing is not for my glory at all but for the Glory of God and His Kingdom.'

The years in Port Elizabeth would prove quite productive for the young Calata family. Among the notable accomplishments during this period is a paper he presented to the Cape African Teachers' conference in 1924 in which he also argued quite strongly for the importance of teaching African songs and hymns. Socially, the family was thriving in Port Elizabeth, but the high-humidity climate wreaked havoc with James's health. During this time in the coastal city, he contracted tuberculosis (TB). In the early stages of his illness, he was forced to slow down, and while this was probably inconvenient for a man like my great-grandfather, who was always thinking of the next item to tick off on his to-do list, it did mean he spent a lot more time at home with his family and on his theology studies. Although he eventually recovered, the TB left him susceptible to infections of the chest.

On Trinity Sunday, 30 May 1926, after serving five years as a deacon in the city, James Arthur Calata was ordained as priest with Rev Richard Beer in the Cathedral Church of St Michael and St George by the Right Rev Francis Robinson Phelps of Grahamstown. Canon AH Cullen, the then warden of St Paul's Theological College, conducted the retreat, which prepared them for ordination. During rehearsals for the ceremony, James had noticed how the choir had struggled with their rehearsals of the hymns, so he offered to assist. His ordination as reverend of the Anglican Church was a big deal for him. He had dreamt of this moment almost all his life, and I imagine he would have wanted it to be perfect – or at least as close to that as is humanly possible. He ditched the hymns the choir was battling with and instead asked them to learn a new set of hymns. These included ones he had composed, as well as older hymns to which he had made slight alterations to the usual or Western tonic sol-fa. The new hymns, some translated, were written in two-, three-, and four-pulse measures with the emphasis on the penultimate syllable. Music scholars and even the church recognised that, at the time, this was quite a departure from the accepted way of composing and performing hymns. The different rhythms of his compositions felt more natural to the predominantly black choir. The rhythms were reminiscent of old African folk songs, which the choir responded to with much enthusiasm[10].

---

10 Calata Papers. Cory Library, Rhodes University.

The day of his ordination was one of the proudest days of James Arthur Calata's life. He had fulfilled his boyhood dream. He was finally an Anglican priest, ready to serve his Creator and his community wherever that might be.

Sadly, James's ordination as a priest meant he would now be lost to full-time teaching. But the church had gained an energetic and very eager servant. Within a few weeks following his ordination, the church transferred the young priest to his first appointment, that of St Ninian's in Somerset East about 180 km northeast of Port Elizabeth. Before leaving the city, however, he and his wife welcomed their third and last child. She too was a little girl, whom they christened Noluthando Mary Elizabeth Calata. Shortly after the birth and just five years after arriving in Port Elizabeth, the young family packed up all their belongings and headed for the town of Somerset East in the Karoo.

Here, the family would spend the next two years. Despite the brevity of their stay in the little farming town, James was said to have been deeply distressed by the living conditions of farm labourers. In 1927, exasperated and desperate to try to address the problem, he organised a conference of the local Vigilance Associations. He also invited ad-hoc bodies representing mostly middle-class Africans in the surrounding towns to lobby their municipalities. The aim of the conference was to force Somerset East's municipality to address the dire living conditions of the impoverished farm workers. The conference later published a statement criticising the poverty that prevailed among the African community[11].

James's health during this period wasn't robust. Although he had left the high humidity of the coastal city behind, the biting cold and dust of the Karoo town wreaked havoc in his chest. So, on the advice of his doctor, the family would be on the move again shortly after arriving in Somerset East.

In a hand-written document, which James had titled 'A Brief History of Churches and Schools in Cradock', he writes: 'My first visit to Cradock

---

11 Tetelman, M. 2012. *We Can! Black Politics in Cradock, South Africa, 1948-85.* Rhodes University: Grahamstown.

(apart from sport) was when a doctor at Somerset East advised me to recuperate at Cradock after a serious attack of pneumonia. I came in February 1928 and stayed here until the end of April. The first month at the Mission House, under Rev. Joe Solilo and later transferred to Mrs Nomanezi Xhallie's house in Mafeking Street. In July 1928 at the suggestion of Rev. Solilo, I was transferred to Cradock when he left for Uitenhage.'[12]

James's arrival in Cradock at the age of 32 is fondly remembered by several community members. Yet, it doesn't seem that his new station made a very good first impression. He writes: 'The Anglican Mission Church was a small tin building used as a church and school, so old that its walls were supported by wooden poles.'[13]

Patrick Mali, a retired school inspector, was one of those who remembered the family's arrival well. The others with memories of that time were Midas Mbuzwana and Nowi Nomavuka. They too are retired teachers. It is inevitable that in Cradock, being the small town it is, I would have come across and even had personal relationships with all three of these people for as long as I can remember. Mr Mali, Ms Mbuzwana, and Ms Nomavuka were Anglican and had attended Tatou's last church, the Church of the Ascension, for several decades. That's where I knew them from – or, should I say, where they knew me from, since I was just a little boy when I first encountered them. Ms Mbuzwana, in fact, had known me for even longer. I was childhood friends with her son, Viwe, who was just a few months older than me. They were our neighbours in Siyabulela Street, iLingelihle. They lived at house number 26, and we at number 30. I doubt many people in the township knew Viwe by his real name; everyone called him by his nickname, 'Porro'. My dear friend, whom I had known practically since we were babies, unfortunately passed away in his early twenties, after a brief illness.

I really wanted to speak in person to Mr Mali and to the two ladies among others. I thought they'd help us piece together the family's arrival and their early years in Cradock. Mr Mali had since moved out

---

12 Rev James Arthur CALATA Papers 1909–1974. University of the Witwatersrand.
13 Ibid.

of Cradock and there was no way of our getting in contact with him – at least it seemed that way. Some would ascribe my chance meeting with Mr Mali in Johannesburg a few days after I had first heard that he no longer lived in Cradock to coincidence, but not me. I don't believe in co-incidences. Coincidence implies the absence of God's will and plan. And, as far as I know, God is omnipresent. So when I ran into Mr Mali and his daughter, Nompilo, outside a restaurant at the Campus Square shopping centre in Auckland Park, shortly after landing in Johannesburg one Sunday morning, I knew immediately that both God and Tatou had ordained this moment. Abigail and I were indeed meant to interview him for this book and subsequent documentary film.

It had been several years since I had last seen him and, although he had aged remarkably well, I was still very proud of myself for having spotted and recognised him. He, of course, had no idea who I was when I approached him. I introduced myself and watched his face light up when I told him I was Fort's son. This revelation was followed by an almighty hug from the old man. I then told him what we were doing in Johannesburg and asked whether we could meet with him for an interview for our book and documentary film. He agreed, and we eventually sat down with him in his home a few days later. When Abigail and I met with him that Wednesday afternoon, it had been at least four months since he'd buried his wife to whom he had been married for over 70 years. Her grave is in Cradock. Mr Mali was now living with his daughters in a beautiful home in Melville. Other than the use of hearing-aids, he looked in good health despite being just four years shy of 100 years.

He was born on 10 September 1921 in Cradock. Although he could no longer recall exact dates and details, I was deeply humbled by his memories of the excitement in his family at the arrival of the new Anglican priest, Rev James Arthur Calata. Mr Mali remembered that he was just a child barely of school-going age then. It was a simple memory, but to me it meant the world. As I sat in front of this old man, I knew right away that I was in the presence of someone who would in his own words help me bring to life the story of my family's genesis in the town of Cradock.

Mr Mali then surprised me with the memory of his first one-on-one encounter with my great-grandfather. In fact, he said it did not even take place in Cradock. The first day they spoke was when he was a pupil in the small missionary outpost of Golden Valley nestled in between Cookhouse and Somerset East just south of Cradock. Mr Mali attended the St Dennis missionary school Tatou had started during the family's brief stay in Somerset East a few years previously. He still regularly visited the school, which had just one teacher who taught from sub-A to standard four. Mr Mali recalled how Tatou would sit in on classes whenever he visited. During these brief meetings, Tatou would request an update on the teacher's health and school requirements. Mr Mali also remembered how Tatou would encourage all the boys to join Boy Scout groups in the area, and that my great-grandfather was elected divisional commissioner of the Scouts. He oversaw the Karoo region, an area stretching from Port Elizabeth to De Aar, Fort Beaufort, Tarkastad, Cradock, Hofmeyr, all the way up to Noupoort.

As he was from Cradock, Mr Mali headed home during the school holidays. While at home, he served as an usher in Tatou's church for many years. I asked him what his childhood impressions were of Tatou. And almost without thinking, he said, 'Tatou was a wonderful, wonderful man. A man who never got tired. He wanted everything he did to be perfect. He treasured excellence.'

Mr Mali remembered fondly how he wanted to be just like Tatou when he grew up. So when he heard that the young priest had been a teacher before he swapped the classroom for the pulpit, that's exactly what the young boy set out to emulate. In Tatou, he had found a role model.

Tatou deeply valued education, Mr Mali said, and always encouraged him and many others in the community to take their education seriously. He would often be invited to speak at schools around the location, where he'd use the opportunity not only to encourage the youth regarding their studies but also to spread the gospel. Again, I found confirmation of this in Manong's book, *If We Must Die*. He writes that a week before he sat for his Junior Certificate examinations in 1970, 'Reverend Calata came to address us in our class with a view to encouraging us and to give us blessings for the tasks that lay ahead.' Manong adds, 'During his moving address, I was pleasantly surprised at his speech. He spoke about the plight of Africans in South Africa generally and about African school children in particular. He said for an African child to sit for Junior Examinations was a great achievement in itself. It was a great achievement against all odds. As students we had to overcome hunger and poverty at home. Our parents were sleeping on empty stomachs sacrificing everything for the sake of our education. Whilst white children were eating food overloaded with vitamins, African children were expected to be content with food overloaded with starch in the form of samp and pap. "Sometimes at my age, I feel like acting rather than talking" – those were his parting words. What an encouraging speech it was.'[14]

As a young boy, I remember how Mr Mali alternated playing the church organ with my grandmother Sis' Ntsiki every other Sunday. I asked him if Tatou had anything to do with his playing the piano. He nodded vigorously, with a big smile on his face. 'Remember,' he said as he shifted his body forward as if to get up, 'uMfundis' uCalata [the Reverend Calata] was my role model. Music was an important part of his life and he loved imparting and sharing it with those close to him.'

The building of St Peter's Church, which the family found on their arrival in Cradock, was quite dilapidated. Simply to fix or renovate it would not have been enough. And anyway, Tatou had much higher aspirations for it. Shortly after the family had settled in Cradock, Tatou once again began to put a school choir together. This, it seems, had become the modus operandi for him. After his successes in Port Elizabeth and Somerset East, why would Cradock be any different? But Cradock *was* different in many other respects. Although not as bad as Somerset East, the little town then had, and continues to this day, to have a unique set of socio-economic challenges. These, in my opinion, are influenced largely by the geographic location of the town itself.

My hometown is named after a Briton, Sir John Cradock. It lies on the banks of the Great Fish River, which makes its way just over 640 km through the province of the Eastern Cape. The river runs throughout the year and is supplemented by the region's summer rainfall. So, with an almost endless supply of water and rich, arable land, it is no surprise that the town is surrounded by a number of farms that draw their sustenance from the Great Fish River. Therefore, Cradock services a large

---

14 Manong, S. 2015. *If We Must Die*. Nkululeko Publishers: Johannesburg.

farming community. In South Africa, large farming communities are synonymous with poverty, and this remains a major problem for my hometown today. In his book, *We Can – Black Politics in Cradock, South Africa 1948–1985*, Michael Tetelman, an American who spent several months researching his doctoral thesis on my hometown, writes, 'In the 1920s, the municipality divided the location into wards. Nearest the river stood "Rooilaer" (Red Camp). To the Xhosa community, this was known as "Esidikidini". This ward referred to a settlement of Africans who often wore traditional clothing and red ochre paint. A ward adjacent to the Rooilaer, where coloured and black people stayed, was named "Stranger". These two wards featured round bee hive huts of wattle and daub, many with petrol tin annexes. Stranger and Rooilaer were poorer wards whose "dark and ill-ventilated" houses epitomized the location's dilapidation.' Tatou and his family, however, had had previous experiences of poverty and lack of resources on such a large scale. Their stint in Somerset East, although brief, had helped prepare Tatou in particular for circumstances such as these. So, after settling in Cradock, the young priest was ready to adopt a different strategy to assist the community.

Tatou, I understand, was much more open and willing compared with other community members to work with the town's white community to improve the conditions and plight of black people in the locations. Despite this, it remains unclear what role he played – if any – in the formation of the Cradock branch of the Joint Council in 1928. This council sought to bring together sympathetic whites and 'responsible' educated black leaders. Its aims, among others, were to 'promote harmonious relations between the races' and 'help towards the development of the non-European races'. Tatou was elected to serve as joint secretary of the council. At or around the same time of his election to the council, he set about to find talent for a second choir. Unlike the church choir, this one would be made up of professional men and women from the location. He named it 'Ikwezi Lomso' or 'The Morning Star' choir. Almost 84 years later, with this fact unbeknown to both Abigail and me, we chose to name our son Kwezi. We chose a similar spelling of the name too – without the 'h'.

Anyway, in 1928, Cradock was a larger community than Somerset

East and despite the intentions of the Joint Council, progress with improving the living conditions in the township over the next year or so was slow – if there was any progress at all.

By 1930, Tatou had realised he would need extra and different help if he hoped to bring about any significant improvement in the plight of the African community in Cradock. At the time, the pre-eminent political organisation for Africans was the African National Congress (ANC). The organisation was formalised in 1912, largely as a response by Africans to the 1910 pact between the British and Afrikaners which led to the establishment of the Union of South Africa. The movement had a proven track record of formidable opposition to the draconian laws that were being passed by the Union government. But by the late Twenties and early Thirties, the ANC was in crisis. At the time, Pixley ka Isaka Seme, who was president-general, faced serious internal challenges. Rev Elijah Mdolomba was secretary-general of the movement nationally and president of its provincial structure, the Cape African Congress (CAC). Despite the problems in the movement, Tatou thought it necessary for him to join the ANC regardless. He approached the Vigilance Association in Cradock in a bid to convince them to become a branch of the ANC. Shortly thereafter, the association agreed to sponsor and host the CAC's provincial conference in Cradock that year. Until the Fifties, ANC conferences were held annually. One of the ANC leaders who attended the conference in Cradock was Rev Mdolomba. He and Tatou would prove to be men cut from the same cloth, and their collaboration was described as one of two very like-minded individuals. In the discussions that ensued over the course of the week-long conference, Rev Mdolomba asked Tatou if he would be prepared to stand for the leadership of the CAC. This, he said, would free him (Mdolomba) up to concentrate on his duties as the national secretary-general.

Tatou was already a busy man. If elected to the position of president of the CAC, he would most likely double his responsibilities and workload almost overnight. He knew he would have to discuss this with his wife first, before making a decision on whether or not he would make himself available for election. Eventually, Tatou stood for election and was duly elected president of the CAC at its Cradock conference in 1930. James Calata had only been a member of the organisation for a few months.

His political ideology and activities were grounded in his faith. According to the *New Dictionary of South African Biography*, edited by EJ Verwey, 'he believed that Christianity could only grow among Africans when their political, social and economic disabilities were recognized and ameliorated. He was an African nationalist with respect for traditional African leaders and desire for African unity. He believed that political goals would be achieved by moderate appeals to government officials and through interracial co-operation.'[15] These beliefs that my great-grandfather harboured so dearly were a foreign concept to the government of Prime Minister James Barry Munnik Hertzog. Earlier in 1930, the government had amended the Riotous Assemblies Act. This meant district authorities such as magisterial offices could at a whim prevent organisations such as the ANC from holding meetings and gatherings. They also had authority to ban political leaders from travelling to certain areas.

After his election, Tatou turned his attention back to his choirs, which had both begun to tour quite extensively, holding a number of fundraising concerts throughout the Eastern Cape. By early 1931, the choirs had raised enough money for Tatou to demolish the old corrugated-iron church and build in its place a new church of brick and mortar, debt-free. The new church, now called St James, was quite an improvement on the previous one. It boasted a beautiful gallery that could accommodate up to 400 congregants and a plaque proudly displaying the motto '*Sinakho* – We Can'. A few months later, a small mission house was built to accommodate the family. A school building followed shortly thereafter, which had a massive hall used largely for recreational purposes. The school was associated with the church and was called St James Higher Primary School. It offered classes from grade one to grade eight.

After Mr Mali qualified as a teacher from Lovedale College[16] in the late Thirties, Tatou would give his young protégé his first teaching post at St James. 'Tatou or uMfundis' uCalata was very strict,' Mr Mali

---

15 Verwey, EJ (ed.). 1995. *New Dictionary of South African Biography*, Volume 1. HSRC Publishers: Pretoria.

16 Lovedale College was a renowned teachers' training college established by missionaries in 1824 just outside the town of Alice in the Eastern Cape.

remembered. 'He wanted every teacher to do his or her work just as diligently as he did.' He added that Tatou was also exceptionally meticulous. To illustrate this, Mr Mali described to me how 'never, not on one single occasion, did uMfundis' miss paying our salaries of eight pounds and fifteen shillings on time'. The Department of Native Education would send the teachers' pay cheques to Tatou and he as manager was responsible for paying the teachers, which, according to Mr Mali, was as regular as clockwork.

Mr Mali's appointment to teach at one of my great-grandfather's schools was not just the realisation of a long-held dream; it was also the opportunity he needed, he told me, upon which to build what would ultimately become a long and distinguished career as teacher, principal, and later school inspector. Mr Mali said that without the presence and influence of my great-grandfather in his life, he didn't think he could or would have achieved half of his life's accomplishments. I could hardly believe the words coming out of Mr Mali. As a young boy, I had witnessed the respect afforded him by the community. But here he was crediting my family for the man he was today. But Mr Mali didn't end there; instead he went on to give Tatou one of the highest honours I had yet to hear one man say about another. According to Mr Mali, 'Cradock, at least the black half of it, is what it is today because of the tireless works and positive influence of James Arthur Calata and his wife Miltha Mary Calata.'

Mr Mali's praise was profound. I was in awe and deeply inspired by the works of my great-grandparents. And now I wanted to know more about them than ever before.

My mother, Nomonde, had been very keen for Abigail and me to speak to Ms Midas Mbuzwana and Ms Nowi Nomavuka. She was convinced that these two ladies would be able to remember and share their own stories and memories of my family with us.

The two ladies were only too happy to oblige my request. Growing up, I had heard a lot about them, particularly how they had served in and been employed by the church, and that they also sang in one of Tatou's choirs, the Congress Choir. My mom arranged that I meet with Ms Mbuzwana.

A few days later, on the night before we were due to interview Ms Mbuzwana, I visited her home. It had been several years since I had last seen her too. I think I must have reminded her of her son Viwe, because she hugged me almost as soon as I set foot inside her home. For a little while, we just embraced, with not a single word spoken. I noticed how tears welled up in my mother's eyes as she stood next to us. I understood why it was hard for Ms Mbuzwana to let go. And we all knew – or at least I think we all knew – that it was okay.

After a few minutes we eventually got to talking about why I was there. I had barely finished explaining the reasons for my request, when she said, '*Mntanam* [my child], I will tell you everything I know about your great-grandfather and family.' She did have one condition: that her lifelong friend Ms Nomavuka could be part of the interview too. She said the two of them would help jog each other's memories not only about Tatou but also the Congress Choir and the many fun trips they had touring as members of the choir. I, of course, was only too eager to agree to this condition; this was after all what I had wanted from the outset. We agreed that Abigail and I would pick them up the following morning and then head to the church where we would conduct our interview. Before we left, Ms Mbuzwana handed me a set of handwritten notes and a few pages which she had compiled. She said she hoped that they would be of use to us.

Abigail and I were up early the next morning. My dear wife is a stickler for punctuality, and I guess she had wanted to ensure we had enough time to finalise our preparations for the interview. Shortly after eight that morning, Abigail and I left to pick up the ladies. On our way, we remarked on the rather pleasant lack of traffic in Cradock, compared to the hustle and bustle of cities like Cape Town and Johannesburg. Unsurprisingly, Ms Mbuzwana was already waiting for us by the time we pulled up in front of her home, and shortly thereafter at Ms Nomavuka's house, just around the corner from her friend. We had been granted permission to use Tatou's Church of the Ascension as the venue for this interview. After all, the church was where the ladies had first met and worked with Tatou. As we drove through iLingelihle, the ladies told me just how excited they were to have the opportunity to share their history and experiences with and of the Calata family. The fact that I was a great-grandchild in the Calata family made it all the more worthwhile, they claimed. Abigail and I were just as excited to have them share their stories with us. We both felt they would help educate us about my family even more. What made this conversation with Ms Mbuzwana and Ms Nomavuka even better is that they also knew Tatou's daughters. Nontsikelelo (my grandmother), Vuyelwa, and Noluthando were older than they were, but they were happy to share what memories they had of Tatou's daughters too.

The church building itself, especially the interior, had changed very little from when I was a child. The pews were unchanged, and while the banners for the various guilds had been modernised somewhat, their colours remained largely the same, hanging where I remembered them. There was one thing out of place, though: the old foot-pedal organ, which my grandmother had played during services, had been moved from the back to the front of the church. The ladies told me it had been serviced recently and the company had recommended that it be relocated to the front if the church wished to keep it for many more years. Other than that, everything felt very familiar. I joked with them that the only thing missing was the incense.

Soon after we started the interview, Ms Nomavuka, sitting almost on the edge of her seat, made it quite clear that she wanted to tell us more about Mamou. Her reasons, she said, were that almost everyone we would speak to – in addition to the books already written about Tatou – would all help shed more light on him. She believed that very few of those people and books would reveal to me the woman whom she argued was behind almost every decision Tatou took.

'They spent very little time together,' said Ms Nomavuka, giving me her thoughts on the couple. She believed this was due largely to Tatou's always being busy, always on the move – as a consequence of his priestly and political commitments. Despite this, Ms Nomavuka described Mamou as the perfect support for her husband. Mamou, she said, was fully cognisant of the fact that her husband was serving a purpose greater than himself and therefore, as his wife, hers was to support and, more often than not, advise him through all of it. She added, though, that Mamou was a leader in her own right, particularly among the women in both the church and community. Ms Nomavuka said Mamou distinguished herself in Cradock's participation in the Defiance Campaign of the early Fifties. Mamou was lauded by her peers in Cradock for her excellent leadership, courage, and humility. Ms Nomavuka argued that Mamou's bravery was at times far superior to that of her husband's, then, almost sheepishly, she added, 'But it wasn't a competition,' a wry smile appearing on her face as she slumped back into her seat.

This extraordinary insight into Mamou was confirmed to me by my uncle, Bangilizwe. We call him Bhut' Bangi. While en route to Limpopo to visit my elder sister, Dorothy, a month or so after our interview with Ms Nomavuka, my uncle recalled just how strict Mamou had been with all nine grandchildren. He said she would demand complete silence from all of them when Tatou arrived home or when he would enter his study. He then shared how, after dinner and devotions, while washing up dishes they would be privy to what amounted to daily debriefing meetings between their grandparents. UBhut' Bangi remembered how, during these discussions, Mamou was always the one who insisted that they discuss a plan of action for the next day. 'She was the leader at home, *bhuti* [that is what he calls me]. Everybody knew she was in charge, even Tatou,' he said, laughing.

Community members (including Ms Nomavuka and Ms Mbuzwana) who witnessed my great-grandparents' marriage, said Mamou had become a model for how a wife, as an equal partner, was meant to support the ministry and, in this case, the political activities of her husband. My mother remembered how Mamou always came to church clutching a straw basket: inside it was a needle and several colours of thread among other things. Mamou, she told me, 'would spend part of the service walking up and down the aisles on the lookout for young girls whose dresses were torn. Once she'd spotted one or two of them, she'd call them to the back of the church, where she would stitch up their dresses right there and then.' In Mamou's basket would also be food, mainly sandwiches, and some fruit, which she would share among the children. For some of them, this was their only meal of the day.

Ms Nomavuka said my great-grandparents' daughters, Nontsikelelo, Vuyelwa, and Noluthando, were close to their mother and attended almost all the church services. During these services, they would always be busy assisting their mother or any of the other older women with various tasks. The sisters, she recalled, also shared a very close relationship, as one hardly ever saw one at church or in the community without either of her sisters present.

As the reverend's wife, Mamou led the St James Mothers' Union, and had the responsibility of writing monthly and sometimes annual reports to the Diocese in Grahamstown about their mission activities in Cradock. In one such letter, dated 23 February 1961, she writes:

'1960 Report of St James Mothers Union

Last year (1960) was another difficult year with us at Cradock.

Death: We lost several mothers through death. Among them was Lizzie Mbuzwana, the wife of our Senior Churchwarden. May they rest in peace.

Imprisonment: Several of our leading mothers were taken to gaol during the emergency, and they all remained there almost to the end. However, we are glad to report that when they returned home they fell into line with the rest of us and carried on the work of the Mothers Union in the usual way. Thanks be to God.

Our Girls: The work among the girls is progressing in two directions. Some are in St Agnes Guild and others, the older ones are in the Anglican Young People's Association all under capable hands.

We were sorry to lose Mr Ernest Tali, the Leader of the AYPA, early last year. His funeral was conducted by Canon Johnson as our Priest was away in prison at the time. This was one of the largest funerals at Cradock at any time.

The Quiet Day: Our Quiet Day was conducted by our own Canon and it was well attended. Over 200 members took part.

Burglary: Our Church has had a burglary and money amounting to 150 pounds and valuable documents and registers which were stored in the safe in the vestry were removed and destroyed.

We are not downhearted. We know that we are engaged in a mighty struggle as we are sure of victory for Christ is on our side.

The mothers are busy repairing the broken doors and windows and replacing the carpets and other lost articles.

Please find five pounds for our subscriptions. The delay in collecting it delayed this report. Please accept our sincere apologies.

Miltha Mary Calata – Enrolling Member'[17]

---

17 Calata Papers. Cory Library, Rhodes University.

Both Ms Mbuzwana and Ms Nomavuka agreed that Tatou was constantly on the road. 'He always had someone to go and see, something to go and do, somewhere else he needed to be,' said Ms Mbuzwana.

As if to emphasise this point, Ms Mbuzwana asked me if I had read the set of notes and few handwritten pages she had given me the night before our interview. When she had handed them over to me, she'd told me she had kept them for decades. The notes, she'd said, were her attempt at documenting some of the details of Tatou's life, and parts of the information were from personal experiences and accounts of Tatou, as she had worked for him as an office clerk.

I had come across some of the details contained in them before, but here I was trying to piece together rough notes of actual events in Cradock at a time when not even my father had been born. And so I was fascinated. My mom was there to discuss certain aspects of the notes with me. She and Abigail also acted as general sounding boards. I truly was engrossed, particularly as Ms Mbuzwana's notes pointed to the sheer variety and scope of my great-grandfather's work inside the community of Cradock. I was so proud of the man whose name I carry.

Chapter Four

A Man of the People and the Movement

LUKHANYO

I thanked Ms Mbuzwana for the notes and particularly for her safe-guarding my family's history. I told her that they had indeed been thoroughly useful as they'd helped shed light on an era which would otherwise have remained largely undocumented. There were some aspects in her notes, however, which either weren't reflected or not properly explained, and which I hoped she could help me answer. For instance, how had Tatou managed to attend to as much as he had, considering his wide range of mostly pressing responsibilities?

Ms Mbuzwana responded by citing an example of his extraordinary organisational capacity. Around 1932/33, she said, shortly after the completion of the new church building, St James, the parish had begun to grow quite rapidly. This meant an increase in the rector's workload. (Ms Mbuzwana often referred to Tatou as the rector.) Soon, he was unable to manage by himself. So, in a bid to delegate and ease his workload, he established the guilds in the congregation. These were divided into the preachers (*abashumayeli*), the Mothers' Union (*umanyano loomama*), the St Agnes Guild, and the servers (ushers), both boys and girls. The servers were taught and trained by the rector himself. The rector also appointed two parishioners to help with funerals and various services.

She added that 'baptismal services were conducted every first Sunday of the month and confirmations were conducted annually, by the Bishop of Grahamstown'.

By 1935, the congregation of St James had a significant number of members, due largely to many 'coloured' families having joined the parish. Among the new members was the Allens family. Ms Mbuzwana remembered that their patriarch, Mr Longway Allens, became the parish interpreter.

Choir rehearsals were held every Sunday, immediately following the morning service. The choir would rehearse both hymns and psalms. Sunday school classes were also taught after services. During *imvuselelo* or Lent services, the various wards (those in the northern and southern regions) held their own services, except on Wednesdays, when services were held in the Cradock parish and conducted by Tatou.

In the Holy Week of Easter each year, Ms Mbuzwana reminisced, 'one could feel the Holy Spirit prevailing in Cradock'. She said bells would ring out from all directions inviting the congregants to services. Good Friday services always started at noon and would end at three in the afternoon. Something rather unusual would happen during these services, she recalled, and, leaning forward, voice almost at a whisper, she told me that 'white parishioners from the St Peter's Parish in town would come to the location and join our service'. I found it odd that Ms Mbuzwana would lower her voice just to share this fact with me, but then I realised that multi-racial worship services might have been the norm for me and my generation in present-day South Africa, but back then in the Thirties, Forties, and Fifties, it was still very much taboo.

The Easter candle Eucharist was usually preceded by an early morning procession led by Tatou to the cemetery. Here, he would conduct a short service in memory of those who had passed away. Ms Mbuzwana described this procession as a 'beautiful and adorable spectacle, particularly when everyone had his or her candle lit'. This, she said, 'reminded us of the Host of Angels as seen by the shepherds when Christ was born'. Christians from other denominations usually joined this service, which she says was testimony to how well loved this procession was by the African and coloured communities of Cradock.

So far, Ms Mbuzwana and Ms Nomavuka, in addition to the notes they'd given me, had helped Abigail and me understand the activities and events on Tatou's to-do-list that had kept him so busy. To make things worse (at least as far as I could tell), these commitments to his church and community were over and above the arduous tasks and responsibilities required by his political office. As if this was not enough, he would over the years add even more responsibilities to his roster, such as when he was elected to serve as president of the Order of St Ntsikana (now known as the St Ntsikana Memorial Association) and again as president of the Cape African Parents Association.

The Order was established in honour of 'Christian Xhosa prophet Ntsikana, who lived between 1760 and 1821. Ntsikana is credited as a young father of the amaRharabe clan of the western borderlands of the Xhosa kingdom. He is said to have experienced visions telling him to convert to Christianity. After one particularly powerful experience, he went down to the river, and washed off his red ochre body paint as a sign of leaving the old ways and taking on the new. Ntsikana's visions also told him to learn to read and write. This he did, and started to travel around the Eastern Cape preaching about Jesus Christ, and telling his followers that they too should learn to read.'[18]

The Cape African Parents Association was formed in 1946 after a major student protest at Lovedale College: 'An estimated two hundred male students damaged school buildings before retreating to the nearby hills for the night. Police arrested 156 of the students who eventually spent up to nine days in jail. In the end only four were acquitted, while the school refused to re-admit over 275 students.'[19] Thirteen of those students came from Cradock. Tatou and Professor DDT Jabavu then called a conference in King William's Town where concerned parents assembled. Here, the Cape African Parents Association was born. Prof DDT Jabavu and Kaiser D Matanzima were nominated and elected as my great-grandfather's deputies.

In addition to these responsibilities, Ms Mbuzwana told me that Tatou was also deeply concerned about the plight of people living on neighbouring farms. 'He was always worried that the people on those farms weren't being exposed to the Word of God,' she said. 'So he decided to visit a few of the farms around here to see if he could obtain permission from the owners for him to hold services for the farm labourers.' Although Tatou was not in favour with some of the farmers – largely because of his political affiliations and office – almost all of the farmers nonetheless gave him permission to hold church services. Ms Mbuzwana then smiled as she recalled a conversation in which one farmer said, 'Calata, teach them the Ten Commandments so they do not steal my stock.'

---

18 Who Was Ntsikana? www.historicschools.org.za
19 Strikes in the Schools. http://www.sahistory.org.za/archive/strikes-schools

Due to Tatou's soft-spoken nature, coupled with the improvement in the discipline and behaviour of the farm labourers, it was just a matter of time before he would win over the farmers. He would then gently persuade them to build the congregation a chapel where church services could be held. These were usually makeshift, built out of corrugated-iron sheets and wooden poles. 'After the church, comes the school for the farm children,' Ms Mbuzwana added. Tatou would supervise and manage the schools.

In a letter titled '1952 Report', and addressed to the Bishop of Grahamstown, Tatou wrote:

'St James Mission comprises of the main station at Cradock and the following Outstations with buildings: St Mark's at Fish River, St Barnabas at Mortimer, St Philip's at Baroda, St Luke's at Drenen, St Matthias at Tarka Bridge, St Paul's at Langford and St Bartholomew's at Hofmeyr. Services are held weekly in these places but I can only visit them once in three months except Baroda, which has over 75 communicants to which I go twice a quarter. I am planning to start evening services and classes at some of the other stations.

Day Schools: Day schools are held at the following places with the following average attendances: Cradock 550, Fish River 72, Mortimer 51, Tarka Bridge 91, Cloverfield 62 Langford 45, and Lansdowne 14. Many children in these schools do not belong to the Church but they receive religious instruction in accordance with the Anglican Faith.

Church Grounds: Our greatest problem is how to influence the farmers to give some security of tenure when they permit us to build a school or a Church on their farms. These properties are put up at great expense but the farmer has a right to take the building without consulting anybody.'[20]

Most of the schools mentioned in this letter still operate to date, although their management now falls under the Eastern Cape Department of Education.

Ms Mbuzwana added that Tatou visited these farms successively, but that he always ensured he was in the Cradock parish on the first Sunday of each month. Two gentlemen were elected from the regions to

---

20 Calata Papers. Cory Library, Rhodes University.

monitor both the morning and evening worship services on the out-stations. The chapels in the north were supervised by Salon Mngqu-shu, who was stationed at St Philip's in Baroda. Tshaka Mntuze was charged with supervision over the chapels in the south. To help keep the management of the schools and churches running smoothly, Tatou appointed administration clerks. Ms Mbuzwana recalled that her two predecessors in this position were Mary Mbayise and Mildred Maki. She believed the clerks were of great help, especially from around 1937, when Tatou was often in and out of police detention.

In 1936, five years after he was first elected president of the Cape African Congress, Tatou once again succeeded Rev Mdolomba, this time replacing him as secretary-general, taking over the movement's national leadership. Much like Mdolomba before him, Tatou too now served as both secretary-general on the national body and president of the provincial structure of the Cape ANC. When Tatou took over the office of secretary-general, the ANC – under the leadership of Pixley ka Isaka Seme – was practically on its deathbed. In his book *Thabo Mbeki and the Battle for the Soul of the ANC* William Mervin Gumede writes, 'Under Seme's conservative leadership, the ANC had become virtually defunct. The ICU (Industrial & Commercial Workers' Union) was on a downward spiral to oblivion, despite pockets of support in Natal. The Communist Party was paralyzed in an orgy of purges. Political activists tried to find avenues in new organisations, such as the All-African Con-vention, the National Liberation League, and the Non-European United Front.'[21] My great-grandfather, however, wasn't demoralised or scared off by any of these issues; instead, he diligently set about turning the organisation's fortunes around.

Tatou and Seme's terms in office would coincide for just one year. During that year, Seme witnessed an internal uprising against him led chiefly by his eventual successor, ZR Mahabane. Tatou wasn't in favour of Seme's continued leadership either, and subsequently became a lead-ing voice in a group that called for a special emergency convention to address deeply divisive issues plaguing the movement. At the end of

---

21 Gumede, WM. 2005. *Thabo Mbeki and the Battle for the Soul of the ANC.* Zebra Press: Cape Town.

1937, ZR Mahabane stood for and defeated Seme in the race for the office of president-general. Now under the leadership of a new president-general, Tatou prioritised the revival of the ailing movement. As soon as Mahabane had taken office, the two set off on a national tour. This tour, which continued through to 1939, saw Tatou and his president visiting all the provinces in a bid to address some of the key problems that had beset the branches. 'This nationwide tour indeed served to revive the organisation and drew younger people into the ANC.'[22]

At the ANC's National Policy Conference held at Nasrec, Johannesburg, in June 2017, I had the opportunity to sit down and discuss this period of the ANC's history with the secretary-general, Gwede Mantashe. He confirmed that when Tatou was elected to office, the ANC was reeling under the 'disastrous' presidency of Seme. Mantashe credited Tatou with rescuing the fortunes of the movement. He added that in the 106-year history of the ANC, the movement, in his opinion, has had three particularly special secretaries-general, namely James Calata, Walter Sisulu, and Advocate Duma Nokwe. Mantashe said that through their brilliant organisational skills, coupled with their tireless work and contributions to the movement, these three men deserve special mention in the annals of the ANC.

During Tatou and Mahabane's travels, Cradock – and particularly the family he'd left behind there so often – was never far from his mind. Ms Mbuzwana said Tatou would ensure that during his absences, his family and parish didn't suffer much. Despite his ascent to national office, Tatou remained a community activist at heart. His role in the community was vital, since escalating levels of crime and gangsterism were becoming a problem in Cradock at that time.

In Ms Mbuzwana's notes, she writes, 'The youth engaged themselves in gangsterism. This was a problem for the community largely because of the deadly results of either gang attacks or fights. Scholars were often intimidated by the gangs, which were named after the areas where they were from (Amasdikidi, Skapu, and Tula). One day the rector stood between two youngsters who faced each other with knives. He talked to them and requested that they give him their knives. They did.'

---

22 Verwey, EJ (ed.). 1995. *New Dictionary of South African Biography*, Volume 1. HSRC Publishers: Pretoria.

Although other areas of general life in Cradock had started to show progress, criminality remained rampant. In a bid to gain the upper hand over the problem, Tatou began to organise sports for the youth. Rugby was the sport of choice, as the location already had an established team, the Blues. Ms Mbuzwana writes that 'almost immediately the youth began to engage themselves in sport, attending regular practices. Soon everybody wanted to be a player, which led to the establishment of two other teams – the Spring Rose and United.'

Local friendly matches were played on Saturdays, while no matches were played on Sundays. On the rare occasion when a game was scheduled for a Sunday, it was played in the afternoon, never during the morning when church services were held. Shortly after the rugby teams were formed, Tatou then set up the St James Lawn and the 'Never Give Up' Tennis Clubs.

Throughout his activism, either in the community or in national office, music remained an important part of Tatou's life, and nowhere was this more evident than at the St James school hall, which was often used as a recreation centre. According to Ms Mbuzwana, this is where they held their ballroom dancing rehearsals and events. The hall also hosted many choir performances. She added that, whenever there was a concert or show in the hall, no gentleman would be allowed inside the venue if he had consumed alcohol. Also, no gentleman was permitted either to dance or sit with a lady while he had his hat on. Smoking wasn't allowed inside the hall.

Two hours of conversation with Ms Mbuzwana and Ms Nomavuka had passed by in a flash. The ladies had both begun to tire by now, and even though I would've liked to continue our interview, it was time for us to take them home. Once again, I was in admiration of my great-grandparents and their hearts for service to the community of Cradock. Even though I had heard of some of their achievements in the community for years, Abigail and I had by now spent hours speaking to people who had direct contact and experiences with Tatou and Mamou, and I still couldn't believe that Tatou, in particular, could achieve all he had in just one lifetime. Ms Mbuzwana and Ms Nomavuka had been extraordinary. For several days following our interview, I found myself reading through Ms Mbuzwana's notes over and over again. I would sit at my mother's lounge table with the notes spread out before me, wondering almost always out loud just how and where Tatou had found the time to do and accomplish so much. I was even more in awe of my great-grandfather when I considered that he had done all this – and so much more – while raising a family.

From 1937, Tatou continued to juggle his time between serving his community in Cradock and the requirements of his office as secretary-general of the ANC. In the three years of Mahabane's presidency, Hertzog's government had introduced several controversial bills, which in essence sought to disenfranchise Africans who had until then enjoyed voting rights on the common voters' roll with whites.

Mahabane would only serve a second term as president-general for three years (his first term was from 1924–1927). By 1940, the leadership potential of a young medical doctor, AB Xuma, who had recently returned from his studies in the United States, had caught Tatou's attention. Gumede writes: 'Calata, an organizational genius, persuaded Xuma to stand for the ANC's presidency in 1940.' Xuma eventually triumphed by 21 votes to 20 over Mahabane, and, Gumede adds, 'Xuma's election set the seal on the ANC's revival.'[23] Tetelman expands on this partnership: 'Xuma and Calata were ideal partners, for both were intellectuals, broad-thinkers, hard-workers and moderates.'[24] But the revival of the ANC, although under way, remained a slow and painstaking process. The biggest challenge facing the new leadership was finances.

Meanwhile, Tatou's political activities, particularly after he was first elected to the presidency of the Cape African Congress, had been an issue of contention for the church diocese in Grahamstown. The bishop and even some of his African colleagues were none too thrilled with one of their own having being elected to serve in the leadership of the ANC.

Their disapproval is evident in a letter Bishop Cullen wrote to JD Rheinallt Jones, whom my great-grandfather knew through his involve-

---

23 Gumede, WM. 2005. *Thabo Mbeki and the Battle for the Soul of the ANC.* Zebra Press: Cape Town.

24 Tetelman, M. 2012. *We Can! Black Politics in Cradock, South Africa, 1948-85.* Rhodes University: Grahamstown.

ment with the Scouts: 'The Reverend JA Calata is not easy to defend. For some time various African clergymen have been saying that he was busily preaching political sermons and engaging in activities which could cause him trouble. One African clergyman told me that he could not invite him to preach in his church as he never preached the Gospel but merely party politics. I do not know how true that is: but it is probably about right. And as a leading member of the African National Congress he was likely to be suspect. And he certainly backed up the passive resistance movement. It would not be easy to defend him publicly too whole-heartedly.'[25]

It is also quite clear that the church's stance regarding my great-grandfather's political activities had led to great tension in his own life. In 1939, he responded to a letter from Bishop Cullen, writing: 'I cannot give up the Church for National work. But I shall do my best to combine the two if the Bishop will permit me. At present my Bishop understands the position, but my situation presents many difficult problems. I am losing influence with Diocesan Synods and Diocesan Missionary Conferences. The younger inexperienced White Missionaries are suspicious of me. The Black Missionaries look upon me as merely ambitious for high positions etc, etc, but in spite of it, I feel it is my call to do my bit at this critical period in our national history. My dilemma is that I cannot give up the Altar but at the same time I feel I have a call to help the African nation.'[26]

The early to mid-Forties was a time of much change for black South Africans. This threatened the ANC's moderate political ideology which it had adopted until that point. Tetelman writes: 'During the Second World War, manufacturing and black urbanisation were booming and powerful black trade unions emerged. The rise of the Council for Non-European Trade Unions (CNETU) and the African Mineworkers' Union (AMU) introduced a politically powerful black urban working class. The increasing influence of the Communist Party also spread working-class militancy.'[27]

---

25 Rev James Arthur CALATA Papers 1909–1974. University of the Witwatersrand.
26 Ibid.
27 Tetelman, M. 2012. *We Can! Black Politics in Cradock, South Africa, 1948-85*. Rhodes University: Grahamstown.

Tetelman goes on to explain, 'The ANC executive responded to the shift in political mood by espousing a slightly more aggressive platform to end segregation. Xuma and Calata resolved that the ANC must respond better to demands from urbanized, working-class Africans while remaining a moderate organisation. In a critical move, the ANC Executive redrafted its constitution in 1943. The new constitution abolished chiefly influence, granted women members equal status, strengthened the central executive and bolstered ANC branches. Most provinces, in particular the Transvaal (Gauteng), increased their membership. With branches finally operating as they should, most provincial leaders could finally call mass meetings.'[28]

The redrafting of the constitution, which was led by the office of the secretary-general, proved to have been a masterstroke – and not only because the ANC, after 30 long years, had finally recognised the role of women as equal partners in the struggles against colonialism and the ever-growing Afrikaner nationalist sentiment.

But 1943 wasn't an entirely successful year for Tatou. Earlier in the year, the Church of the Province had nominated him for the Bishopric of the Transkei. Many white clergymen, however, did not approve of a black bishop, particularly in the form of Tatou, and prevented his election. According to Tetelman, 'White clergy also disliked Calata's efforts to empower black clergymen.' Just a few months before his nomination for the Bishopric, Tatou was elected president of the Interdenominational African Ministers' Federation (IDAMF). Tetelman notes, 'This organization sought to educate African clergy and give them a larger role in church affairs. Senior clergy especially disapproved of Calata's role in the ANC.'[29]

The ANC continued their upward trajectory throughout 1944. On 2 April 1944, the Youth League of the African National Congress was established, with Anton Lembede elected its first president. Also among its leadership ranks were Nelson Mandela, Ida Mtwa, Lilian Ngoyi, Duma Nokwe, Walter Sisulu, and Oliver Tambo. For many observers and historians, the seeds of the Youth League could be found

---

28 Ibid.
29 Ibid.

in the countrywide tour Tatou and former President-General ZR Mahabane undertook in the years between 1937 and 1939.

From around 1940 onwards, Tatou had begun to utilise the Ikwezi Lomso choir, which he had by now renamed the Congress Choir, to raise funds in aid of the ANC's dire financial situation. The Congress Choir, despite featuring fewer members than when it had started, due to some of them having passed on over the years, is still relatively active to date. Its performances, though, are limited mostly to within Cradock and surrounds. For those still alive, such as Ms Mbuzwana and Ms Nomavuka, the memories of the Congress Choir in its heyday were precious. Smiles as broad as the Great Fish River simultaneously appeared on their faces as soon as I asked them to talk to me about the days of the Congress Choir. Ms Nomavuka remembered the travels with the choir most of all. If it weren't for the choir, she doubted she would've had the privilege to see and experience as much of the Eastern Cape as she did back then. Ms Mbuzwana concurred, highlighting in equal measure the fun they had had as members of the choir and the extraordinary discipline Tatou had demanded of them, particularly when they travelled. She said that, even though they were all young men and women, they never engaged in undesirable activities such as having sexual relationships with one another. They all knew that Tatou wouldn't approve of such behaviour and none of the choir members wanted to disappoint him.

By 1945, the ANC was still on the up. Work done in previous years had begun to yield results for the organisation. But all this was threatened by the government's introduction of the amended Natives Urban Areas Consolidation Act. This piece of legislation imposed 'influx control' on black men.

This, and several other repressive Acts weren't well received by the younger, more militant Youth League. Between 1946 and 1947 the young lions, as they were called, were harshly critical of the ANC's executive, and espoused radical politics. On more than one occasion, the Youth League slammed Tatou and Xuma – and the rest of the executive for that matter – for being 'passive and elitist'. The Youth League insisted that Tatou and his fellow office bearers act upon 'mass-based African grievances', demanding mass protests particularly against the more repressive laws.

Seeking to respond to the pressure of the Youth League, Dr Xuma asked Tatou to 'help him devise a broader-based strategy. One that would somehow help them bring their plan to the rank and file and let the rest of the world know of their capabilities.' Xuma's request, however, could not have come at a worse time for my great-grandfather. By 1947, Tatou had served as secretary-general for eleven years. He was tired, his health had begun to suffer once more, and he was considering stepping down from the position. Towards the end of that year, Tatou was again diagnosed with TB. He would spend several months recovering in a Durban hospital[30].

In 1948, the National Party under the leadership of Daniel Malan won the national election, having campaigned on a policy of apartheid. This was the proverbial red flag to the Youth League's bull, who used the new government's policies to push for a more militant response to whatever 'apartheid' was. Where Xuma remained unmoved by the Youth League's militancy, Tatou (even while in hospital) had begun to soften his stance towards them. According to Mantashe (the secretary-general to whom I spoke at the ANC's National Policy Conference in June 2017), Tatou had tried to calm the Youth League's militancy by appealing for patience and time, in order for the ANC to first see what the proposed 'apartheid' policies would actually be, before the ANC considered its response.

Those policies became clearer in 1949, when the Malan government introduced several repressive laws. Nelson Mandela, in *Long Walk to Freedom*, lists the key Acts as follows: 'The Separate Representation of Voters Bill, [which] eventually robbed the Coloureds of their representation in Parliament. The Prohibition of Mixed Marriages Act was introduced in 1949 and was followed in rapid succession by the Immorality Act, making sexual relations between white and non-white illegal. The Population Registration Act labelled all South Africans by race, making colour the single most important arbiter of an individual. Malan introduced the Group Areas Act – which he described as the "very essence of Apartheid" – requiring separate urban areas for each

---

30 Tetelman, M. 2012. *We Can! Black Politics in Cradock, South Africa, 1948-85*. Rhodes University: Grahamstown.

racial group. In the past, whites took land by force; now they secured it by legislation.'[31]

The Youth League grew more uninterested in Tatou and Xuma's wait-and-see approach with the introduction of each law. Tetelman writes: '[T]o militant Congress members, especially those in the Youth League (ANCYL), Calata and Xuma were out of touch with the mass-based urbanized black politics of the post-war era – politics that demanded confrontation rather than accommodation.'[32]

The stand-off between the ANC and the Youth League's leaders came to a head at the 1949 National Conference in Bloemfontein. The Youth League, in the lead up to the conference, had drawn up a Programme of Action which would form the basis of its campaign of mass mobilisation.

Once in Bloemfontein for the conference, Tatou – as a delegate and despite his reservations – signed the Youth League's Programme of Action, which called for 'boycotts, strikes, stay-at-homes, passive resistance, protest demonstrations and other forms of mass action'[33]. Xuma, on the other hand, remained totally unconvinced by the Youth League. Mandela recalls how, a few weeks before conference, he, Walter Sisulu, and Oliver Tambo had visited Dr Xuma at his home. The purpose of the visit, he writes, was to solicit the president's support for their Programme of Action, which Xuma declined: 'We gave Dr Xuma an ultimatum: we would support him for re-election to the presidency of the ANC provided he supported our Programme of Action. If he would not support our programme, we would not support him. Dr Xuma became heated, accusing us of blackmail and laying down the conditions on which we would vote for him. He told us that we were young and arrogant and treating him without respect.'[34]

The Youth League would eventually sponsor Dr James Moroka to stand against Xuma for the position of president-general, and Xuma was defeated. Meanwhile, Tatou had declined re-election as secretary-general.

---

31 Nelson, M. 1994. *Long Walk to Freedom*. Macdonald Purnell: Randburg.
32 Tetelman, M. 2012. *We Can! Black Politics in Cradock, South Africa, 1948-85*. Rhodes University: Grahamstown.
33 Nelson, M. 1994. *Long Walk to Freedom*. Macdonald Purnell: Randburg.
34 Ibid.

According to one source, he 'cited as reasons his long service, many responsibilities, and the fact that he believed a younger man should be appointed to the position'.[35]

Tatou was 54 years old when Walter Sisulu replaced him as secretary-general, and Oliver Tambo was elected to serve on the National Executive. Tatou had earlier in the year also relinquished the position of president of the Cape African Congress. He was replaced by ZK Matthews.

Because of his long years of political service, Tatou had become a marked man in Cradock, and saw frequent visits from the police. These mostly ended with either his home being raided or his detention. By 1952, the ANC had begun to roll out its Defiance Campaign against Pass Laws on a national level, while Tatou was now back at home, serving house arrest. The family's mantle during the ensuing strikes and stayaways was assumed by Mamou. Tetelman writes: 'One evening, a new round of volunteers, mostly Anglican and led by Mrs Calata, were arrested for breaking curfew regulations. They sang freedom songs as police marched them into the station in town.'[36]

Throughout this time, Tatou was either placed under house arrest or banned from attending any other meeting outside of Sunday morning church services. This was despite the many requests to have him attend and at times travel for certain gatherings and meetings for which the magistrates almost always refused to grant permission.

In August 1953, Cradock hosted what would turn out to be a crucial conference for the ANC. It was here in the dusty streets of my hometown that Prof ZK Matthews, who had taken over from Tatou as president of the Cape ANC in 1949, first mentioned the idea of a 'Charter for all the people of South Africa'. Matthews proposed the summoning of a 'national convention at which all groups might be represented to consider our national problems on an all-inclusive basis to draw up a Freedom Charter for the Democratic South Africa of the future'.

Matthews's idea was endorsed at the ANC's annual conference in

---

35 Verwey, EJ (ed.). 1995. *New Dictionary of South African Biography*, Volume 1. HSRC Publishers: Pretoria.

36 Tetelman, M. 2012. *We Can! Black Politics in Cradock, South Africa, 1948-85*. Rhodes University: Grahamstown.

September of the same year. Other organisations, among them the South African Congress of Trade Unions (SACTU), South African Congress of Democrats (COD), South African Indian Congress (SAIC), and the South African Coloured People's Organisation (SACPO), also took up the idea and participated in the Congress of the People. In Kliptown on 25 June 1955, delegates from groups throughout the country met to present their vision for a just ordering of South African society. This was the culmination of the Freedom Charter Campaign, during which thousands of volunteers went into townships, factories, and rural areas, organising people into groups to discuss their grievances and set out their demands.

The Charter was formally adopted the next day on 26 June, with Cradock officially recognised as the 'Cradle of the Charter'[37].

The Freedom Charter reads:

'We, the People of South Africa, declare for all our country and the world to know:
that South Africa belongs to all who live in it, black and white, and that no government can justly claim authority unless it is based on the will of all the people; that our people have been robbed of their birthright to land, liberty and peace by a form of government founded on injustice and inequality; that our country will never be prosperous or free until all our people live in brotherhood, enjoying equal rights and opportunities; that only a democratic state, based on the will of all the people, can secure to all their birthright without distinction of colour, race, sex or belief; And therefore, we, the people of South Africa, black and white together equals, countrymen and brothers adopt this Freedom Charter; And we pledge ourselves to strive together, sparing neither strength nor courage, until the democratic changes here set out have been won.

The People Shall Govern!
Every man and woman shall have the right to vote for and to stand as a candidate for all bodies which make laws; All people shall be entitled to take part in the administration of the country; The rights of the people shall be the same, regardless of race, colour or sex; All bodies of

---

37 Rev James Arthur CALATA Papers 1909–1974. University of the Witwatersrand.

minority rule, advisory boards, councils and authorities shall be replaced by democratic organs of self-government.

All National Groups Shall have Equal Rights!
There shall be equal status in the bodies of state, in the courts and in the schools for all national groups and races; All people shall have equal right to use their own languages, and to develop their own folk culture and customs; All national groups shall be protected by law against insults to their race and national pride; The preaching and practice of national, race or colour discrimination and contempt shall be a punishable crime; All apartheid laws and practices shall be set aside.

The People Shall Share in the Country's Wealth!
The national wealth of our country, the heritage of South Africans, shall be restored to the people; The mineral wealth beneath the soil, the Banks and monopoly industry shall be transferred to the ownership of the people as a whole; All other industry and trade shall be controlled to assist the wellbeing of the people; All people shall have equal rights to trade where they choose, to manufacture and to enter all trades, crafts and professions.

The Land Shall be Shared among Those Who Work It!
Restrictions of land ownership on a racial basis shall be ended, and all the land re-divided among those who work it to banish famine and land hunger; The state shall help the peasants with implements, seed, tractors and dams to save the soil and assist the tillers; Freedom of movement shall be guaranteed to all who work on the land; All shall have the right to occupy land wherever they choose; People shall not be robbed of their cattle, and forced labour and farm prisons shall be abolished.

All Shall be Equal before the Law!
No-one shall be imprisoned, deported or restricted without a fair trial; No-one shall be condemned by the order of any Government official; The courts shall be representative of all the people; Imprisonment shall be only for serious crimes against the people, and shall aim at re-education, not vengeance; The police force and army shall be open to all on an equal basis and shall be the helpers and protectors of the people; All laws which discriminate on grounds of race, colour or belief shall be repealed.

All Shall Enjoy Equal Human Rights!

The law shall guarantee to all their right to speak, to organise, to meet together, to publish, to preach, to worship and to educate their children; The privacy of the house from police raids shall be protected by law; All shall be free to travel without restriction from countryside to town, from province to province, and from South Africa abroad; Pass Laws, permits and all other laws restricting these freedoms shall be abolished.

There Shall be Work and Security!

All who work shall be free to form trade unions, to elect their officers and to make wage agreements with their employers; The state shall recognise the right and duty of all to work, and to draw full unemployment benefits; Men and women of all races shall receive equal pay for equal work; There shall be a forty-hour working week, a national minimum wage, paid annual leave, and sick leave for all workers, and maternity leave on full pay for all working mothers; Miners, domestic workers, farm workers and civil servants shall have the same rights as all others who work; Child labour, compound labour, the tot system and contract labour shall be abolished.

The Doors of Learning and Culture Shall be Opened!

The government shall discover, develop and encourage national talent for the enhancement of our cultural life; All the cultural treasures of mankind shall be open to all, by free exchange of books, ideas and contact with other lands; The aim of education shall be to teach the youth to love their people and their culture, to honour human brotherhood, liberty and peace; Education shall be free, compulsory, universal and equal for all children; Higher education and technical training shall be opened to all by means of state allowances and scholarships awarded on the basis of merit; Adult illiteracy shall be ended by a mass state education plan; Teachers shall have all the rights of other citizens; The colour bar in cultural life, in sport and in education shall be abolished.

There Shall be Houses, Security and Comfort!

All people shall have the right to live where they choose, be decently housed, and to bring up their families in comfort and security; Unused housing space to be made available to the people; Rent and prices shall be lowered, food plentiful and no-one shall go hungry; A preventive health scheme shall be run by the state; Free medical care and hospitalisation shall be provided for all, with special care for mothers and young children; Slums shall be demolished, and new suburbs built where all have transport, roads, lighting, playing fields, crèches and social centres; The aged, the orphans, the disabled and the sick shall be cared for by the state; Rest, leisure and recreation shall be the right of all: Fenced locations and ghettoes shall be abolished, and laws which break up families shall be repealed.

There Shall be Peace and Friendship!
South Africa shall be a fully independent state which respects the rights and sovereignty of all nations; South Africa shall strive to maintain world peace and the settlement of all international disputes by negotiation - not war; Peace and friendship among all our people shall be secured by upholding the equal rights, opportunities and status of all; The people of the protectorates Basutoland, Bechuanaland and Swaziland shall be free to decide for themselves their own future; The right of all peoples of Africa to independence and self-government shall be recognised, and shall be the basis of close co-operation. Let all people who love their people and their country now say, as we say here: THESE FREEDOMS WE WILL FIGHT FOR, SIDE BY SIDE, THROUGHOUT OUR LIVES, UNTIL WE HAVE WON OUR LIBERTY.'[38]

In September 1954, Tatou was honoured by his parish for 25 years of service to the community of Cradock. They surprised him with the gift of a car. Tetelman writes: 'His poverty-stricken outstation congregants were among the most generous donors. The crowd sang "Siyabulela". A representative of Chief Sandile, the paramount chief of the Gaika, praised Calata. Prof. ZK Matthews extolled Calata's long service to the community and predicted that "when the story of African liberation came to be written, his name would be prominent."' Tetelman continues: 'Calata did not disappoint in his speech. He stressed that he would never give up fighting to ensure that "the Black man will ultimately achieve the position God wanted him to attain".'[39]

Despite no longer holding office, Tatou continued to serve on the ANC's national executive as its senior chaplain in the Fifties. By then, a young

38 Luthuli, A. 2006. *Let My People Go: The Autobiography of Albert Luthuli*. Tafelberg: Cape Town.

39 Tetelman, M. 2012. *We Can! Black Politics in Cradock, South Africa, 1948-85*. Rhodes University: Grahamstown.

man by the name of Albert Sachs was a member of the COD which, alongside the SAIC, SACPO, and SACTU, constituted the Congress Alliance, together with the ANC. Sachs recalled several personal encounters with Tatou and the likes of iNkosi Albert Luthuli, who had by now taken over from Dr James Moroka as president-general of the ANC.

I was fortunate to interview Albie Sachs, as the former Constitutional Court judge is known, for this book and subsequent documentary about his interactions with Tatou. A friend and fellow filmmaker, Adam Asmal, the son of the late ANC stalwart Kader Asmal, directed the interview with Albie. We sat down with the former judge in his home, situated on the slopes of the beautiful Clifton Beach along the Atlantic coastline. I was pleased to have Adam with us that morning, as he and Albie knew each other quite well, which made the set-up of cameras, lights, and everything else associated with film interviews a much more pleasant experience. Albie was very gracious in his description of my great-grandfather, telling us: 'In my memory, Calata and Luthuli were cut from the same cloth, almost literally from the Cross. They were both religious leaders, but it was a religion that wasn't simply striving for perfection of the soul, for an afterlife. It was a religion very immersed in the pains and energies and strivings of the people today; it was a religion that paid enormous attention to the theme of equality of everybody under their skins in the eyes of God.'

The ANC, having unshackled itself from the conservative leadership and ideology of the Forties, became a true mass movement in the Fifties, helped largely by the success of the Defiance Campaign and other mass-based protests. The results of these campaigns, which included boycotts (mostly of government amenities such as buses and trains), also affected white-owned businesses, as black people (inclusive of Indian and coloured communities) were encouraged not to buy from white-owned shops. The businessmen who were losing thousands of rands every day – due to their products such as meat, dairy, and other foodstuffs going bad from not being sold and consumed – then began to apply pressure on the apartheid government to break the back of these campaigns.

By late 1956, the ANC boasted not only several successful campaigns but also the Freedom Charter. So, in response, the National Party government authorised and conducted simultaneous raids, throughout the country, early one December morning. The Security Police rounded up and arrested 156 prominent anti-apartheid leaders and charged them with treason. Tatou was among those charged. Tetelman describes Tatou's arrest as having 'traumatized many in the location. One organiser recalls that as a child "seeing him [Calata] dragged by the police, some of us used to cry. It was very painful and we didn't like it all."'[40]

It was during his stint at the Old Fort Prison that Tatou would first meet his latest grandson, whom he christened Fort.

---

40 Ibid.

Chapter Five

'Son of a Preacher Man'

– Aretha Franklin

ABIGAIL

Fort and Nomonde's love story is a real South African story. In my opinion, it is a testimony to the power of love and strength of the human spirit. I am amazed at how their love for and commitment to each other wasn't quashed by the horrendously oppressive circumstances they found themselves in during their relationship in Cradock.

Fort's story is so inextricably linked with that of Nomonde's that his story is her story too. I was curious about the roots of this love story, so for a period of about seven days, while Lukhanyo, Kwezi, and I were in Cradock in March 2017, I sat down for several interviews with Nomonde. Some of these lasted two to three hours as she shared with me the story of how a young, thin, dark-skinned boy with big ears swept her off her feet.

It was a Sunday, late afternoon in March 1974, barely two days after heavy rains had caused the Great Fish River to burst its banks. Nomonde was among a group of friends, which included her sisters, who had attended a dance commonly referred to as an 'afternoon spend' at the iLingelihle community hall. At these afternoon spends, local bands played mostly cover versions of American funk and soul music. They provided one of the main forms of recreation for the town's poor African and coloured communities. The week before, Nomonde and her friends had attended a similar 'spend', where Fort's band, The Heartbreakers, performed. This was Fort's second band after The Ambassadors, which he joined in 1972 as a guitarist and drummer[41].

Nomonde was there to dance and have a good time. She wasn't really

---

41 Notes provided by Jo-Ann Bekker.

into boys, so remained unaware of him. Fort, on the other hand, had had his eye on her for at least two years by then. On more than one occasion, he had asked Mabhudlela, the son of her elder half-sister, Nobantu, about her. Nobantu lived near the Calata home in iLingelihle, so whenever Nomonde had to go there either on an errand or just to visit, she had to pass Fort's home in Mongo Street. By then, Tatou and his family had relocated to Mongo Street after the forced removal of eMagqubeni's black residents in the late Sixties. My mother-in-law suspected it was probably on one of these visits that Fort first saw her. Even as young as he was, Fort clearly knew the value of patience. He bided his time before finally making his move at the 'spend' that Sunday afternoon. He was seventeen years old, while she was only fifteen.

Her memories of their first meeting had anything but faded; instead my mother-in-law relived and recalled them as vividly as if they had happened just the day before. With a glint in her eye, she remembered dancing in a group with her sisters and friends when, towards the end of the spend, this 'short, pitch-black boy with big ears' took her by the hand and began to dance with her. She laughed, recalling how he hadn't made a great first impression, as her first thought about him was, *Tsk! This one is trying his luck with me.*

Up to that point, her experience with boys was limited to innocent hand-holding with another musician, Peter, a coloured boy who was playing the drums that afternoon. During their first dance, Fort never told her his name. He simply said, 'I'm gonna walk you home.' Nomonde's reaction was one of dismissal; she remembered thinking, *Huh? I don't even know you. You don't know me, yet you want to take me home?*

When the song finished, the skinny, big-eared boy disappeared. I asked her if she still remembered the song, which to my disappointment she did not. Anyway, Nomonde found herself without a partner for the inevitable slow dance at the end of the spend. I'm convinced she was looking for him when she scanned the hall in search of a dance partner. A boy called Monde came to her rescue.

But Fort was waiting for her outside next to the gate when she and her friends left the hall to go home. The sun had just set, and the weather in Cradock was still unsettled following the rains just two days before, so this autumn evening in the Karoo town was uncharacteristically cold. Again, Fort took Nomonde by the hand and asked if he could explain his sudden disappearance. 'He told me he had gone home to fetch a jacket,' she said. And then he began to walk with her. His friends, as silly teenagers often do, shouted encouragement, calling him by their nickname for him, 'Go, Hettie! Go, Hettie! Go, Hettie!' My mother-in-law remembered wondering who this 'Hettie' was that they were going on about. Fort had still not told her his name. Her sisters and friends, on the other hand, were less enthusiastic about this guy. They kept on telling her to hurry up and stop holding his hand.

The skinny boy with big ears eventually introduced himself. 'He said his name was Fort, Fort Calata. He asked if I knew Tatou, and I said, "Yes, I know Tatou." He said Tatou was his father. And my heart started beating faster; I thought, *No, this can't be. The reverend's child? No, it can't be. I come from a very poor family and who am I? No, no, no, this can't happen.*'

On that first walk down Sikhulu Street, as they headed in a north-westerly direction towards the old location of eMagqubeni, Fort revealed to Nomonde that he had seen her several times before, but that he had been too shy to come over and speak to her. 'He also said that he thought I was still too young for him to ask to be my boyfriend, but now he could see that I'd grown up. He told me he saw me at the spend the weekend before, and knew that I went out at night also.' Even though Fort asked a couple of times how old she was, Nomonde would not tell him. He would eventually learn that she was fifteen years old from her sister Fundiswa.

'I thought he was gentle and sweet, not like the other boys,' Nomonde told me. Fort was soft-spoken, something his cousin Mandisa confirmed: 'Fort was a quiet and sweet guy. As we grew up, I noticed that Fort was very private, very private.' She added, 'He would only talk about something if it was necessary. I liked that about him.' And so did Nomonde. She was immediately attracted to his gentle nature. But then, as most guys tend to do when they sense that maybe, just maybe, the girl likes them too, they say or do something stupid. In this case, he became a little too confident. 'You know, he then had the nerve to ask me what I think of him. I cut him down immediately. I told him I thought nothing of him,' Nomonde recalled, a gentle smile lifting the corners of her mouth.

My mother-in-law was and still is a beautiful woman. And so Fort was undeterred by this response. As they neared her home at 81 St James Street, he asked when he could see her again. 'I agreed to see him again the following weekend at the big tank [the water reservoir] near the clinic,' she said.

Even though she'd agreed to see him again, Nomonde hardly thought of Fort again that week. Strangely, I had a very similar experience with Lukhanyo. Our story is different from that of his parents, but there are also some striking similarities. I think, just like his father, Lukhanyo knew very early on what his intentions with me were. At the time I met him, I was still smarting from the pain of divorce. My first marriage lasted four years, and when I met Lukhanyo, I had been separated from my ex for about a year. The day before we met, my close friend Asyia Sheik-Ojwang and I had partied up a storm at the J&B Met. So that Sunday morning at the Fezeka High School in Philippi, I was certainly not looking for a relationship, never mind the love of my life. I think I even forgot his name mere seconds after he rudely interrupted my conversation with fellow journalist Chantall Presence to introduce himself. I recall thinking of him as that black guy with the Spanish-looking surname from eNews because, despite having lived in South Africa all my life, back then I was quite ignorant of the clicks in isiXhosa.

My introduction to his mother a couple of months later proved to be quite extraordinary. Lukhanyo was by then working as the news editor at Heart FM and had left my apartment earlier that morning for work. While I was putting the finishing touches to my morning routine before heading to parliament, where I worked as a reporter for *Beeld*, an Afrikaans daily newspaper, I felt a presence in the bathroom with me. Simultaneously, I was also overcome by an indescribable sadness, which I could not connect to any of my circumstances. It dawned on me that I had a message for Lukhanyo's mother from his father. I had never had an experience like this, but had been told before that I am very intuitive, and that I choose to shut down my intuition. I knew the presence with me in the bathroom that morning was Fort. I also knew I had to make contact with Lukhanyo's mother, whom I'd never spoken to before then.

As soon as I got to the office, I called Lukhanyo to ask for his mother's telephone number. Nomonde's children are very protective of her and his first, rather defensive, question was what I wanted with her. I told him I had a message for her from his father. The questioning by Lukhanyo came to an abrupt end and he promptly gave me his mother's telephone number. Looking back, I'm surprised at my lack of nerves when dialling her number. This was after all my first conversation with my boyfriend's mother and one would think there would be a fair amount of agonising about making a good impression. Nomonde's impression of me was the last thing on my mind, though, as I waited for her to answer. At that time, my only concern was that I had a message to deliver, but what that message entailed was not clear to me at that moment. When she answered, I introduced myself to her. She graciously said that she knew about me and was very pleased to hear from me.

I told her I had a message for her from Fort and immediately had her full attention. It was only at that moment that it became apparent to me what I had to say to her. I told her that Fort wanted her to know he was terribly sorry for the way he had left her and that it was never his intention to leave her like that. She cried. If this conversation took place these days, the tears would also be streaming down my face. She proceeded to tell me that Fort had appeared to her in a dream the night before in which he'd told her that he was going to Cape Town to attend to some matters there. And so the bond between Nomonde and myself was established. I cherish this connection with my mother-in-law. I'm also grateful to my mother, Mary Isaacs, with whom I share a very loving and open relationship – a consequence of which is the ability to relate lovingly and respectfully to other women.

Back to Nomonde and Fort's love story. When they eventually met up again, the spark of love ignited the week before was fanned. 'It started very strongly, you know. It was as if we had known each other for years,' Nomonde told me. 'He could not live without me and I could not live without him. I sort of abandoned my friends and he became my best friend. He had abandoned his friends, but not his band, and I became his best friend.' In those early years, the bands Fort played in performed quite regularly in Cradock and the surrounding towns. He always took Nomonde with him when his band played at various afternoon spends. 'When the band played, which happened every weekend in towns like Cookhouse, he'd take me with. We'd go to Middelburg, Bedford, Adelaide, and Graaff-Reinet,' she recalled.

Thandiwe Mahangu, Fort's friend at that time, confirmed that when his relationship with Nomonde started, Fort had no interest in other women: 'Fort was in love with Nomonde.' Mahangu, a very colourful, expressive, and loud personality, added for emphasis, 'They were madly in love. We always accompanied Fort to fetch Nomonde at her home. It was an everyday thing, and as a result, the late Shwele one day asked, "Oh Fort, don't you see any girl except this Nomonde? We are also beautiful, why don't you see us?"

'Fort responded, "*Hayi suka!* Don't tell me that. I just love Nomonde."'

But who was this young girl, whose life was so intertwined with Fort's, that more than three decades after his brutal murder she was still unable to let him go? Who raised this woman, whom I see selflessly sacrificing herself to provide the best she can for their children and now grandchildren, in honour of the man she still loves so deeply and so completely? To me, Nomonde is the real hero of this story. I believe if marriage is the coming together of two to form one, Fort will agree that Nomonde was and still is the best part of him. He lives on through his children, Dorothy, Lukhanyo, and Tumani, but more than anything it is Nomonde's quiet passion for the love of her life that has birthed and sustained all the efforts to keep his memory alive through the efforts of their children. I might not be her biological daughter, but I am her spiritual daughter, and when she is no longer with us, I will continue her work to ensure that the sacrifices we Calatas have made and the monumental loss we have suffered will not have been in vain.

Nomonde Liza Maclean was born in 1959, to William Nthandazo (Oom Willem) and Nothobile Vivian Maclean. They lived in eS'dikidini, part of the old location also known as the Red Location.

This was where the poor, working-class black and coloured residents of Cradock lived. The Macleans lived in the only brick house in this part of the old location. At the time of her birth, the Calata home was just a few hundred metres away, in the more affluent part of the old location known as eMagqubeni.

Oom Willem was from Cradock. Her mother was born on the farm Jakkalsfontein, which lies around 60 km outside of Cradock. By the time Oom Willem met Nothobile in the early Fifties, they had both been married, had children, and lost their respective spouses. Oom Willem was 20 years older than the woman he would make his second wife. He took a liking to her when she, as a young woman of about 22, moved to town to look after the children of a white family. He worked as a milk delivery man at the time, and had to assure her 'madam' that he had the means to look after her before he was allowed to court her.

Shortly after the couple were married in a traditional ceremony, Nothobile fell pregnant with their first child and only son, Zwelinzima Victor Ralawe (1955), followed by a daughter, Fundiswa (1957), and then Nomonde (1959). Zwelinzima or Pa, as her brother was known, was born a Ralawe and not Maclean. Oom Willem was originally Ralawe. With the introduction of the *dompas* in the late Fifties, however, he applied to be reclassified as coloured in 1959. He was fair-skinned and, maybe because of that, his application was successful. He chose the surname Maclean, an anglicised version of the isiXhosa name Makeleni, the name of a distant relative. Nomonde was the last of her six siblings to be born Ralawe in 1959, before they were reclassified and registered under Maclean. The three sisters born after her, Nomzamo Iva (1961), Ntombiyomzi Veronica (1962), and Nomathamsanqa Charmaine (1967) were all born Maclean.

Nomonde's actual date of birth is a matter of dispute in the family. On both her birth and baptismal certificates, her date of birth is recorded as 10 April 1959. But her half-sister, Nobantu, from her father's first marriage, recalled it was bitterly cold on the day Nomonde was born. She said she and a cousin were sent by Nomonde's mother to collect money owed to her by railway workers. These workers were paid on either the 27th or 29th of each month. Nobantu also contended that Nomonde was born in June and not April. There has so far been no way of corroborating this information, so the family continues to celebrate her birthday each year on 10 April.

Life for the Macleans was not easy. Oom Willem's employer, for whom he had worked for several years as a milkman, relocated back to England, leaving Oom Willem without employment. Fortunately, he knew how to read and write, and quickly found employment again as a general worker for a firm of land surveyors based in Cradock. His new job meant Oom Willem was away from home a lot. Nomonde wryly remembered that they called her elder brother Pa because he was in fact the man of the house. 'When my father worked for those people,' she said, 'he only came home to make a baby and then he would leave again.'

While Oom Willem would be out of town for months at a time, his family was left vulnerable and suffered extreme harassment at the hands one of his sisters, Nompinzi, better known as Titi. My mother-in-law recalled this abuse at the hands of her cruel aunt with great sadness and despair. Nomonde's mother, Nothobile, received a *dompas* only after legally marrying her father sometime in the Sixties. Before that, she could not legally live in the location. According to Nomonde, Aunt Titi would arrive at their home with municipal officers in tow. Her mother would then be forced to pack up all her children and most of her possessions and move to the farm of her birth. This to and fro, which Nomonde said happened as regularly as every three months, not only disrupted their lives but also their schooling. The harassment continued even after Nomonde's parents were legally married. It eventually came to an end when Oom Willem's daughters, Nobantu and Mporose, took matters into their own hands. Nomonde recalled it was around the time her mother was pregnant with her last child in 1967 that the confrontation with their cruel aunt resulted in a physical fight. After the beating she suffered from her own nieces, Aunt Titi never again bothered Oom Willem's family. Nomonde believed her aunt's actions were motivated by jealousy and envy: 'My mom could sew really well. She also loved beautiful things, and this was reflected in the way she decorated our home.' She recalled that her half-sisters had lived with this aunt after their mother's death, saying, 'They were neglected in that house, but my mother took them in when my parents married. She cleaned them up and raised the two girls as her own.' Incidentally, this same aunt was the one who registered Nomonde's birth with Home Affairs, which in part explains why there is such confusion around her date of birth.

The Maclean children started school quite late. Thus, my mother-in-law was only in standard five (grade seven) when she first met Fort at the age of fifteen. She told me that she didn't like the academic side of school that much, but excelled at sport. She was particularly good at athletics and gymnastics, and appreciated the attention she received from her teachers for her sporting abilities. She understood the value and importance of education, dreaming of one day qualifying as a nurse.

This dream, however, was shattered when she fell pregnant in late 1974, aged fifteen.

In those first few months of Nomonde and Fort's relationship, they practically saw each other every day. Bangi had a few stories to tell about Fort and Nomonde's early relationship. He and his sister, Mandisa, recalled that Mamou used to lock the outside gates at six in the evening and at eight o'clock, everyone had to sleep. Mamou would personally switch off all lights at the main switch. The Calata home was one of the very few houses in the area that had electricity.

One evening while locking up, Mamou became worried about Fort. She hadn't seen him for a while and no one knew where he was. Bangi smiled, remembering that the boys shared a large communal room where each had his own bed. Fort wasn't in bed; he had taken the wooden coat-hanger that usually stood by the door, placed it under his blankets, and jumped out of the window to go see Nomonde. Later that evening when Mamou checked to see if all the boys were in bed, she discovered the coat-hanger in Fort's bed. Bangi didn't quite remember what happened to Fort when he eventually returned home that evening.

Nomonde and Fort's physical relationship began towards the end of 1974. Fort's friend and band member who played the electric guitar, Kura, served as a witness to their 'marriage' in front of the local clinic, which wasn't too far from the Maclean home.

'It was summer and we were standing there by the clinic,' Nomonde told me. 'There was a wall by the clinic. It was me, him, and his friend, Kura. I was just about to go home because it was late – it was after eight – and we were standing there by that wall. Fort said to his friend, "Kura, come and stand closer. Why are you standing so far?"

'Kura replied, "I don't want to listen to your things when you are talking."

'Then Fort said, "No, come. Come closer." Kura came.

'He said to him, "Kura, I want you to be a witness today. Nomonde and I just got married. So, you are a witness that me and Nomonde are husband and wife." And we laughed about it.

'Kura said, "Yes, I am a witness."

'When I ran home from him, he said, "Nomonde, don't forget that we are married now." I said, "Ja, okay," and I ran home.'

I find it difficult to determine whether Fort was motivated by a sense of propriety or whether this occasion was arranged as a ploy to convince Nomonde to sleep with him. My mother-in-law was so in love with him by then, she probably would have done anything he asked her to anyway. It also doesn't square with many people's impression of him as being an honest and forthright young man. I must therefore assume that, as one who grew up so closely connected to his grandfather, a clergyman, and who also served in the church, Fort felt compelled in some way to formalise things before commencing with their physical relationship.

In January 1975, Fort left Cradock for Cala, a town in the former Bantustan of the Transkei. This is where he would complete his high school education. One afternoon while back home for the school holidays in March, he began apologising profusely to Nomonde. She remembered his saying that he didn't know how it had happened. She thought Fort was apologising for something he'd done while in Cala. He wasn't. He was in fact apologising for getting her pregnant. Although Nomonde had noticed her widening midriff, ignorance combined with denial had prevented her from recognising what had actually happened. 'Even after Fort had told me that I was pregnant, I kept on hoping that it was not so,' she said.

While Nomonde was hoping against hope, Fort got on with the business of preparing for the baby's arrival. 'I thought maybe he'd come back home and be ashamed,' Nomonde said of her mind-set at that time. Instead, Fort told his mother, who was by now teaching in the neighbouring town of Aberdeen, about Nomonde's pregnancy, adding she could expect Nomonde's family to come and officially report her pregnancy as is custom in Xhosa culture. Fort meanwhile assured Nomonde that he would marry her as soon as he had completed his studies. 'He told me not to worry,' she said. 'What could I do? I was pregnant, I just had to go on.' She agreed to marry him. 'I loved him. I really loved him. And he loved me.'

Fort was very supportive of Nomonde during her pregnancy. He even sent her money to buy things for their baby. Nomonde did not spend the money on the baby. The needs at home were so great that she considered it far more prudent to spend the money on her family instead of providing for her unborn child.

Vakele, an elder brother from Nomonde's mother's first marriage, led the delegation to the Calatas to report her pregnancy and begin the arduous negotiation for the 'damages' due to the Maclean family because of the pregnancy. She recalled that Vakele was very proud of the way they were received by the Calatas. 'We didn't have difficulties there,' Nomonde remembered her brother saying. 'When we got there, these people already knew about us. They were expecting us. Even Tatou was there. He welcomed us.'

Fort ensured he was at home too when the Maclean delegation visited. He was called in to the meeting, where he acknowledged that he knew Nomonde, that he knew she was pregnant, and that he was responsible for her being pregnant. Her brother was pleasantly surprised by Fort's frank admissions. 'My brother said, "You know sometimes when you go to people and you say you have made my sister pregnant, they'll say, *Who is your sister? I don't even know your sister?* But Fort said, "I know your sister. I know that she's pregnant and it's me [who made her pregnant]."'

Fort's response to the pregnancy is extraordinary, firstly because of his age (he was only eighteen years old) and the times they lived in. Children born out of wedlock to teenage parents were not welcomed with open arms into the community – not today and even less so in the Seventies. Furthermore, there was the shame of having fathered a child out of wedlock, while being the 'son' of a now-retired Anglican priest, responsible for the building of at least two churches in the community. Despite this, the young Fort readily acknowledged and supported Nomonde with scant regard for what others in the community might have thought. But this did not mean he strutted around the location arrogantly as if he'd done nothing wrong. He still submitted to the authority of his (grand)parents and Nomonde's parents. He did the honourable thing, when he could have done as so many others have before and after him, denying paternity of Nomonde's child, sure in the knowledge that very few people would hold it against him.

Nomonde had to leave school as her pregnancy advanced. She was also not allowed to return to school once the baby was born. Her life, she said, 'became very difficult'. She had to deal with the stigma and shame of being a pregnant teenager alone as Fort spent most of the year at school in Cala. She could not expect any support from the nurses at the clinic or Cradock Hospital. Worse still was the fact that none of her family members accompanied her to the hospital when Dorothy was born. She was all alone when Dorothy emerged on the first chime of the town clock at five on the morning of 11 July 1975.

Nomonde described the coloured nurse who attended to her as 'very negative and racist'. 'When I came to the hospital, I was sixteen, just a child. I don't say what I did was right, but with that said, I was young and it was my first time,' she explained. 'Even for an older person, when it's your first time you don't know what is going to happen. She just put me in that thing [stirrups] and did a little bit of assessments and said, "You are not very far." Then she left me all by myself. All alone. During contractions I was on my own. When the baby eventually came, I was still on my own. I rang the bell [to call her], but she never came. She eventually showed up when she heard the baby cry. And the first thing she did was to shout at me for not calling her earlier.'

By ten o'clock that morning, Nomonde was home with her new baby. One of her first visitors was Fort's elder sister, Sisana, who arrived with baby clothes. In the afternoon, his mother visited with more gifts for the newborn. Nomonde was not sorry that she hadn't bought clothes for her baby because the little girl received a lot of clothes from her father's family.

July was school holidays, and Fort arrived back from Cala on the day Dorothy was born. 'I should think he was very scared, but he wanted to see the child,' Nomonde said, explaining his state of mind on the day. It would be the first time he'd visit inside the Maclean home. Ironically, Nomonde had visited at the Calata home and was known by Mamou. Iva, Nomonde's younger sister, opened the door for him. She gestured to Nomonde, who was in a bedroom with her parents, that Fort was at the door and what should she do? Nomonde didn't know and shrugged. Their father saw this exchange, and went to the door to greet Fort and invite him in. Fort accompanied her father to the living room, where they talked before Nomonde was called in with the baby. 'My father came to me and said [Fort] wants to see the child, but my father made him pay to see the child. I think maybe R10,' Nomonde told me. 'I took the child to him [Fort] and we sat there for a while. He was very proud of his baby girl.'

Despite his earlier promise to finish his studies, Fort offered to leave school. But Nomonde's father, Oom Willem, refused Fort's offer and instead encouraged him to complete his education. 'My father told Fort that they would take care of me and his daughter until he finished his studies,' said Nomonde. Again, I find Oom Willem's handling of the situation quite extraordinary. This was not what normally happened, particularly as some families – once they had an acknowledgement of guilt, so to speak, from the father – would insist he started taking responsibility for his child almost immediately, and quite often this meant the young men were forced to leave school and start working to support their children.

Although Nomonde's parents were upset by her falling pregnant out of wedlock, they came to accept it. 'I think they were disappointed, but they were supportive,' she told me. 'I had great parents. Any parent would be disappointed when something like that happened to their child. At a later stage, they accepted it. I should think the fact that Fort didn't make a lot of trouble by denying it also put them at ease.'

Nomonde had the responsibility of naming the baby. Under normal circumstances, it would be a family affair, as illustrated by Lukhanyo's naming six years later. The young mother had determined, however, that her daughter would not have an isiXhosa name. Fort had told her that his sister Peggy's second name was Dorothy. Nomonde looked up the meaning of the name and liked what she saw. Dorothy means gift from God. She did not tell her parents what name she chose. After their first clinic visit, her mother asked what name she had registered on the child's clinic card and Nomonde answered, 'Dorothy Maclean.'

Nomonde knew she had to start working and provide for her child. Although Fort sent money, it was not nearly enough to raise a child. She was fortunate to find work at a local butcher. She was the successful candidate out of five hopefuls vying for the job. While working at the butcher, she heard they were recruiting at the government hospital and she submitted an application to serve as a general worker there. Nomonde had been working at the butcher's for a year when she was appointed to the hospital. Once there, she worked her way up the ranks, eventually becoming the head cook in the hospital kitchen. She held this position until her dismissal in April 1984.

My mother-in-law described Fort as 'very involved in Dorothy's life'. His nickname for her was Nana. When he was home from school, he would fetch her from Nomonde's home and, as she grew older, Dorothy would spend up to a week at a time with the Calatas. Tatou was well into his eighties by that time, and he clearly enjoyed having the young child in the house, becoming upset when she came to fetch Dorothy after work. It was clear from a very young age that Dorothy had a talent for singing, so from early on Fort would put a microphone in her small hand and let her sing with his band at rehearsals. Dorothy herself also remembered how, whenever there was a new popular song, Fort would have her learn it from a cassette tape recording he made from the radio before she performed it with the band.

In June 1976, Fort was in matric in Cala. Nomonde, who was now raising their daughter in Cradock, remained largely unaware of his political involvement at school. On 16 June, the day of the Soweto Youth Uprising, iLingelihle's pupils largely steered clear of mass protests. Many would read about the revolt in newspapers, with *The World*, a progressive publication, a popular choice among them. The sporadic acts of resistance that flared up only flattered to deceive, and nothing much came of them. A few months later, though, while at home for the September holidays, Fort resorted to sabotage. He was almost 20 years old by now, and had been rather frustrated by the lack of response from the municipality to several letters he had written. In these letters, he had complained about the state of public transport, taking particular issue with the old, rickety bus service used to transport the older black workers to and from the location. He also highlighted the road hazards presented by the giant boulders strewn around iLingelihle's streets. Finally, he complained about the social impact of the municipal beerhall in the township. Mystery surrounds the typewriter Fort used to type these letters. It's unclear whose it was and who had sent it to him. Nomonde's younger sister, Iva, did remember that Nomonde had asked her on behalf of Fort to collect a travelling case from the Cradock train station one day. Iva recalled that the 'red case was incredibly heavy' and that she had no idea what she and a friend of hers, Sarel, were carrying. Fort had hoped that the police would be unable to trace the typewriter back to him. Nomonde delivered the letters by hand to the owner of the bus service, the municipal offices in town, and in iLingelihle. The two of them, Nomonde said, 'were naïve enough to believe that if we covered our hands with clothes, they would not leave fingerprints on the letters or envelopes'. So whenever they handled the letters, they covered their hands with items of clothing.

Despite their precautions, it was only a matter of time before the police came looking for both Fort and Nomonde. Her youngest sister, known as Toekie, recalled a funny incident during one of these searches by members of the police's Special Branch. 'As they were searching our house looking for Fort and Nomonde, one of the officers, probably in a moment of desperation or absent-mindedness or both, asked if they were hiding in one of the pots on the stove. He then opened it and looked inside,' Toekie said with a deep chuckle. It was at this point that their father, Oom Willem, lost his temper. 'He thought they had gone too far and began to shout at the officers, ordering them to leave his home.' Although this particular search was unsuccessful, the Special Branch eventually tracked Nomonde down. When she arrived at the police station, Fort and fellow activist Aubrey were already there. Nothing came of this investigation, as they couldn't find the typewriter and therefore could not establish a link between Fort and Nomonde.

After those letters, though, the bus service improved – slightly. The council did the bare minimum to the streets in iLingelihle by removing the boulders and 'resurfacing' them with more gravel. The third letter, which concerned the beer hall, was simply ignored and its doors stayed open. It was at this time that Nomonde's political consciousness was awakened. 'Fort started to brief me a lot more on what was going on politically,' she said. 'Also, it was the time of Black Consciousness.' Fort often suggested reading material to her.

Nomonde had now joined the ranks of the politically conscious and active youth in Cradock. Such was their activism that throughout the Sixties several young men from and others connected to Cradock, such as Jamani Jacques Goniwe, Stanley Manong, Sindiso Mfenyana, and Charles Nqakula, who had all received their education in the Karoo town, fled into exile to join uMkhonto weSizwe. So, the introduction of the Black Consciousness (BC) ideology, eloquently espoused by Steve Biko, quickly took root in iLingelihle.

Tetelman writes: 'Students at Sam Xhallie School began to translate frustration into action. They first established firmer connections with the BC movement. A cadre of young activists, including Nceba Gqasana, Vuyisile Goniwe and Thando Tuku, met with Biko in nearby King William's Town. On their return the group formed a Black Consciousness branch under the auspices of the Black People's Convention. The group reflected BC's masculinist approach: Male organisers did not allow their female counterparts to visit Biko, which resulted in few women joining the fledgling group.'[42]

Tatou is believed to have linked up with the BC activists, allowing organisers to use his home for their political discussions. He also helped them reorganise the youth choirs to connect students to Congress themes[43].

The worsening political tension in Cradock would culminate in Fort's actions around September 1976, some weeks after the Soweto Uprising. He must have felt ignored by the municipality on the beer hall matter, so he led a small group of young people to burn a municipal vehicle and iLingelihle's library in protest. The saboteurs escaped detection, and protest subsided during the rest of the year.

It is difficult to say why Fort would have resorted to violence in this case, but I suspect his heightened emotions also stemmed from the death of his grandmother, Mamou, on 9 June 1976. She passed away after having bravely battled pneumonia. Nomonde recalled that Fort was still at school in Cala at the time. One afternoon he called to ask her please to go and buy medicine from the pharmacy to take to Mamou. One of his siblings (probably Roy, his younger brother) had told him that her chest had got worse. My mother-in-law did as Fort asked, recalling that when she dropped off the medicine at the family home, she heard Mamou cough from inside the room. Nomonde said she became very concerned as 'that cough wasn't good for a 76-year-old woman'.

Mamou died a day or so later. Her death was a tremendous loss for the family, particularly her husband. They'd been married for 53 years,

42 Tetelman, M. 2012. *We Can! Black Politics in Cradock, South Africa, 1948-85*. Rhodes University: Grahamstown.

43 Ibid.

raised three daughters and eight grandchildren. Bhut' Bangi recalls that after Mamou's passing Tatou would lock himself up in his room for hours, with curtains drawn, and they'd often hear him read Scripture and pray. She was buried several days later.

The murder of Steve Biko on 12 September 1977, while in police custody, led to the first major shift in the political dynamic and power relations in iLingelihle. As black people around the country mourned his death, the grief felt by the youth in iLingelihle quickly turned to anger. This manifested itself at Biko's funeral held in King William's Town in early October. BC activists from Cradock attended his funeral and returned from there ready to avenge Steve Biko's murder.

Although there was no coherent plan, they decided to launch a school boycott. By mid-October, activists of the Black People's Convention (BPC) executed their plan, led by Nceba Gqasana and Thando Tuku among others. Tetelman writes: 'The young men walked into the classroom (Cradock Bantu Secondary School) and ordered students who were about to sit for an examinations paper to forgo their exams and march instead in protest against Biko's death. From there, the marches moved to the Solomon Akena School and took on more students as teachers watched helplessly.'[44]

A police van which had followed the march was forced to hastily retreat when the marchers, who had by now been joined by older residents, hurled stones at it. From there, the angry crowd made their way to the home of an alleged student informer, where they burnt his home and furniture. Next they headed to the home of Henry Maqhina, a police officer serving in the Security Branch who lived in iLingelihle. By the time Maqhina arrived at his home, flanked by an army of police, it was too late – his house was already engulfed by flames. Enraged by this act of arson on his home, Maqhina discharged his service pistol in the air, sending the marchers running for cover in all directions. Police then launched a search for the alleged ringleaders. In the ensuing violence, Tatou is said to have come out of his home to try and stop the unrest, but a resident told him to keep quiet and go home. Sadly for Tatou, his time of leading peaceful protests iLingelihle had come to an end.

---

44 Ibid.

With night-time approaching, the youths regrouped, but a heavy police presence in the location forced them into a different strategy. Now, they divided themselves into smaller, more nimble groups. Under the cover of darkness, they managed to set fire to the post office as well as the local office of the Bantu Affairs Administration Board located in one of the higher primary schools in iLingelihle.

Police were determined to break the back of the demonstrations, so they moved in, hundreds of them wielding shotguns and sjamboks, and conducted house-to-house searches looking for the youths. Residents who got in their way were either beaten or arrested. One student, Rocky James, was shot in the back and killed as he tried to escape the attentions of the police. Almost all of the organisers and close to 30 other students and residents were arrested that night. Many of them were convicted and imprisoned. Tetelman writes: 'iLingelihle's schools stayed closed for several months. The primary schools re-opened in early 1978, and the secondary school re-opened soon after.'[45]

When the Lovedale Teacher Training College, which had helped countless black students obtain their qualifications, shut its doors in 1979, Fort went on to complete his training at the Lennox Sebe Teachers' Training College in the Ciskei. He was the recipient of a bursary from the Ciskei government, which obliged him to teach for two years in the homeland upon his qualification. In 1980, Fort began to teach accountancy, business economics, economics, and Afrikaans at Kuyasa Senior Secondary School in Dimbaza for standards six to nine. He would make sure he was home in Cradock, a nearly 500 km round trip, almost every weekend to be with his family and perform with his band.

It was during his time in Dimbaza that he started paying lobola, the bride price he was required to pay in order to marry Nomonde. His sister Peggy recalled that there was a great deal of excitement among the Calatas in anticipation of this wedding. But she did not understand why. She'd never approved of Nomonde because she came from a poor family and therefore wasn't good enough for her brother. My mother-in-law, who today is known for her skill in organising weddings, made all the arrangements for her own wedding. She not only chose her dress but also bought the brown suit her bridegroom wore.

---

45 Ibid.

Fort and Nomonde were married on 25 October 1980 at the St John's Catholic Church in Michausdal, the coloured township in Cradock. Father John Clarke conducted the ceremony. The reception was held at the Maclean house, and attended by 50 family members and friends. Fort bemusedly observed to Nomonde, 'Look at how happy these people are about this wedding and this paper that Father Clarke gave us. We're long married. They just didn't know about it. We are just celebrating with them.'

My mother-in-law's one regret about her wedding day is that there are no photos of their white wedding. The photographer she hired for the occasion never arrived. The pictures the family has were taken the following day, when the Calatas welcomed their new daughter-in-law into the family during a traditional wedding ceremony. In each photo, Fort is sporting his trademark sunglasses, while Nomonde has the demure stance of a good Xhosa *makoti*. She told me the sunglasses had caused her huge frustration in the days leading up to the wedding. Fort, as with most musicians, thought wearing sunglasses made him cool, but his bride did not agree. She requested him not to wear sunglasses on both their wedding days. 'He agreed not wear them at our white wedding,' she said. But Fort argued that the traditional wedding was on his home turf and therefore he could wear his sunglasses for the ceremony.

After just fifteen months teaching in the Transkei, Fort returned to Cradock in March 1981 to take up a teaching position at Sam Xhallie Secondary School. Here, he taught isiXhosa and Afrikaans for standards six and seven. Shortly after he arrived back home, Lukhanyo was conceived, but it would be another month before Nomonde found out. Neither my mother-in-law nor I like milk very much. Yet, from around April/May of 1981, she found herself having to start each morning with a glass of milk, which would be followed by nausea and vomiting. Over 30 years later, Lukhanyo knew something was going on when yoghurt became a staple in our home. Nomonde's friend, who was also a nurse at the hospital, noticed that something was wrong with her and they did a pregnancy test, which delivered a positive result. When she told Fort she was pregnant again, he only showed surprise at Nomonde's not knowing she was pregnant, saying, '*Hayi*, Nomonde, till now you still don't know these things?'

Her answer to him was: 'No, I didn't know.'

Fort decided that in view of Lukhanyo's imminent arrival, the family would get its first car. He bought a red-and-white Volkswagen kombi, which could transport his family, his band and their instruments. Lukhanyo loves cars, and although his allegiance has since shifted to Japanese car manufacturers, he still has a special affinity for German-engineered cars. In 1981, the young family's future seemed bright. Both husband and wife were gainfully employed. Although they still lived with Fort's grandparents, they were on the waiting list to rent one of the new council houses that were being built in iLingelihle. This new neighbourhood, named Calata after the Canon, was the latest housing development in iLingelihle, which was established under the Natives Urban Areas Act in the early Sixties.

In a report, I found evidence that the community of eMagqubeni (the old location) had been vehemently opposed to its initial establishment. To them, the new location, iLingelihle, meant they would lose the homes in which many of them had lived for decades. Also, residents of eMagqubeni were wary of the social impact of the relocations. They were right to be wary too, as, according to my mother-in-law, residents of eMagqubeni had their own societal norms and lived according to certain customs. 'The majority of the youth back then were disciplined and raised to accept their place in our society,' she told me. 'The removals, the old people feared, would jeopardise that sense of family, belonging, and discipline.' The minutes of a meeting held on 27 June 1956 in Cradock confirm that the community did not approve of the removals. They read as follows:

'A meeting of the Vigilance Association held on Wednesday 27th June 1956 at St James Hall elected the following persons to be a Committee to present their case against the proposed implementation of the Group Areas Act at Cradock. Messrs: Joe Alfred Ncaca (Convenor), Peddy Luhabe, William Mongo, Henry Tukani, Richard Vara, Sam Xhallie, William Notwala, William Majokweni, and Mrs Rosie Phono. Questions To Be Asked:
1. Why must the African inhabitants be the ones to move?
2. If Racial separation is compulsory, what dangers are anticipated against the present position?

3. If the object is to provide better amenities, why not create the amenities near the Bantu Secondary School, which is sufficiently segregated from the schools of other racial groups?
4. If the object is to provide extra land, why not extend the present Location eastward beyond Wilken Township?

Arguments Against the Proposed Removal of African Inhabitants.

Our people have built their homes to suit their family needs out of meagre means. It would be impossible for many of them in these difficult times to build new homes.

Sondag's Hoek, the place proposed for the new site and service scheme, is quite unsuitable and undesirable in many ways. We have been made to understand that it had previously been offered to the Coloured people. We do not want it too.

We have also been made to understand that the chief reason for applying the Group Areas Act in the way suggested is, that the 41 Coloured families who live among the Europeans, must be sent out of town. If they are willing to go why not send them to a new place? Why move 1200 families to make room for 41? The suggestion is ridiculous.

The Africans have not complained against the present position, neither can it be said they have misused the privilege of staying where they are now. Which is already outside of town. Further they have not asked for new land other than an extension of the present Location so as to meet the growth and expansion of the people.

If the local authorities are compelled by Law to implement "Apartheid" in this way, we beg to submit that "The law is made for *man* and not *man* for the law": and we are convinced that our circumstances at Cradock do not require the assistance of this Law which will spoil the happy relations that now exist.

The Community of Cradock cannot be compared with other urban areas where this grouping has been applied, because Cradock has not got a sufficient Labour Market to hasten the rise of wages nor has it got the factories.

Last, but not least, the Removal of the Mission Churches and Hall will create an adverse sociological effect on the Christian inhabitants of this town. These institutions are rallying places for the congregations of the town and districts, and it would require, at least, some 40,000 to 50,000 Pounds to rebuild them [. . .] as they are in another area. Who will provide the money? It has taken these Congregations many years to build them and now they are Religious Centres and Social Centres for thousands of people. Just think of an alternative if they should go. Besides that, a good portion of land on which they stand is freehold. There is no guarantee of Freehold Tenure elsewhere.

SIGNED: William Mongo (Chairman), & William Notwala (Secretary)'

The petition failed. This saw the forced removal of the 1200 African families from the old location eMagqubeni to the new site called iLingelihle from 1964 onwards. Therefore, the new neighbourhood was merely an extension of iLingelihle.

Meanwhile, the family tale about Lukhanyo's birth tells of a heavily pregnant Nomonde who spent part of the hot summer's afternoon before his arrival riding a bicycle up and down the street. Her parents and neighbours at 4 Rietbok Street in Michausdal (the family was relocated there in 1976) were anxious on her behalf. Nomonde began to have contractions later that afternoon, while taking a bath. By eight o'clock that evening she was in hospital waiting for the arrival of her new baby. He only arrived at seven the following morning, on 18 November 1981. Nomonde was discharged from the hospital on the same day. She warmly recalled the argument between Fort and one of her aunts, Sis' Darkie, who was a nurse at the hospital: 'So my aunty was very fond of her grandchild. When Fort came to get us from hospital, she said to him, "Okay, Fort, you are going to carry [Nomonde's] bags and I'm going to carry the baby."

'Fort said, "No, Sis' Darkie, that is my son. I'm going to carry my child and you are going to carry your sister's daughter's bags. I'm going to carry my son." My aunt was very upset, but Fort carried his son to the kombi and we went home.'

Their first stop was at the home they shared with Fort's family on Mongo Street in iLingelihle. Tatou looked at the new baby and said, 'His name is Lukhanyo. He shall be the light of this family.' *ULukhanyo* means 'the light' in isiXhosa. My mother-in-law was shocked because in the car on the way there she and Fort had been discussing what they should name the child. 'Tatou was very old by then,' she said, 'and we were surprised he could come up with such a beautiful name.'

For me, there is a wonderful continuity between Tatou's naming first his grandson, Fort, and later his great-grandson, Lukhanyo. This continuity also lay in his choosing their names to illustrate what role each boy, and later man, would play in the family and, by extension, their community. Lukhanyo's grandmother, Sis' Ntsiki, wanted to get in on the baby-naming too. She named him Bruce, after the Anglican bishop in the Eastern Cape, Bishop Bruce Evans. The baby who would become my husband was then taken to meet his maternal grandparents, where he was given a third name, Matthews. By giving him this name, Oom Willem, whom his grandchildren called Da or Dada, expressed the wish that Lukhanyo would one day grow up to be like a very successful lawyer in Cradock at the time, who had the surname Matthews.

Lukhanyo spent his first ten days living at his maternal grandfather's house. His mother had to return to work and the family moved back to Tatou's house in Mongo Street. The love Fort felt for his son was unmistakable. He was involved in his day-to-day care and, as Lukhanyo began to interact more and more, Fort became his playmate. Lukhanyo, the family, and his band became Fort's refuge, particularly as he had grown frustrated with the hesitancy of – or in some cases outright refusal by – some teachers at Sam Xhallie to entertain political discussions of any kind.

It is therefore so much more heartbreaking for me that Lukhanyo's only memory of his father is his funeral. My mother-in-law and I frequently discuss the fact that there must be other memories locked up in my husband's subconscious, but in blocking the pain associated with the loss of his father, Lukhanyo is also blocking the emotions that could trigger those good memories he has of his time with Fort. My prayer is that the painful loss of his father will one day lose its sting, and he will allow himself to feel that pain so he can also access the joy he felt in his father's presence during those brief three years they had together.

Chapter Six
'Feed the Spark, It Becomes a Flame'
– Cus d'Amato

LUKHANYO

The beginning of 1983 saw the arrival of a new deputy principal named Matthew Goniwe at the Sam Xhallie Secondary School where my father was teaching. UBhut' Matthew, or Mzala as my mother calls him, was a science and mathematics teacher who arrived on transfer from the Nqweba Senior Secondary High School in Graaff-Reinet, a town 142 km from Cradock. Until Matthew's arrival at Sam Xhallie, Fort had grown disillusioned with his fellow teachers. Despite several attempts to engage with some of them on several issues affecting the community, none, it seemed, displayed an appetite for political activism. Matthew, however, was different. Although he was around nine years my father's senior, the two of them connected almost immediately.

I remember my mother sharing the story with me of how excited my father was one afternoon when he came to pick her up after work. He told her, 'Monde [that's what he used to call her], our [new] deputy principal finally arrived at our school today. It's Matthew Goniwe, my former boxing coach. I think we're going to work well together.'

When Fort and Matthew met that January morning, they were 27 and 36 years old respectively. The older Goniwe had been politically active for a few years. In fact, he had already served a four-year prison sentence after he was convicted under the Suppression of Communism Act in 1977. Much like my father, the new deputy principal was also from a political family in Cradock. Matthew Goniwe was born on 26 December 1946. He was the last of eight children born to David and Nomakula Elizabeth Goniwe, who both worked as farm-labourers on the farm Elandsberg in the district of Cradock. His siblings were Alex, (known locally as Chief), Evelyn, Tetesi, Alie, Samuel, Velile, and Jacques (pronounced Jakes) Jamani[46].

Matthew began his schooling career in 1953 when he was enrolled at St James Primary School, a school Tatou had founded in Cradock in the Thirties. Matthew displayed above-average intelligence at school, which saw him promoted from standard two to standard four. At around the same time, the young Matthew, who loved music and sports (particularly rugby and boxing), joined the Cradock Male Voice Choir, in which his elder brother Jacques was a leading member. Shortly after the Sharpeville massacre on 21 March 1960, the year Matthew passed standard six, Jacques – who had been politically active under the leadership of Tatou in a highly politicised Cradock – fled the country to join the ANC's armed wing, uMkhonto weSizwe (MK). The event and circumstances of his brother's eventual departure sparked Matthew's political consciousness[47].

In 1963, Matthew wrote and passed his Junior Certificate while still at the Cradock Bantu Secondary School. He eventually matriculated at Healdtown near Alice in 1965. From there, he enrolled at Fort Hare University, where he obtained his teacher's qualification in 1967, majoring in science and mathematics.

He began his teaching career at his alma mater – the Cradock Bantu Secondary School. From the outset, Matthew would prove a dedicated teacher. He conducted himself in a manner which set him apart from the other teachers. In most African schools, pupils are almost always referred to by their surnames, but Matthew didn't do this; instead, he learnt the first names of all his students. Although he prized discipline, he hardly ever used the cane or corporal punishment when pupils had not met his expectations. In addition to his academic responsibilities, Matthew also conducted the school choir.

The young teacher – now nicknamed 'Bullet' by his students due to his boxing ability – would make a life-changing difference in the life of one Stanley Manong, a student who came to further his education in Cradock from Victoria West in 1968. In *If We Must Die*, Manong, a former

---

46 Cupido, AB. 1991. *Matthew Goniwe, 'n Biografie.* (unpublished).
47 Ibid.

uMkhonto weSizwe commander, recalls sitting in Matthew's classroom as a student. He writes: 'After a few days at school, I realised that Mr Goniwe was very popular among students. He was a very young teacher not even wearing a beard as he was only twenty years old [. . .] Bullet never entered a classroom without having prepared meticulously for a lesson. The absence of textbooks did not deter him from doing his work. After each lesson, he would dictate notes to the class. He made General Science not only interesting but he made it look easy. Among students, General Science was by far the most popular subject.'[48]

Cradock, at this time, still boasted a highly active and politicised community. Manong describes Cradock as 'a different kettle of fish' when compared to his hometown in political awareness and activism: 'Africans in Cradock had a long history of political resistance as embodied in the persona of Rev. Calata who first came to Cradock in 1928.'[49]

Matthew, having grown up in this community, realised that his responsibilities as a teacher and contributing member of society stretched far beyond the borders of the school. So he often visited the homes of his students to apprise himself of their family environments.

Around October 1968, the Goniwe family and community in Cradock heard that four young MK soldiers, Jacques Jamani Goniwe, Gangathi 'Gandhi' Hlekani, Lennox Melani, and Ben Ngalo (part of the guerrilla force known as the Luthuli Detachment), three of whom were from Cradock, had died in battle with the Rhodesian security forces near the border with Rhodesia (Zimbabwe) during the Wankie and Sipolilo campaigns. Writing about this time, Manong says: 'I heard the news on the evening bulletin of Radio Bantu that four "terrorists" were killed trying to enter South Africa through neighbouring Rhodesia. At school the following day, I was told the truth by my classmates that one of the four fallen heroes, Jamani Goniwe, was the elder brother of Matthew Goniwe. In my class, we had two cousins of Matthew Goniwe's, Stanley and Margaret. After the news broke about the death of the (first) Cradock Four, Margaret did not attend school for a week as she was mourning the death of Jamani.'[50]

---

48 Manong, S. 2015. *If We Must Die*. Nkululeko Publishers: Johannesburg.
49 Ibid.
50 Ibid.

A few years later, in 1972, Matthew, following an invitation from John 'Oom Jan' Hlekani, resigned from his position and got ready to leave Cradock. Oom Jan, a former Cradock resident and prominent ANC activist, was school principal at Dalindyebo Senior Secondary School in the Transkei.

In the weeks leading up to his departure, Matthew kept busy by coaching standard six pupils in boxing at his former school. Among the participants in his boxing class were Fort Calata and his friend, classmate, and sparring partner, Sipho Majombozi. Majombozi vividly recalled Matthew's instructions, particularly when they did squats training as part of physical conditioning: 'He [Matthew] would sing, *"down slowly, down slowly and then up slowly, up slowly."'* Majombozi, who hailed from Hofmeyr, also shared a desk with Fort in class. Matthew eventually left Cradock later that year and began teaching at Oom Jan's school.

In 1973, Matthew and Oom Jan opened a new school, Holomisa High School, in eMqanduli. By then, a beautiful young woman who had once been a pupil of his, Nyameka Puwani, had caught Matthew's eye and he began to court her. Matthew and Nyameka married in January 1975.

In the same year, while still teaching in the Transkei, Matthew joined a reading or study group led by the brothers, Lungisile and Dumisa Ntsebeza. The Ntsebeza brothers had been among the leaders of the 1975 strike at Fort Hare University. The group is said to have studied Marxist texts, and Matthew fully embraced their teachings. By the end of that year they, Matthew in particular, had begun recruiting students into the study group. Tetelman adds that 'the group members were doomed to be caught, especially when they began raising funds publicly'.[51]

On 17 June 1975, Nyameka gave birth to their first child, a little girl she and Matthew called Nobuzwe.

The beginning of 1976 saw an optimistic Matthew ready to take a step forward in his political activities. By now, the study group had several additional cells in parts of the Transkei and as far as Fort Hare in the Ciskei. One of Matthew's biggest influences during this period was a book called *The Other Face of China*. It dealt with the reconstruction

---

51 Tetelman, M. 2012. *We Can! Black Politics in Cradock, South Africa, 1948-85*. Rhodes University: Grahamstown.

of China, its manufacturing sector, and how the communist state had combatted illiteracy and instilled a sense of pride and self-respect among its people. In a letter to his brother Samuel, Matthew writes: 'We are planning something big and I have thrown my all in it.'[52]

In addition to educating himself on international affairs, Matthew also kept in regular contact with Steve Biko, whom he often visited in King William's Town, and other prominent activists.

But his optimism was misplaced. The growth of the cells left them more vulnerable to forces looking to infiltrate them. This would prove to be the case with the Fort Hare cell. One of its founders and most dedicated members turned out to be an informer for the Security Police. In his confession to the group after they'd grown suspicious of his activities, the informer detailed how he 'had been targeted by his cousin before he had even enrolled at Fort Hare University. His handlers had paid his tuition fees and pocket money. He also told them he usually met his "handler" while jogging on the national road between Alice and Dimbaza'[53]. The cell was disbanded immediately.

In a letter the Fort Hare 'cell commander' sent to Matthew to inform him of the developments, he writes: 'Brace yourself for something dreadful [. . .] one of our core members [. . .] is a spy.'[54]

On 11 June 1976, just five days before the Soweto Uprising, police acting on the information from their spy swooped in and detained the Ntsebeza brothers, as well as Godfrey Silinga and Michael Mgobizi. Fortunately, Matthew was in Cradock during the raid. He had gone home for the June school holidays, using his time there to establish a similar cell. And so he only became aware of the arrests when he read about them in the *Eastern Province Herald* newspaper under the headline 'Transkei Swoop'. During the few days he spent in Cradock, Matthew reconnected with Sicelo Mhlawuli, an old childhood friend[55].

Despite the wise counsel of many in Cradock, who advised Matthew not to return to the Transkei for fear he too would be arrested, Matthew

---

52 Cupido, AB. 1991. *Matthew Goniwe, 'n Biografie.* (unpublished).
53 Ibid.
54 Ibid.
55 Ibid.

travelled there on 19 June. He was arrested around eight o'clock that very evening, just minutes after his arrival, and charged alongside the Ntsebeza brothers under the Suppression of Communism Act.

His wife, Nyameka, was by now a student at Fort Hare University. She would often hitch-hike the 590 km round-trip from Alice to Umtata and back to see her husband during his detention and trial[56].

During the trial, which only began in 1977, Matthew contracted tuberculosis of the spine, and at times had to attend court proceedings walking with the aid of crutches. In September 1977, almost a year after they were first charged, the court found the defendants guilty of 'propagating communism'. All but Michael Mgobizi were handed four-year prison sentences. While in prison, Matthew would spend his time rather productively. He enrolled at the University of South Africa, where he studied towards a Bachelor's degree in political science and education.

After his release from prison in 1981, Matthew headed back home to Cradock. Here, he remained unemployed for a few months. Nyameka, having qualified as a social worker, became the family's breadwinner, while Matthew was at home looking after the couple's young daughter, Nobuzwe. He took up yoga classes (long before yoga had become fashionable among black communities) to help combat a spell of depression. Towards the end of 1981, another teacher from Cradock, Mr Wilson John, helped Matthew obtain a teacher's position at the Nqweba Senior Secondary School in Graaff-Reinet. He would spend just a year teaching there as he was far from his young family in Cradock, where Nyameka was by now nursing their second child, a boy born on 15 June 1982 whom they christened Nyaniso.

In January 1983, at Matthew's request, the Department of Bantu Education transferred him back to Cradock, to the same Bantu Secondary School where he had begun his teaching career over a decade previously, now renamed Sam Xhallie Senior Secondary School. This time, however, he had returned as the school's deputy principal.

Within a week of Matthew's arrival back in Cradock, Fort started negotiating with my mother. 'Look, Nomonde,' he would say to her, 'my (deputy) principal and I are going to have a meeting here at home, so tonight please could you go and keep my mother company until we

---

56 Ibid.

are finished.' My mother, never one to just accept anything, told me she would remonstrate, asking him, 'Why don't you hold your meetings at school?' He would respond, 'We can't, not at school. I'm going to use my room.' Tatou's home, where my parents, Dorothy, and I still lived at that point, was about 500 m from the school where my father and Matthew taught. It wasn't long after their first meeting that they began having regular meetings. At first, it was only the two of them. Whenever Tatou, who was quite old and frail by then, had had a good day, they would meet and consult with him. 'Almost every evening, Fort and Matthew would meet for discussions in the outside room where we slept, and I would have to sit with my mother-in-law inside the house for hours in order not to disturb their meeting,' my mother said.

Tetelman writes about this partnership: 'Goniwe found a committed partner in Canon Calata's grandson, Fort. He was fortunate, for Calata was a dynamic leader. Like his grandfather, he had inexhaustible energy and fiery commitment.'[57]

It was around this time that Matthew, Mbulelo Goniwe (Matthew's nephew), and my father were first approached by Makhenkesi Arnold Stofile, an ANC underground activist based at Fort Hare University. Stofile asked them to build an organisation in Cradock and other Karoo towns[58].

Within a month or so after the first meetings between my father and Matthew, Mbulelo, Sparro Mkonto, Madoda Jacobs, Moppo Mene, and Mtutu Ntombela began to join these meetings. According to Mbulelo, whom Abigail and I met with in Cradock, 'they discussed and debated many issues; chief among these was how to organise the township youth to stop the decline in discipline, curb rampant delinquency, and reduce the escalating rate of teenage pregnancies.' They also sought out other older men, like my mother's father, Oom Willem, for advice, as they considered these men as having first-hand experience and knowledge of Cradock's history of struggle against oppression.

---

57 Tetelman, M. 2012. *We Can! Black Politics in Cradock, South Africa, 1948-85*. Rhodes University: Grahamstown.

58 Declassified National Intelligence Agency Document. Briefing Notes: '"The Cradock Four" – Fort Calata, Matthew Goniwe, Sparro Mkonto, Sicelo Mhlawuli.'

At school, Matthew and my father prioritised discipline and the well-being of their students. My mother recalled that at times the school children would visit our home when they had problems with their parents: 'They would come and talk to Fort and tell him their problems. He [would] go to their parents and talk to them to try to solve some of the problems between the child and the parent.

'I also remember the time when Fort was teaching at Sam Xhallie. Every end of the month, he [would] ask me for money and say, "Monde, you know I must have money – I have to buy bread, peanut butter, and juice for my classroom. Some of the children there don't have food, and there must be food in my class, so that those who don't have food at home can eat".'

Matthew also highlighted my father's efforts among other teachers to emphasise to them the need for a more active role in society. He stressed that they needed to co-operate with the parents of their students to address the prevailing social conditions affecting the youth in particular[59].

Moppo Mene, describing my father and Matthew's friendship and leadership, said, 'the two of them, uBhut' Matthew Goniwe and uBhut' Fort Calata were different. We had in them a leadership that boasted two intellectuals [who] were highly intellectual when we sat and discussed issues. Then you add to that uBhut' Sparro Mkonto, who was more a trade unionist, [and] more pragmatic in terms of what was supposedly to happen.' Mene continued: 'uBhut' Matthew, though, wasn't very close to us young people but uBhut' Fort was. Even now, today, you can go to chaps who were ten to fifteen years [old] at the time. They will tell you about uBhut' Fort Calata. He even charged the toyi-toyi in some instances because of his militancy. But at the same time, he had a very substantive voice of reason when we debated issues. For us, we felt that we can't then have any other leader who might not display these complementary leadership qualities. He began to converge us, because among us youth, you had people like myself, who wanted to theorise, then you had Lulamile Jojiyasi, who was very vocal, and you had Madoda Jacobs, who was always trying to keep everybody else together. Mbulelo Goniwe was a very good organiser, then you had Zenzile Blou

59 Tetelman, M. 2012. *We Can! Black Politics in Cradock, South Africa, 1948-85*. Rhodes University: Grahamstown.

Top: The Ikwezi Lomso Choir, 1930, with Rev James Calata as conductor. The choir's concerts helped fund the new St James Church and associated school in Cradock. *Reproduced with permission courtesy of Rev James Arthur Calata Papers, Historical Papers Research Archive, the Library, University of the Witwatersrand, Johannesburg.*

Bottom: Rev Calata in 1948 with some of the members of the Congress Choir, which sung around the Eastern Cape to raise money for the ANC. *Reproduced with permission courtesy of Rev James Arthur Calata Papers, Historical Papers Research Archive, the Library, University of the Witwatersrand, Johannesburg.*

Top: Treason trialists sing at Gandhi Hall in Johannesburg in 1959. James Calata – by now a canon of the Anglican Church – is second from the left while others in the choir included Vuyusile Mini, Sonia Bunting, Elias Moretsele and Frances Baard. *Reproduced with permission courtesy of Rev James Arthur Calata Papers, Historical Papers Research Archive, the Library, University of the Witwatersrand, Johannesburg.*

Bottom: Miltha Mary Calata, or Mamou as she was affectionately called.

Top: Canon Calata's life commemorated by the September 1983 edition of *Sechaba*, the ANC journal that was published in London from 1967. *Image: ANC Archive/Africa Media Online.*

Bottom: The Canon – affectionately known as Tatou – at home on his birthday in 1974.

Top: Fort, at the back, with his band on a trip to Namibia.

Opposite page:
Top left: Fort Calata in 1976, aged 20, shortly after his return
from initiation.

Top right: Fort Calata, on the right, in 1976.

Bottom: Fort and Nomonde were married in 1980 in Cradock.

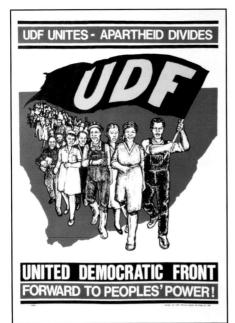

UDF UNITES - APARTHEID DIVIDES

UDF

UNITED DEMOCRATIC FRONT
FORWARD TO PEOPLES' POWER!

DETENTIONS!!!!
UDF LEADERS DETAINED
BANNINGS!!!!!!
MEETINGS IN 22 AREAS BANNED
REPRESSION!!!
PEOPLE SHOT DEAD IN TOWNSHIPS
HARASSMENT!!!

UDF

WE WILL NOT BE
SILENCED

Above: Matthew Goniwe's burnt-out car that was discovered on the road between Grahamstown and Port Elizabeth in June 1985 after the four went missing. *Picture: Jack Cooper/The Herald.*

Opposite page:
Top: The iconic picture, believed by many to be the Cradock Four, shot in October 1984 but two of the men – Mbulelo Goniwe, far left, and Madoda "Dopla" Jacobs, second from left – were not on the ill-fated trip to Port Elizabeth that saw Matthew Goniwe, Fort Calata, Sparro Mkonto and Sicelo Mhlawuli killed by security police. Calata is second from the right; Matthew on the far right. Jacobs, a political activist and former student of Matthew's, survived on low-paying odd jobs until he died in 2003 while Mbulelo, Matthew's nephew and the only one of the men still alive, went on to become the ANC's chief parliamentary whip. *Picture: Colin Urquhart/The Herald.*

Bottom left and right: The formation of the United Democratic Front (UDF) in 1983 revived the spirit of political activism in townships across South Africa. UDF posters, banners and T-shirts were produced cheaply and quickly – the 'viral campaigns' of an earlier era – as they publicised events and messages of the movement. *Images: ANC Archive/Africa Media Online.*

Top: The funeral of the Cradock Four was a crucial turning point in the struggle as it prompted PW Botha's regime to declare the 1985 State of Emergency, which started in 36 of the country's 260 magisterial districts and mostly in the Eastern Cape. *Picture: Jimmy Albertus.*

Bottom: More than 60 000 people attended the funeral on 20 July 1985. The headline in the *Sunday Times* the next day was 'Priests march under the red flag'. *Picture: David Goldblatt/Africa Media Online.*

Opposite: Mourners carrying a South African Communist Party banner to iLingelihle cemetery. The Church of the Ascension is in the background. *Picture: Gille de Vlieg/Africa Media Online.*

Top: Dr Alan Boesak and Rev Beyers Naudé were borne aloft on the shoulders of the funeral-goers at the stadium while the crowd chanted, 'Boesak, Boesak, Boesak!' *Picture: David Goldblatt/Africa Media Online.*

Bottom: Nomonde and Tumani, who was born nineteen days after Fort's funeral, with Molly Blackburn.

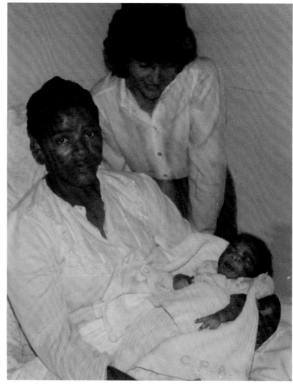

Top: The graves of the Cradock Four in the days after the funeral in 1985. *Picture: David Goldblatt/Africa Media Online.*

Bottom: Lukhanyo, Tumani, Nomonde and Dorothy (obscured) in the cemetery about a decade after Fort's death.

Top: From the left in the front row, Nomonde, Tumani, Charles Nqakula, Bantu Holomisa and Fort's mother, Sis' Ntsiki, in 1994. Holomisa and Nqakula joined Nelson Mandela, who is missing from the photo, on this visit to pay their respects to the Cradock Four.

Bottom: The simple memorial stone for the Cradock Four.

Top: Nomonde receiving Fort's posthumous Order of Luthuli in Bronze from President Thabo Mbeki in 2006.

Bottom: Three of the Cradock Four widows at the 2006 ceremony for the Orders of Luthuli and Baobab. Nomonde is second from left in the back row, Nombuyiselo Mhlawuli second from left in the front row and Sindiswa Mkonto second from right in the front row. Among the other recipients were Constitutional Court Justice Albie Sachs and Prof Barney Pityana.

TUESDAY JUNE 28 2016   www.capeargus.co.za
Cape Argus
AM EDITION   R7.00   Country R7.00   **Page 2**

WII
Pick n Pa
vouchers
valued at
R2 50(

'Is this what Fort Calata died for?'

Slain activist's son and SABC staffer hits out at his bosses

Lance Witten
DEPUTY NEWS EDITOR
lance.witten@inl.co.za

IN THE wake of acting chief executive Jimi Matthews's resignation, SABC TV parliamentary reporter Lukhanyo Calata, the son of Cradock Four member Fort Calata, has spoken out against its censoring policy implemented by chief operating officer Hlaudi Motsoeneng.

"For anybody to try and tell me, you can't say this, you can't cover this, you can't write this, you can't do this, in a democracy, to come and tell me this, when literally thousands of people died in the Struggle for me to have the right, the constitutional right, to have an opinion and express myself.

"How can we then sit back and allow somebody to come and be a dictator. Not in a democracy, it doesn't work like that."

Calata's father was one of the Cradock Four murdered by an apartheid police hit squad on June 27, 1985 – 31 years to the day yesterday.

"I don't know what awaits me by speaking out like this. But my father, and thousands like him, gave up their lives for what they believed in.

"All I have to lose is my lifestyle. Life versus lifestyle.

"We have to do what is right and what is going on is not right.

"Is this what my dad died for?"

Earlier yesterday, Calata issued a statement on the latest movements at the SABC.

"I made the decision to become a journalist after years of watching journalists coming to our home as part of their drive to tell the story of my father and his comrades," he wrote.

"Thirty-one years later, I now work as a news reporter, with the sole purpose of telling stories of my people with dedication, truth and freedom.

"A freedom that many like my father either died or were imprisoned for.

"It is therefore with great sadness that I am confronted with the disturbing direction taken by my employers.

"A direction I believe flies in the face of what many have sacrificed.

"The decisions taken recently by the SABC cannot be described in any other way but as curbing media freedom.

"A freedom to report ethically, truthfully and without bias."

Yesterday marked the 31st anniversary of the death of the Cradock Four.

Fort Calata, Matthew Goniwe, Sparrow Mkhonto and Sicelo Mhlauli were picked up by the hit squad en route to Port Elizabeth to attend a UDF meeting in June 1985.

To page 2

WON'T BE QUIET: SABC reporter Lukhanyo Calata with son, Kwezi, after he broke his silence on sentiment at the public broadcaster's decision to black out coverage of violent public protest.   PICTURE: DAVID RITCHIE

1985 – SILENCED BY THE STATE

FORT CALATA
BORN 05-11-1956
DIED 28-06-1985
REST IN PEACE
NOBLE SON OF AFRICA

FORT CALATA

2016 – SILENCED BY THE STATE BROADCASTER

NOT IN OUR NAME

LUKHANYO CALATA

FRIDAY JULY 01 2016

www.capeargus.co.za

Cape Argus

LATE FINAL

R7.00
Country R7.00

JUST A
Low Mainter
"Tillandsies"
"Urs
Largest se
Weste
Starke Ayres
T.

Scores say no to SABC censorship

SUPPORT: Motorists driving past the SABC office in Sea Point hooted in support of scores of protesting journalists. Among the protesters was SABC journalist Lukhanyo Calata, not pictured, who spoke out against his employer earlier in the week. PICTURE: HENK KRUGER

Journalists around the country picket on #BlackFriday

ABOUT 200 journalists and social activists gathered outside the South African Broadcasting Corporation's (SABC) studio in Sea Point this morning, to heed the #BlackFriday rallying call to protest against the censorship of some of the broadcaster's news content.

There was a buzz of conversation as protesters, some dressed in black to mark "Black Friday", stood in Beach Road and discussed the controversial situation at

Staff Reporters and ANA

SABC. Some members in the crowd held up posters which read "#Free Journalists" or "#Black Friday".

The pickets in Joburg, Cape Town and Durban were organised by the SA National Editors Forum (Sanef). Many Independent Media staffers, editors and journalists, including some from the Cape Argus, attended the pickets this morning.

Sanef is concerned at the impact that the "corrosive atmosphere" at the SABC is having on the public's right to know.

"Recent editorial policy directives are a direct assault not only on the journalism profession, but on media freedom as a whole," it said in a statement. "Sanef warns against the SABC being turned – once again – into a state broadcaster that only serves the interests of the ruling party. The SABC is accountable to the South African public, so what is going on at the public

broadcaster is of concern to everyone."

Scores of protesters also gathered at the Auckland Park premises of the SABC in Joburg and at its Durban offices this morning, chanting slogans calling for free media. In Joburg journalists chanted "journalism is not a crime", "no to censorship", "the SABC is a public broadcaster" and "reinstate them". Some of the placards read "Hlaudi with no chance of news" and

To page 2

Top: Journalists protested against the treatment of the SABC 8 outside the broadcaster's offices in Cape Town, Johannesburg and Durban. *Front page courtesy of Cape Argus.*

Bottom: The SABC 8: Thandeka Gqubule, Krivani Pillay, Lukhanyo Calata, Foeta Krige, Busisiwe Ntuli and Vuyo Mvoko at Suna Venter's memorial service in July 2017 in Johannesburg. (Missing from the picture is Jacques Steenkamp.) SABC staff members honoured Venter with white balloons as a symbol of her fight against censorship. *Picture: Gallo Images/Beeld/Wikus de Wet.*

Nomonde Calata (seated) with her and Fort's grandchildren, children and their spouses. Back row from left: Lukhanyo and Abigail Calata, Lukhanyo Dombo, Tumani Calata, Dorothy Calata-Dombo and Alugumi Dombo.
Front row from left: Kwazi and Kwezi Calata, Nomonde, Junior and Pumudzo Dombo. *Picture: Charles Pullen.*

and Mtutu Ntombela, very intellectual also. But uBhut' Fort would pull us all together and then make sure he gave us guidance in terms of what needed to happen. He would relay this information to the Civic Association. That was his character and we felt he was the best of us to lead the Youth Association at the time.'

Mene laughingly added, 'He [Fort] was another character. Yoh! He was just another character. Matthew used to say, "Fort, what do you want among these young boys?" And he would say, "No, no, no, look it's my responsibility. I'm leading them. I must lead them by example."'

As winter approached in 1983, Tatou's health had begun to deteriorate. I suspect Tatou'd realised by then that Fort had finally found in Matthew a partner who could help him advance the struggle of the African people, both in Cradock and the country at large. Tatou must've been comforted by this: he had successfully passed on the baton and revolutionary spirit to my father and Matthew. On 16 June 1983, just six months after Fort and Matthew began working together, Canon James Arthur Calata passed away. He was 88 years old.

My mother recalled that Thursday as if it were yesterday. She was still employed at the Cradock Hospital at the time. As it turned out, she would be the last family member to see Tatou alive. He had been admitted to hospital a few weeks previously due to chest problems. My mother worked in the hospital kitchen, which meant she usually cared for him during his admission. 'I often helped him eat his lunch,' she said. 'That day I went to his ward to help him with his food. He didn't eat much. After just a few spoons, I cleaned his mouth, wiped his face, and changed his pyjamas. Tatou said thank you, but his voice was very faint. I could hardly hear him. He said thank you and he held my hand and I held his back, and he just nodded a little bit. I thought he was saying goodbye, since I had told him I was going home for lunch and that Fort had said he would come back with Sis' Ntsiki in the afternoon to visit him. He just nodded his head.'

Fort was waiting for her outside, to take her home for lunch. 'Normally,' she told me, 'he would come into the hospital to see his grandfather, but that day he didn't. He said he would visit later that evening when he came to pick me up from work.' They went home for lunch and when she returned, the nurses told her Tatou had died.

Tatou's death and subsequent funeral would prove a pivotal point in the political education and activism in iLingelihle.

Fort, naturally, was devastated by the loss of the man who had raised him and whom he had considered his father. But he did not have that much time to mourn, as he, with the help of Matthew, began to organise Tatou's funeral. There were two very strong opinions and differences in my family regarding how Tatou should be buried. The one opinion led by Vuyelwa (the middle daughter) advocated for a solely religious funeral ceremony. The other two daughters, Nontsikelelo (my grandmother) and Noluthando (the youngest), with the support of most of the grand-children, wanted the funeral to acknowledge his role in politics within the ANC.

Tetelman writes: 'Calata's funeral was a complex and significant per-formance, embodying his multiple political and social identities. The Anglican church looked to play a large part, with St James congregant and school principal Mr Patrick Mali scheduled to give the introductory speech. The banned African National Congress was also prepared to play a major, if implicit, role via United Democratic Front organisers, who were to speak of Calata's political contributions. The goal was to unite theological and oppositional politics, but days before the funeral began, political organisers and clergy clashed over the burial proceed-ings. The clergy, especially the local Anglican minister, Reverend Dume-zweni, wanted Calata buried out of the Ascension Church.' Tetelman adds, quoting my mother, that 'the Church wanted to bury Tatou, like a priest, at the Church, singing hymns and saying nothing about his involvement in Politics. Fort objected, arguing that his "grandfather cannot be buried like this. He was involved in the ANC also and it needed to play its role, in paying its respects."' [60]

My mother remembered how relieved Fort was when the matter was finally concluded just two days before the funeral. He told her that 'the pain of losing Tatou was somewhat softened by being able to send him off with a funeral befitting his legacy'.

The ANC took its cue from the family. My mother recalled that when a family delegation arrived at the funeral undertakers, they were told that a coffin had already been paid for, and that it would be transported

---

60 Ibid.

to Cradock from Queenstown that same day. Fort then arranged for the construction of a stage in front of the open plot of land outside Tatou's home. The band's equipment, including microphones, amplifiers, and speakers, served as the public-address system. At around two o'clock that Friday afternoon, the church began to circulate its programme for the funeral. My mother told me that my father was very annoyed by this move from the church. He, Matthew, and the ANC had been in discussions, but had not yet finalised their programme for the funeral. I suppose my father must've felt very sheepish at being pipped at the post by the church. Despite this setback, they forged ahead, and at around seven that evening, about an hour after Tatou's night vigil had started, they distributed a different programme, this time printed on yellow paper. Thereafter, Fort approached and informed the Reverend Dumezweni, who was now stationed at the Ascension Church, that his grandfather's remains would be transferred to the Ascension Church only after the ANC had concluded its programme the next day.

Tetelman writes: 'Among the three thousand who attended and spoke at the funeral were older ANC activists, such Archie Gumede, who would later become the first president of the United Democratic Front, Popo Molefe, the future General Secretary of the UDF, Steve Tshwete, a leading underground activist from the border region and Nonyamezelo Victoria Mxenge, the widow of slain Durban activist Griffiths Mxenge.'

Gumede, who was the keynote speaker, 'above all lauded Calata's unswerving commitment to oppressed people. Calata, he concluded, "paid particular attention to the welfare of the people he served which influenced him to fully participate in efforts to achieve the total freedom of the individual in South Africa regardless of colour, creed or religion."'

Mxenge, in her turn at the podium, stressed that: 'Calata had realised that the Kingdom of God is an extension of a freedom realisable in this world and consummated finally in heaven. Calata,' she said, 'refused to divorce Christianity from the liberation struggle.'

Dr Simon Gqubule, the former president of the Methodist Church, said: 'Church groups should not be gatherings where people get together to cry over their sins, but to be active and make themselves useful to the community.'[61]

---

61 Ibid.

For some of the Anglican clergy gathered there, the words spoken from the podium were the cause of quite significant discomfort.

After the ANC had paid its respects at the memorial, Tatou's remains were eventually transported to the church for the funeral service. He was buried in the same grave as his wife, Miltha Mary (Mamou), who had passed away seven years previously.

Fort, my mother recalled, did not properly mourn his grandfather's death. She said it was hardly a few days after Tatou was buried when he and Matthew began meeting regularly once again. Although they taught at the same school, spending several hours in each other's company, they would still meet again after school, and sometimes, she said, 'the meetings would go on late into the night'.

Indeed, as Tetelman explains, "Tatou's funeral became a critical moment in crystalising a national opposition movement. For many UDF organisers, the funeral marked the first time that they had congregated openly. According to COSAS organiser and future leader of the Port Elizabeth Youth Congress (PEYCO), Mkhuseli Jack, the funeral "gave the opportunity for national activists to build up something. It was a core gathering where all the activists came to canvass."'[62]

Cradock's revolutionary flame was re-ignited. The funeral proved to be the perfect platform from which my father and Matthew could begin to mobilise residents of iLingelihle. .

At around the same time as the funeral, the Cradock Municipality had begun to circulate notices in the location of iLingelihle. These notices informed the community of its soon-to-be introduced sliding scale rent policy, which would be implemented in the new ward of about 500 council houses nearing completion in the southeast part of iLingelihle. Residents had called this new neighbourhood the Calata ward, in honour of my great-grandfather. These rent proposals were from the Eastern Cape Administration Board, and rental rates per home would be calculated on the monthly income of the tenant. This meant paying rent ranging between R37,91 and R84,73 'for houses that were similar to houses in the old section. Although these were houses built in 1983,

---

62 Ibid.

they lacked such bare essentials as electricity, bathrooms, and a flushing toilet.'[63]

The rent policy had become a major point of debate and frustration for the community.

In a speech delivered at the Black Sash National Conference in 1985, Matthew described Cradock as 'a dusty, rural town situated in the Eastern Cape. According to official statistics, its (black) population is 24,000. A characteristic feature of Cradock is a lack of places of employment. There are no industries. The bulk of local residents survive on the meagre wages earned by women working as domestic servants in town. The only major means of employment for men is working as labourers in the South African Railways. A small number work in shops and supermarkets. Cradock thus has a huge army of unemployed people. It is no exaggeration to say that a significant number of local people eke out a lingering existence, plagued as they are by the dire economic straits.'[64]

My father and Matthew redoubled their efforts in the weeks to come, beginning to mobilise the youth in particular. Teachers at Sam Xhallie were facing severe disciplinary challenges from their pupils. So on Sunday, 7 August 1983, just weeks after they had buried Tatou, my father and Matthew called a community meeting in the hall at the Ascension Church. Hundreds of community members attended the meeting, during which they first called for the launch of a new youth organisation called the Cradock Youth Association (Cradoya). Residents, mostly parents, were apprehensive and many even rejected its formation for fear that this Youth Association would be a political organisation. Many parents recalled the events of October 1977 and did not want their children involved in a repeat of that. Matthew assured them that Cradoya would not be a political formation; instead, it would be a cultural organisation. Based on his assurances, residents relented and the Cradock Youth Association was born.

Its first executive included, among others, Rev Leslie Pezi of the AME Church (who was elected its chairperson), prominent teacher Ruben Mahangu, and his sister, Nolungile Martha Ralawe. In its first meetings,

---

63 Goniwe Papers. Cory Library, Rhodes University.
64 Ibid.

Cradoya duly discussed critical issues affecting the community, such as the abuse of alcohol and marijuana among the youth. Also on the agenda was the apparent lack of political leadership in the community now that Tatou was no longer there. His death had in some ways highlighted the leadership vacuum in the location. True to form, Cradoya began to organise youth-based programmes such as musical rehearsals and drama classes in the community. My father was asked to assist the youths who could play a musical instrument and 'see what he could do' in turning them into a band.

But this apolitical Cradoya was of little interest to the youth. They did not share the same fears as their parents and clearly wanted the organisation to address political issues of the day. The year 1983 also saw the release and return to iLingelihle of many arrested in the October 1977 revolt.

My mother told me that Fort too was growing frustrated with the cultural and indoor-sports activities, and recalled how Matthew often had to 'calm him down' before they attended Cradoya meetings. Fort then caucused a plan to hijack the agenda of the next Cradoya meeting with Mbulelo Goniwe, Madoda Jacobs, Moppo Mene, and Victor Puwani, among others. My mother said that Fort thought it would be the ideal time to strike, as Matthew wouldn't attend this particular meeting due to travel arrangements. My father only revealed the plan for the takeover to Matthew a day or so before he was to travel. Although uncertain, Matthew gave it his blessing.

It was shortly after the Cradoya executive had tabled their reports in the meeting when Jacobs, Mene, Goniwe, and Puwani set their plan in motion. They began to sing struggle songs and were almost immediately joined by those attending the Sunday afternoon meeting. Hearing the singing, chants, and commotion coming from inside the hall, nearby residents who had initially stayed away from the meeting began to make their way towards the hall. Inside, they joined a particularly vociferous crowd, who grew more emboldened with each individual who walked through the hall's doors. Their excitement was palpable, and 'the executive was shocked and bewildered'.[65]

Mbulelo Goniwe would come to their rescue, as he 'calmed the

---

65 Cupido, AB. 1991. *Matthew Goniwe, 'n Biografie.* (unpublished).

tensions' by assuming the role of chairperson for the duration of the meeting, which adopted a more radical agenda and at the same time proposed the election of a new leadership. The new executive included my father, elected as the new chairperson, and Mbulelo Goniwe as secretary, in addition to Madoda Jacobs (the head boy of Sam Xhallie), Moppo Mene, Mtutu Ntombela, and Mzimkhulu Zenzile.

Fortunately for the new executive, Rev Pezi, the ousted former chairperson, did not take his removal personally. In a handover discussion with Matthew and my father a day or so after he was deposed, Matthew told the reverend: 'It is time to take the struggle to the white man, but before that, we must mobilize the people, teach them about themselves, then they will realise their potential. It's high time for structures to be formed, to organize the people to know each other. The people must stop report[ing] misdemeanours to police.'[66]

When my father and his colleagues established the more radical and politically inclined Cradoya on 12 August 1983, they were in fact reflecting a national sentiment. Just a few days later, on 20 August, a new national organisation called the United Democratic Front (UDF) was established. Thousands of activists representing over 500 different civic and youth formations from around the country descended on the Rocklands community hall in Mitchell's Plain for the official and historic launch of this new organisation. Among the delegates was Rev Allan Boesak, who had in January that year called for a united front of civil-, business-, and faith-based organisations to combat apartheid.

Boesak was elected patron of the organisation while Archie Gumede, who had been a guest speaker at Tatou's funeral just weeks before, was elected as the new organisation's first president. In Gumede's maiden address, he quoted Peter Bowen who had during Tatou's funeral used the biblical story of Moses as an analogy of the times. Gumede said: 'Much like Moses had led the children of Israel out of Egypt [. . .] there is simply no reason why the UDF could not lead the people of South Africa out of the apartheid state and into a state in which all shall be free and the people shall govern.'[67]

---

66 Ibid.
67 Tetelman, M. 2012. *We Can! Black Politics in Cradock, South Africa, 1948-85*. Rhodes University: Grahamstown.

Back in Cradock, the 'new' Cradoya almost immediately began to bear positive fruits, where the most significant changes were in the attitudes and discipline of the youth. My mother remembered that one of the first tasks my father had set the organisation was to secure the safety and relative comfort of pensioners at pension and social grants payout points. Mene recalled how they would often supervise the payouts, which were conducted at the community hall.

This had two spin-offs: the first was a tangible decline in petty crimes such as robberies in iLingelihle, and, secondly, it served to protect the pensioners from unscrupulous loan sharks and 'shebeen queens' who preyed on some of them[68].

The Cradoya executive bore the hallmarks of the cells and study groups Matthew had set up in the Transkei several years before. 'We would listen to Radio Freedom with your father and Matthew, at six o'clock in the morning, then again at six o'clock in the evening,' Mene told me. 'That would be followed by Radio Namibia at seven o'clock and nine o'clock. Immediately after that, there would be discussions in terms of what the message was that had been put through.'

At the beginning of September 1983, my father, mother, sister, and I eventually moved out of Tatou's home and into our new house at number 30 Siyabulela Street in the Calata ward. My family was one of several hundred others who moved into these 'mere shells of houses'. Our new house had four rooms, which according to my mother, was a far cry from Tatou's home: 'It had only windows and doors and no other fittings. The walls were not plastered and there were no ceilings.' Residents were expected to turn these empty shells into homes. Due to the sliding-scale rent policy, my family (because my father was a teacher) paid rent of R68 per month, while the Damoyi family in the identical house next door were only expected to pay about R13 because their father, Teddy, was a railway worker. It was these discrepancies in rent and the appalling living conditions black people had to endure which angered the iLingelihle community, and which made sure that whenever a meeting was called, many residents attended.

In the intervening days, Matthew and my father travelled to Port

---

68 Cupido, AB. 1991. Matthew Goniwe 'n Biografie. (unpublished)

Elizabeth for a briefing with Mrs Molly Blackburn, a prominent member of the Black Sash who also served as a member of the Provincial Council. The Black Sash comprised mainly white women who sympathetically took up and supported black people's struggles. They briefed Molly, as she was known in iLingelihle, about the sliding-scale rent issue and requested that she 'please make an official inquiry' with Mr Louis Koch, the chief director of the Eastern Cape Administration Board, into the structuring of the rents and rent formula. Matthew also asked her for advice on running a civic association[69].

Koch had not been to Cradock in several years. In fact, the last time he had visited the town was in 1979, when he came to address the community on the introduction of community councils. The Community Councils Act of 1977 replaced the Advisory Boards and Urban Bantu Councils, instituting a new system of elected black officials under the supervision of the Bantu Affairs Administration Board[70].

The state, of which Koch was a fervent proponent, promoted the community councils as a new semi-autonomous system of government, which they claimed 'allowed black people far greater control over township housing and services'. The councils came into effect in 1978, and the Cradock Community Council was supervised by the Cape Midlands Administration Board[71].

In Cradock, however, the composition of the community council wasn't determined by an election, as was required by law and (hopefully) practised nationally. In my hometown, that decision was made by officers of the South African Police (the Special Branch, as they were known in iLingelihle). They decided whether or not an aspirant councillor was apolitical enough to be appointed onto the council. And, as with most things under the diabolical apartheid regime, the Special Branch did their job rather well. The Cradock Community Council comprised mostly 'middle-class' residents who had refrained from political protests.

In 1978, the council had enjoyed brief support from the community

---

69 Goniwe Papers. Cory Library, Rhodes University.

70 Tetelman, M. 2012. *We Can! Black Politics in Cradock, South Africa, 1948-85*. Rhodes University: Grahamstown.

71 Ibid.

in its early months, but that had begun to wane by 1980 when residents realised that it lacked the actual power to deliver on any of its promises. Community councils, it turned out, were not what the authorities, in particular Louis Koch, had led the residents of iLingelihle to believe.

A few days after the September meeting between Molly, Matthew, and my father, Molly wrote to Koch, requesting a copy of the sliding scale used to determine rentals and service charges in the Eastern Cape townships. Numerous aspects of his reply, received on 3 October, were thought to be confusing[72].

The very next day, on 4 October, during what had now become regular mass meetings, the community resolved to form a new organisation, which they called the Cradock Residents' Association (Cradora). Matthew was elected its chairperson, my father its treasurer, and Mbulelo Goniwe its organiser. Also on the executive were Zenzile Blou, Thami Hani, Lulamile Jojiyasi, Monwabisi Gladwell Makhawula, Moppo Mene, Sparro Mkonto, Mtutu Ntombela, Victor Puwani, and Wekens Soga.

Those in attendance debated how to fight the sliding-scale rent plan. Gilgashe Skweyiya, or 'Oom Gillie' as he was known, proposed that the community appoint an attorney to help them challenge the matter legally. Residents not only approved his motion, but also agreed that each household would pay R5 towards legal fees. In the end, the community raised over R2000[73].

The various community meetings had been relatively peaceful until then. Despite this, they had nonetheless come under the attention of the Security Branch in Cradock. Lieutenant Henri Fouché, the Special Branch commander at the time, began to monitor the meetings from around 4 October 1983, the day Cradora was formed.

An article in the *Eastern Province Herald* quoted Matthew speaking at a follow-up meeting of Cradora: 'Professional persons in the community should remember, they too were members of the oppressed, and should therefore not join dummy bodies. We call on church ministers,

---

72 Goniwe Papers. Cory Library, Rhodes University.

73 Tetelman, M. 2012. *We Can! Black Politics in Cradock, South Africa, 1948-85*. Rhodes University: Grahamstown.

doctors, lawyers, teachers and other professional persons in our community to ignore the temptation to serve on bodies which do not represent our community in the true sense.'

In one of Fouché's police reports, he writes: 'The last meeting in a church was on November 4 (1983) and the community came out vehemently against the concept of community councils and the recent increases in rents.'[74]

By November of that year, Matthew had been appointed principal of Sam Xhallie Secondary School. A letter dated 7 November 1983 from the office of the Circuit Inspector of Education and Training had also assured him that he would continue as principal of the school the next year. Then, on the morning of 10 November, after dropping me off at her mother's for the day, Nomonde took the bus into town from Michausdal to travel to work at the Cradock Provincial Hospital. She remembered it was a hot morning and once on the bus she took off her jersey. Little did she know that the bottle-green T-shirt she was wearing, which bore the slogan 'FREE MANDELA', had caught the eye of police officer Adam 'Akoer' Ackerman, who was also on the bus.

Minutes after her shift started at eight o'clock that morning, my mother was called into Matron Nieuwoudt's office. She recounts that, as she walked in, a male police officer who had been standing behind the door slammed it shut behind her. 'It startled me,' she said. 'I didn't expect that he would be there, and I wasn't expecting the door to bang like that. A female officer then immediately grabbed my work overalls and ripped the buttons [snap fasteners] open, to reveal my T-shirt [underneath]. She started shouting, "Take off this T-shirt, take it off!" I said, "No! I am not taking my T-shirt off, and who are you?" I then asked the matron if this was why I was called into her office.'

The matron didn't answer, deferring instead to one of the two male officers. He told her a fellow officer had seen her on the bus wearing this T-shirt. 'He asked if I knew that wearing a T-shirt with Mandela's name on it was against the law. I said, "No, I didn't know." He then told me that I would have to go with them to the Sanlam building.' The only thing her matron said was, 'Nomonde, you are now in big trouble.' My

---

74 Henri Fouché. Affidavit. 31 January 1985.

mother told me, 'I just looked at her and kept quiet.' The cops then detained my mother. Shortly after she was booked, an officer called my father's school to ask him to bring another top for my mother, as well as her identity document and their marriage certificate.

Minutes later, my father and Matthew walked into the Sanlam building in Adderley Street. This building housed the offices and holding cells of the Special Branch in Cradock. For activists in iLingelihle, the Sanlam building was a notorious space: this was where many of them were detained, interrogated, beaten, and tortured to within an inch of their lives. It represented hell on earth to them and the Security Police were only too happy to reinforce that notoriety every time they detained any of iLingelihle's youth or community activists. My mother, however, recalled that she wasn't fazed throughout her time there in both the holding cells and while she was interrogated. She said she remained absolutely quiet. My mother knew many people had seen her being led inside the building, and that my father was there because he had indeed brought her a different blouse to wear. She was eventually released five hours later, shortly after one o'clock that afternoon.

An article in the *Eastern Province Herald* on 11 November 1983, the day after her detention, quotes my father as saying: 'They wouldn't let me see her but said she was being detained for wearing the T-shirt. I asked what the charge was, but they said it would eventually appear on the charge sheet. They also would not let me take her back to work but said they would do so themselves.' The same article quotes Matthew as saying: 'The Calatas are leaders and held in high esteem in Cradock's community life and social circles. We understand three policemen went to the hospital to arrest Mrs Calata and we view the whole affair as a form of intimidation.' Colonel Harold Snyman, acting chief of the Eastern Cape's Security Police division in Port Elizabeth, is quoted as saying: 'The T-shirt was banned by the Publications Board and the slogan was believed to have ANC (African National Congress) connotations. Police were investigating the matter and a charge would probably be laid against Mrs Calata.'[75]

Then, about a month after the arrest, on the morning of 7 December,

---

75 Jongbloed, B. 11 November 1983. *Eastern Province Herald.*

my mother remembered 'a highly irritated Matthew, who, unusually for him, knocked on the door just once, before he opened it and walked inside'. He had come to see Fort, and she could tell something was wrong. Matthew was holding a letter received in the post a few hours earlier. It was from the Department of Education and Training, informing him (allegedly on the orders of national-level officials in Pretoria) of their decision to transfer him back to Graaff-Reinet. The reason stated in the letter was that 'Graaff-Reinet was short a mathematics and science teacher'. He told my parents that he believed the transfer was politically motivated, and that he would decline the transfer. My mother then asked that he sit down, in a bid to calm him. After a few minutes, while Matthew was able to catch his breath, my mother left the two of them in the sitting-room to tend to me. My father and Matthew discussed how they were going to respond to the department's decision on the transfer. Among their resolutions was for Matthew to table the matter before the Cradora executive and then before residents at a community meeting. Matthew would also have to telephone Molly Blackburn in Port Elizabeth to alert her to the letter and its contents.

Indeed, a meeting was called a few days later, where Matthew informed the residents of the department's decision to transfer him back to Graaff-Reinet. The residents objected and pointed out that this very need for a mathematics and science teacher would arise in their own community should Matthew be transferred. It was clear to them too that the department's order to transfer him was politically motivated. Residents of iLingelihle were not going to accept what they deemed an irrational decision. The final outcome of the meeting was that Matthew must stay in iLingelihle. Cradora then addressed a letter to Molly Blackburn expressing their support for Matthew, both as a teacher and valued member of the iLingelihle community.

Towards the middle of December, the UDF in the Eastern Cape – which had struggled to get off the ground (when compared to provinces such as the Western Cape and the Transvaal) – finally held its inaugural conference in Port Elizabeth. Fort (Cradoya chairperson), Matthew (Cradora chairperson), Mkonto and Mene (executive members of both organisations) attended and immediately registered both Cradoya and Cradora as affiliates of the national organisation.

Chapter Seven
'Tata, uYaphi?'

LUKHANYO

At the beginning of the school term in January 1984, Matthew did not report for duty at Nqweba Secondary School in Graaff-Reinet. Nor did he show up at the recently opened iLingelihle High School, to which my father had been transferred from Sam Xhallie Secondary School.

In the first few days and weeks of the new school year, Cradora wrote to the department, urging the authorities to reconsider their decision. Matthew then personally wrote to the department in an application for re-instatement as a teacher in Cradock, making it clear that he 'did not expect to be considered for the Vice-Principal position of the school and that he would accept even the lowliest post'.[76]

But the department, through its regional director, Günther Merbold wasn't interested in all their pleas, even after a Cradora delegation had travelled to see him in Port Elizabeth. Merbold stood firm, ensuring that Matthew was dismissed through a letter sent to him on 6 February 1984. It read:

'Termination of Service

Due to the fact that you did not assume duties at the Nqweba Secondary School, Graaff-Reinet, within 14 days from the re-opening of schools on 9 January 1984, the Department has approved of the termination of your services as teacher with effect from 1 January 1984 in terms of Art. 21 (2) (a) of the Act on Education and Training, 1979 (Act No 90 of 1979) as amended. According to the said Act, it is regarded that you dismissed yourself by not reporting for duty within 14 days from the date of re-opening of schools.

---

76 Goniwe Papers. Cory Library, Rhodes University.

Kindly furnish this office with the address to which your pension contributions must be forwarded.

Yours faithfully
P A Nortjé
Regional Director: Cape'[77]

In a bid to force their hand to reinstate Matthew immediately, my father privately caucused a plan (with Madoda Jacobs, the school's head boy, and Moppo Mene) to launch a school boycott if their demand to re-instate Matthew wasn't met. They also called for democratic Student Representative Councils (SRCs), more textbooks, and more qualified teachers. My mother remembered that this meeting took place at our home. With agreement among the three of them, the decision was put into action.

A few days later, on 8 February, pupils from the recently opened iLinge-lihle Secondary School, under the leadership of Madoda, set in motion the first day of their school boycott. Madoda and Nomsa Frans (the head girl) solicited the support of their school's deputy principal for Matthew's re-instatement. When he refused, they led a boycott with close to 800 pupils from their classes. Four days later, due to the continued boycott, classes at iLingelihle Secondary School were suspended.

The next day, a large group of students from Sam Xhallie (Matthew's former school) began to boycott classes too. Pupils who refused to participate in the boycott were intimidated and threatened. Five pupils were arrested in the scuffles and charged with intimidation, assault, malicious damage to property, and public violence. Two days later, all classes were suspended at Sam Xhallie Secondary School, due to the non-attendance of pupils. After this, the boycotts began to gather pace. Just four days later, the Nxuba Higher Primary School was forced to shut its doors, as pupils failed to show up for classes.

During a Residents' Association meeting held on 8 March 1984, and addressed by both Matthew and my father, residents whole-heartedly endorsed the call for a general boycott of all schools in iLingelihle.

---

77 Ibid.

The next day, a group estimated at about 500 strong forced pupils out of classes at the Ncaca Lower Primary School. They then turned their attentions to the Solomon Akena Primary School and E Macembe Junior Primary School, which are in close proximity to each other. But police had anticipated their intentions, and a stand-off between residents and police ensued. Police fired several rounds of teargas at the protesting group, which had by now swelled to about 800 pupils and residents[78].

On 6 March, the regional director of the Department of Education and Training through the office of the Circuit Inspector sent letters to the parents of boycotting pupils in iLingelihle. The letters – which the parents tore up – warned them of the likely expulsion of their children if they continued to boycott school.

Matthew was now officially unemployed. Angry at his treatment at the hands of the state, he used the time to officially organise a resistance movement. In that month, when not leading the school boycotts, Cradora began to consolidate the extent of its fledgling influence beyond iLingelihle. This started with a 'CRADORA meeting held on March 10th which was attended by a number of organisations from Port Elizabeth and surrounding areas. Among these was the UDF, United Women's Organisation (UWO), Students for Christian Action (SUCA), Uitenhage Youth Congress (UYCO), Port Elizabeth Youth Congress (PEYCO), Port Elizabeth Black Civic Organisation (PEBCO) and the General Workers Union of South Africa (GWUSA).'[79]

In his address to the delegates, Matthew urged them to continue the school boycotts until the authorities reinstated him as a teacher. My father iterated Matthew's call, imploring all pupils to consider launching similar offensives in their towns to send the government a message of unity. Tetelman explains: 'CRADORA then sought to establish strong links with civic organisations, particularly in the Border Region. This was in large part due to (Matthew) Goniwe's close ties with Charles Nqakula from Cradock and Steve Tshwete – ties solidified by Canon

---

78 Henri Fouché. Affidavit. 31 January 1985.
79 Tetelman, M. 2012. *We Can! Black Politics in Cradock, South Africa, 1948-85.* Rhodes University: Grahamstown.

Calata's funeral. CRADORA organisers travelled to Grahamstown regularly to help its activists, who had formed their own Grahamstown Civic Association (GRACA) on October 10th 1983. CRADORA also formed close ties with activists from Port Alfred, which lies around 60 kilometres from Grahamstown.'[80]

With the boycotts further consolidated in March, teachers including my father continued to go to class, albeit merely to sit there with little to do. Some of their pupils were involved in daily skirmishes with the police, and several relatively small incidents of violence occurred, with residents hurling stones at police vehicles and the officers retaliating by shooting the protesters with rubber bullets and teargas canisters. My mother recalled how my father complained about having to sit in class while he could hear the commotion outside between his students and the police. Security Branch officers often visited the schools to check up on the teachers' whereabouts, and in particular whether my father was at his desk.

With the boycotts in full swing and community meetings growing ever larger as increasing numbers of residents turned up for meetings, 'Cradock, according to Nyameka (Matthew's wife) now boasted mass-based protest movements – movements that were disciplined and powerful.'[81]

The situation in iLingelihle had become an embarrassment for local authorities, and their attempts at a clamp down – mostly through violent force – weren't yielding the desired results.

Molly Blackburn, who had grown concerned by the reports, particularly of police brutality coming out of Cradock, convinced her Progressive Federal Party (PFP) to press the government to negotiate with the residents of iLingelihle. She and a colleague even visited Cradock in a bid to mediate the stand-off, but the state was not interested. Tetelman writes: 'iLingelihle had embarked on a bold, unprecedented resistance campaign, and its residents now waited for the state to make its next move.'[82]

The government, never one to disappoint, responded with great

---

80 Ibid.
81 Ibid.
82 Ibid.

determination to break the back of the boycott before it spread to other townships.

Most Cradora meetings took place in local churches in iLingelihle. The Security Branch were almost always looking for ways to destabilise and infiltrate not only the meetings but the Cradora executive. So they approached local clergy and ordered them not to make their facilities available to the 'agitators', Goniwe and Calata. The clergy, who mostly sought to avoid conflict with the police, acceded to the order, while some began to charge the cash-strapped Residents Association for the use of their facilities. In one instance, my mother recalled at least one clergyman, Rev George Njozela from the AME Church, and a teacher, Boyce Magadu, coming to see my father at home. She was in the kitchen preparing supper while he sat in the sitting room reading the newspapers. They told my father that they had come to urge him to cut his friendship and working relationship with Matthew. After they had presented their case, my father, ever combative, made it clear to them that his friendship and working relationship with Matthew were his business and that he would 'most likely die wherever Matthew dies'. My mother said Fort, much to her embarrassment, then swore at the older men, before threatening to beat both of them up if they didn't leave our home at once – 'which they did,' she told me, laughing.

State officials, however, were undeterred by this rejection by some of the ministers, and set about to undermine Cradora. Among their tactics, the Special Branch then began to spread a rumour that Matthew was plotting to kill my father out of bitterness for his taking over the leadership of Cradoya. This too failed. Instead, it had the adverse effect on the community, as it served to unite the residents against the 'enemy'. One organiser said: 'It gave the organisation credibility, most particularly in the eyes of the youth.'[83]

Until this time, Cradora had posed a strong challenge to the government, but the challenge had been relatively moderate and, significantly, free of any violence – an influence from Tatou's era, no doubt. In its early days, Cradora had relied on tactics like petitions to push for lower rents, using non-violent means to do so. And this non-confrontational style was one of Cradora's greatest strengths. Indeed, Cradora wasn't

---

83 Ibid.

alone: most civic organisations employed peaceful tactics to challenge the state[84].

But this peace would be shattered in Cradock on the Sunday afternoon of 25 March 1984. Jacobs, Mene, and some of the Cradoya executive had called a youth meeting to be held at the Ascension Church to discuss the lack of progress in their demands to the government, which included, among others, Matthew's reinstatement, democratic SRCs at local schools, and better-qualified teachers. Just two days before, however, the government had hoped to prevent this meeting from taking place, responding to rumours of its occurrence by tightening the screws. It banned all planned Cradora and Cradoya meetings. In the order in which he invoked the Internal Security Act of 1982, Magistrate André Groenewald declared:

> 'Whereas I, André Groenewald, magistrate for the district of Cradock, have reason to apprehend that the public peace would be seriously endangered by meetings to be held in the iLINGELIHLE TOWNSHIP and MICHAUSDAL TOWNSHIP at CRADOCK on the 21 March 1983 in the district of CRADOCK. I, in terms of section 46 of the INTERNAL SECURITY ACT, 1982 (ACT 74 of 1982) hereby prohibit for the period beginning at 14H00 on Friday the 23rd day of March 1983 and ending at 14H00 on Sunday the 25th day of March 1983 the following gatherings:
> All gatherings in the iLingelihle Township.
> All gatherings in the Michausdal Township at which residents of the iLingelihle Township are present,
> Except any such gathering which at any time is expressly authorised by me as the Magistrate for the district of CRADOCK.
> Signed at CRADOCK on this 21st day of March 1983.
> MAGISTRATE/CRADOCK
> GROENEWALD
> It is ordered that this order be served personally on:
> Mr Matthew Goniwe
> 44 Qhina Street
> CRADOCK
> 5880
> This prohibition will be published in the said Townships by announcing it orally by means of a loudspeaker.'[85]

---

84 Ibid.
85 Goniwe Papers. Cory Library, Rhodes University.

The Cradoya meeting, originally planned for the Friday night, was postponed, but tensions between the residents and police were escalating. So, in a bid to keep a lid on the bubbling agitation, hundreds of police officers were deployed in iLingelihle on the Saturday evening to conduct a massive peace-and-order patrol. Small groups of protesters set up roadblocks of boulders and burning tyres at each of the entrances to the location in a bid to prevent or at least delay the police from entering iLingelihle. The police responded by firing teargas and several rounds of rubber bullets at the youths. By this time, Cradoya had begun to spread word across iLingelihle that its previously postponed meeting was rescheduled for the next day, Sunday, 25 March 1984. With tensions this high, some in the Cradora executive felt this meeting would be viewed by the police as an act of provocation, particularly in light of the proclamation to extend the ban on meetings in both iLingelihle and Michausdal. My father, however, was of the view that the meeting should take place as scheduled, and it was reported as such to the community.

Day break on Sunday, 25 March, revealed evidence of the overnight skirmishes between the police and the Cradoya activists, who by then had retreated, living to fight another day. My mother remembers that morning, saying it started out as most other Sunday mornings in our home, as she and my father got Dorothy (my eight-year-old sister) and me ready for church. Fort had mentioned to her the previous day that he and Matthew were due to travel to Bedford and Adelaide that afternoon to meet with members of the newly established youth associations in the two towns. Matthew then came to collect my father around noon before they set off. At around three o'clock, exactly an hour after the end of the ban on meetings in iLingelihle, a group estimated at 2000 boisterous but peaceful young men and women gathered at the Ascension Church for a Cradoya meeting. Madoda Jacobs, who would chair the meeting in my father's absence, had already sought the permission of Mr Wilson John (a church elder) to hold the meeting at the church. The members were meant to discuss and assess the state of their on-going schools boycott. But even before the official programme of the meeting commenced, a number of Special Branch vehicles, with close to 20 officers, began to gather on the large open veld opposite the church.

Mene still remembered the events of that afternoon, telling me that 'uBhut' Matthew and uBhut' Fort were not in town for that meeting. Madoda and I were delegated to lead it. We were meant to facilitate the discussion on the boycotts, as well as a possible way forward. We would then relay the resolutions back to the rest of the executive when they return. Shortly after the meeting got under way, Mr Wilson John walked in. He had just spoken to Henri Fouché (the branch commander in Cradock), who had wanted to know who had given us permission to gather at the church. Mr John told him he had granted us the permission to do so, on the understanding we would not antagonise or in any manner agitate the police. And, as far as he could see, that was indeed the case. Fouché, although he agreed that the meeting had thus far been peaceful, said it was, however, an illegal gathering, as the ban on meetings in iLingelihle was still in effect. Mr John told us that he negotiated with Fouché to allow him to come in and ask us to halt the meeting.' Madoda consented to halting the meeting, and Mr John left to inform Fouché that the youths had agreed to disperse quietly and peacefully. Madoda also urged the members not to give the police a reason to attack them: 'Go straight home, he told them, 'do not run or sing.'[86]

The youths then turned and began to disperse as instructed. It's unclear what provoked the police's next actions. As Mr John made his way to inform Fouché of the decision, despite no provocation of any kind, police fired several teargas canisters at the exiting crowd. Mene remembered standing at the front of the church, shouting instructions to those still inside to leave quietly and in an orderly fashion, when he was startled by the sound of teargas being fired. Those outside started running back inside the church for shelter from the teargas. 'I then heard a window break – the police had shot a teargas canister into the church,' Mene said. By now the pupils were running in all directions, including the rectory and the courtyard. 'Then one, two, three more canisters were fired in those areas of the church too. All hell broke loose in that church that afternoon. Police literally smoked us out of the church as if we were nothing,' he added.

I can just imagine how some of the young men and women still inside the church started jumping onto the pews in their desperate rush

---

86 Ibid.

for safety, their orderly exit now in complete chaos, with many choking from the thick smoke. It's a miracle (at least to me) how they avoided a deadly stampede. Those who made it outside barely had time to breathe in the fresh air when police began to open fire, this time shooting at them with rubber bullets. Although hundreds of students were injured, there were no fatalities, thank God.

Mene didn't quite remember how he managed to escape the smoke-filled church building unharmed, but he said once outside his only thought was to hit back at the police: 'They had tried to kill us when they shot at us like that – for no apparent reason.' While still struggling to breathe and see due to the effects of the teargas, the battered young men and women retaliated by pelting the police with stones or anything else they could find. Hearing the ruckus, neighbours had come out, and many were shocked by what they were seeing – scores of young people, running, desperately looking for the nearest stone to hurl back at the police. They couldn't match the police's superior fire power, though, and the police eventually managed to force the majority of them away from the church. This battle had lasted around 30 minutes. When the smoke in front of the Church of the Ascension (which was once Tatou's pride and joy) eventually cleared, it was evident that the open veld in front it and its surroundings bore the scars of a battlefield.

This sight would greet my father and Matthew as they drove down eLuxolweni Street into iLingelihle just an hour or so after the carnage. The church building is among the first landmarks you see when you enter iLingelihle. I can only guess what went through their minds as they were confronted by the first signs of that afternoon's unprecedented attack. Despite being tired, my father and Matthew immediately investigated the events of that afternoon. They drove around the location not only to survey the extent of the damage, if any, but also to search for the Cradoya executive for an urgent briefing on the events of that afternoon. Mr John had sought refuge from the shooting and ensuing violence at a house nearby. One of the residents who saw him there then began to shout at him, accusing him of being a police informer and sellout. She said she had seen him talk to the police before they opened fire on the youths. Despite Mr John's denials of any impropriety, she maintained that he was an informer, and in her anger she threw a stone at him. The small group of pupils she was with joined in the attack. Mr John fled to another nearby home, with the crowd in pursuit. They managed to force the door open and dragged him into the street where he was assaulted. Defiantly, he managed to escape to a third home. Shortly after this, my father, Matthew, and Cradora executive member Monwabisi Makhawula came across this attack, which they immediately diffused, rescuing a battered Mr John from a highly charged and dangerous situation. There was still no sign of the Cradoya executive anywhere though. This was because many of them were either in hiding or part of a group of 29 residents arrested that afternoon. Among them were Thandeka Bholani (32), Roy Calata (my uncle, 27), Daluxolo Dywili (24), Mpumelelo Faxi (19), Dinah Malgas (47), Siphiwo Stemele (22), and Wekens Zondiwe (25)[87].

The events of the afternoon of 25 March 1984 marked an historically significant shift in the political dynamic in Cradock.

Henri Fouché, it seems, recognised this too. In his report sent to the Joint Management Centre (which sat in Port Elizabeth) about the violent confrontation, he recorded the incident as the 'day unrests and riots were unleashed in Cradock'[88].

The Joint Management Centre (JMC) comprised senior members of the South African Defence Force (SADF) and Security Police in each province. It was chaired by the military commander, and deputised by his Security Police counterpart. JMCs reported to the secretariat of the State Security Council (SSC).

The SSC, when first established in 1972 as a permanent committee of cabinet, was an advisory body on intelligence matters. But when PW Botha became prime minister of the republic in 1978, the SSC gradually became a major policy-making body. The secretariat usually convened directly before each meeting of the cabinet, and often took decisions which were then simply rubber-stamped by cabinet. Its operational arm was the clandestine National Security Management System (NSMS), established in 1979. It was made up of a network of regional and local

---

87 Ibid.
88 Henri Fouché. Affidavit. 31 January 1985.

bodies such as JMCs, which co-ordinated the actions of the SADF, the SAP, and civil defence units[89].

On Wednesday, 28 March 1984, just three days after the violent standoff between Cradoya and the Security Police, the Special Branch detained Madoda Jacobs under Section 28 of the Internal Security Act. They accused him of being the ringleader of the banned meeting which had preceded the violent standoff with police. Mene recalled that upon receiving news of Jacobs's detention later that day, my father and Matthew bravely marched into the notorious Sanlam building, to demand firstly to see him and secondly his immediate release. By the time they got to him, Jacobs had been severely assaulted and was lying in one of the cells. Unfortunately, my father and Matthew were unable to secure his release.

The 29 arrested were eventually charged with 'endangering public peace and security by erecting road barricades which prevented the Police from entering the Cradock African township'. They also faced charges of 'throwing stones which injured two police officers and two civilians, including Mr John and damaging both Police vehicles and the Church of Ascension's Hall'.[90]

On the afternoon of Friday, 30 March 1984, my father arrived home from school. For the better part of that first school term, he and all the teachers in iLingelihle had spent their days mostly twiddling their thumbs in class as there were no pupils to teach. My mother had the afternoon off too, so the family spent some time at home, before my father had to attend a Cradora executive meeting in the early evening. Dorothy remembered how much fun she and my father had on days like this when he could spend some time at home with his family. Even as an eight-year-old, my sister had an amazing singing voice. My mother remembered that Fort would often brag to her, saying, 'Monde, *uya chul' unana* [Monde, our daughter can sing],' and 'She gets that from me.' Dorothy, my father, and I shared a deep passion and connection through

89 Padraig O'Malley Archives. https://www.nelsonmandela.org/omalley/index.php/site/q/03lv01508.htm
90 Bekker, J. 8 August 1984. Teargas Was Fired 'While Pupils Were Leaving Hall'. *Eastern Province Herald.*

music. Dorothy recalled that he often played me Peter Tosh albums whenever we drove in his red-and-white VW kombi. She said our father had also assigned to her the responsibility to record (on Beta tape back then) a weekly television music programme called *Pop Shop*. Once recorded, Dorothy said, 'Tata would make time not just to watch it with me but also for us to dance to the music.'

At around five o'clock that afternoon, though, Matthew came to our home to pick up our father for the meeting. 'Strangely, Fort didn't ask me if you could go with him to this meeting,' my mother said. Through the years, she'd told me stories of how my father often took me with him to community and Cradora executive meetings. Once there, I would bide my time, playing either on stage or close to it, under the supervision and company of two older community members, Doctor Mbanda (who wasn't a doctor – instead, he owned a fleet of taxis) and his best friend uTat' uMaqegu.

In any case, on this Friday afternoon I did not accompany my father to his meeting. Matthew dropped him off back home just after seven o'clock that evening. We had supper together. Dorothy and I were then put to bed just after eight. At about ten o'clock, my father switched off our electric generator outside and brought it into the house. My mother remembered that he took two tablets (prescribed to treat pain in his right shoulder, caused by adhesive capsulitis, commonly known as a 'frozen shoulder'). Just as he was about to get into bed, there were multiple heavy knocks on both the front door and bedroom windows. She said, 'We looked at each other and wondered out loud what the police were doing at our home that time of the evening.' Ever feisty, my mother cheekily remarked that if they were not going to knock decently on the door, she was not going to open and let them in. A more polite knock at the front door eventually followed. The second she opened the door, my mother was nearly knocked over as members of the police and army swarmed into our tiny home. They had come to detain my father, and handed him a warrant document granting them the right to do so under Section 28 of the Internal Security Act. Under this provision, the Security Police had the legal right to detain a person of interest (my father in this case) without charging him/her for up to 180 days (six months) at a time.

After Fort read the warrant, my mother told the officers that they would have to wait before they could take him away: 'I said Fort was just about to get into bed and would need time to get dressed before he left the house at that time of night. When I looked around, the house was packed with police and soldiers carrying these huge guns. They were everywhere.' My mom recalled that Dorothy and I woke up, due to the commotion in our tiny two-bedroom home. I asked, '*Tata, uyaphi?* [Father, where are you going?],' to which he replied, '*Ndiyabuya, kwekwe* [I'll be back, my boy],' before they led him out of the room.

'When they got to the front door,' my mother said, 'I asked the police not to handcuff his hands behind his back because of the pain in his shoulder. But those careless bastards showed me that as soon as they reached the gate, they handcuffed his hands right behind his back. Just there by the gate right in front of me, [after] I had asked them not to handcuff him like that.' She watched as they put him in the back of an Orange Ford Cortina XR3. 'When I saw the street, it was packed with police and army vehicles. They stretched from one end to the other end [of the street], there were many, many cars. I could not believe that all of them had come just to detain one man.' After the police had gone, my mother then asked our neighbours the Damoyis for the assistance of their two eldest daughters, Thoko and Joyce. At thirteen, Joyce, who was the younger of the two sisters, would look after Dorothy and me, while my mother and Thoko would make their way to the Goniwe home, a 20-minute brisk walk away. 'When we got there, the first thing I said was, "*Mzala, bazok' landa uFort* [They took Fort]," and *mzala* said to me, "*NoMatthew bazok' mlanda* [They took Matthew too]."' My mother and Nyameka Goniwe call each other *mzala* too, because of my mother's clan relation to Matthew.

In any event, when my mother arrived at the Goniwe family home that night, they, much like her, were still a little confused, maybe even shocked about what had just happened. 'Where's uMbulelo?' some family members asked. Nyami then asked my mother to sit down as she tried to relay what had happened when they came to detain Fort. 'They told me the same thing had happened to them. They took Matthew at the same time as they took Fort. While I was still there, more policemen came looking for uMbulelo.

'I remember, the one remarked, "You came here quickly. Do you have a car or did you run?" I said, "No, I walked." He said, "Yoh, you walk fast." I looked at him and responded, "Yes, I walk fast."'

Mbulelo then returned home. 'I think he had jumped over the fence at the back to come and eat at his grandmother's house. I don't think he knew that the police would be waiting for him when he walked through the back door. They took him almost immediately. The following morning, we heard they had taken Madoda too.'

The four, all of them strategic leaders of both Cradora and Cradoya, were driven to Mortimer, a farm about 35 km outside of Cradock. There, they were separated. Fort (president of Cradoya and treasurer of Cradora) and Mbulelo (convenor of both Cradora and Cradoya) were then driven overnight to Johannesburg's Diepkloof Prison, while Matthew (chairperson of Cradora) and Madoda Jacobs (former Cradoya executive and head boy of iLingelihle Secondary School) were driven in the opposition direction to Cape Town, where they would be held at Pollsmoor Prison for the better part of their detention.

Chapter Eight
The Epicentre of the Revolution

LUKHANYO

The state had hoped that the removal of the key 'agitators' would restore a sense of law and order, and help return iLingelihle to some semblance of normality. The next morning, on 31 March, Louis le Grange, the Minister of Law and Order, imposed a 90-day ban on all Cradora and Cradoya meetings in iLingelihle.

A young *Eastern Province Herald* reporter, Jo-Ann Bekker, was interested in the unfolding political situation in the location. She was assigned to the 'Cradock beat' by her editor, JC Viviers, who was commonly known as 'Koos'. She began to follow and report on the activities of Cradora and Cradoya, and of course the resultant standoffs between them and the Security Police. In one of her articles, published on 2 April under the headline 'Cradock Meetings Banned' shortly after Minister Le Grange had imposed the ban, she quoted Molly Blackburn who 'had visited the area on four occasions since October last year. Blackburn believes the three-month ban was timed to silence protest against these detentions'[91].

On 10 April 1984, my mother's 25th birthday, she had very little to celebrate. She had not seen her husband, who had been in detention in Johannesburg, for ten days. To make matters worse, the magistrate, Mr A Meintjies, who had presided over her 'Free Mandela T-shirt case', called her to court that day to deliver his judgment in which he found her guilty of 'publicising a banned person' under the Internal Security Act. He sentenced her to a three-month prison term. My mother's lawyer, Mr Boyce Moerane, lodged an immediate appeal against this

---

91 Bekker, J. 2 April 1984. Cradock Meetings Banned. *Eastern Province Herald*.

sentence, and she was granted bail of R300, which meant my mother could come home to Dorothy and me instead of spending the first of many nights behind bars. The next day, she got ready for work as usual. On her arrival, she was once again called into Matron Nieuwoudt's office. There, the hospital's secretariat informed her that they were terminating her employment – with immediate effect. With tears in her eyes, my mother told me, 'I tried to argue against it, even pointing out to them that my matter was on appeal.' The matron, however, would have none of her pleas. Instead, she ordered hospital security to assist my mother in collecting her personal belongings before escorting her off hospital grounds. As she walked home, feeling like a criminal 'because of the way I was treated', my mother was stopped by police officers several times along the way. 'Although I was distraught and still in shock at what had just happened,' she said, 'I was determined not to show the police any weakness.'

Inside, though, her heart was racing – and understandably so, as she was daunted by the prospect of having to raise two children, with no salary, her husband in prison, and no idea when or if he would return. 'I walked straight to uSis' Nyami's [Matthew's wife] home to inform her about my dismissal,' she said. Once safely inside the Goniwe home, my mother was overwhelmed by emotions and broke down in tears. She remembered Nyami asking her, 'What are we going to do now?' My mother told her that she would have to think of something – 'Maybe a small shop, which I could run from home,' she remembered saying. Nyami helped her buy the first stock for the small spaza shop which she began to operate out of the dispensary at our home a few days later. The two also notified Molly Blackburn about my mother's dismissal.

I don't know if it was coincidence or fate, but violence escalated in iLingelihle from the day my mother was dismissed. The violence, which had begun to engulf iLingelihle's everyday life, was most probably not what the government had expected when they detained my father, Matthew, Madoda, and Mbulelo. Those most at risk of the residents' ire – other than the police of course – were members of the iLingelihle Community/Town Council residing in iLingelihle. Residents, the youth in particular, targeted these councillors on the basis of their alleged participation in and collusion with the repressive apartheid state. Several homes where councillors lived were stoned and petrol-bombed in different incidents aimed at intimidating them. These incidents took place over a two-week period, and most of them ended with running battles which at times lasted several hours between the community and the trigger-happy police.

Meanwhile, at Diepkloof Prison, a young Methodist priest named Paul Verryn had begun to visit my father and Mbulelo at the request of Molly Blackburn shortly after the two arrived there. Mbulelo recalled that in those early days and weeks it was always a relief to see Paul's caring face. 'Even if it was that of a white man, at least it wasn't of a pissed off Afrikaner,' he said, chuckling. Matthew and Madoda (in Pollsmoor) would receive regular visits from Di Bishop and Molly Blackburn, among others. Helen Suzman and Andrew Savage also visited them from time to time.

Permission for these visits, especially if you weren't family of the detainees, had to be sought from and granted by the commissioner of the SAP. In one letter, Di Bishop wrote:

> 'Dear Sir,
> I herewith wish to apply for permission to visit the following persons who are being held under Section 28 of the Internal Security Act of 1982 at Pollsmoor Prison:
>   Mr Matthew Goniwe
>   Mr Madoda Jacobs
> I have been requested by Mrs N. Goniwe, wife of Mr Matthew Goniwe and the Misses Jacobs, the two sisters of Mr Madoda Jacobs to visit and would like to accede to their requests as soon as possible.
> Thank you for your attention to this matter.
> Yours faithfully
> D. Bishop (MPC)'

To which Commissioner JC Broodryk responded:

> 'Dear Madam,
> Re: Application for permission to visit persons detained in terms of Section 28(1) of the Internal Security Act (Act. 72 of 1982)
> With reference to your written application to visit Section 28 (1) detainees Mr Matthew GONIWE and Mr Madoda JACOBS who are at

present being detained at Pollsmoor Prison, the Commissioner of the
South African Police has granted the necessary permission. In terms
of Section 28 (8) (a) of the said Act the visits will take place as stipu-
lated by the Commissioner, under the following conditions:
In the presence of an officer of the South African Police, and
Only matters regarding family problems or personal requirements can
be discussed.
You are advised to make arrangements for your proposed visits with
the Officer in charge of the Pollsmoor Prison in conjunction with the
divisional Commander of the Security Branch of the South African
Police at Cape Town.
Yours faithfully
Brig S A POLICE / Commissioner
J C BROODRYK'[92]

For my family, the beginning of May marked at least one month since
we'd last seen Fort. The only comfort was that my mother had at least
by then been informed that her husband was detained at Diepkloof
Prison. And so, with the financial assistance of the South African Council of Churches, through Rev Sithile Zondani, my mother made arrangements for us to travel to Johannesburg to visit him. She remembered
that, before travelling, she first had to obtain permission to visit her
husband from Lieutenant Henri Fouché. His office was located in the
Sanlam building in Adderley Street. 'The first time I had to go and ask
him [Fouché] for permission to be able to travel, I was so upset,' she told
me. 'I felt humiliated. Imagine having to ask for permission from him,
of all people, just so that my children could see their father. He had the
power to decide whether you guys [Dorothy and I] could see your father.
But what else could I do? I had to go into that building and be completely dehumanised, otherwise I couldn't travel and see my husband.'
My mother's voice then began to crack and tears welled up in her eyes as
all the emotion of those trips to the Sanlam building came flooding back.

Fouché, she said, 'would take his time to sign the documents'. She
added that he would delay doing so until she had answered a series of
questions, most of which had nothing to do with her planned trip to

---

92 David Forbes Archives.

Johannesburg. My mother, Dorothy, and I usually travelled to Johannesburg by train and, while there, we stayed with my aunt Sisana (Fort's eldest sister) in Tsakane near White City in Soweto. This would become our usual mode of transport and accommodation for the monthly trips to and from Johannesburg for the duration of my father's detention. Visiting hours were between eleven and twelve o'clock each day for fourteen consecutive days every month, which we observed as regularly as clockwork. My mother still recalled how the excitement of our first visit, coupled with all the travelling, must have exhausted me. She said that when we finally got to see my father at the Diepkloof Prison that first time, all I could manage was '*Molo, Tata* [Hello, Father]' before I fell asleep on her lap. She added that, although he was happy to see us, he lamented the fact I fell asleep just minutes into the visiting hour. After that first visit, Dorothy refused to accompany my mother and me on our trips to see my father. The prison's visitors' section had a glass partition, which meant that my mother spent the entire hour speaking to my father through a telephone, unable to touch or hug him. 'I told him that I had been dismissed from the hospital, but that he shouldn't worry, as family and friends, particularly Nyami and Molly [Blackburn], had all pitched in to help me start a small shop in [our] house, which residents were generously supporting. He then told me about the conditions in prison, which he said weren't bad. I had a sense that he wasn't telling me everything or even the truth about the conditions inside there.' She then said, 'You know, all those months when Fort was in detention, I used to worry about whether he would come back home. I was scared, what the government could do to him, to uBhut' Matthew, uMbulelo, and Madoda while they were in detention. I always kept going back to what the state did to Steve Biko . . .'

Mbulelo remembered that he and my father had initially shared an entire prison floor between the two of them: 'My cell was on one side of the floor and his on the other. Most of our time there, we spent in solitary confinement, locked up in our cells. Fort and I had one hour's exercise in the courtyard every day. Sometimes, the wardens would let us exercise together, but most days we exercised separately and at different times of the day.' This, Mbulelo suspected, was to prevent or at least restrict private conversations between them as much as possible.

He also added that 'after the second or third month in detention, a third "activist", claiming to be AZAPO, was put in a cell on the same floor with us. But a week after his arrival, during a rare joint exercise with Fort, he whispered to me that he suspected that guy was an informer and that we should not engage with him any more.' A week or two after that, Mbulelo said my father's suspicions were vindicated when they fortuitously spotted the third detainee (whose name he couldn't remember any more) having what they considered an inappropriate conversation with one of the prison warders. The 'detainee' was eventually removed from the cells a week or so later when it became clear to him that my father and Mbulelo would no longer speak either to him or each other in his company. In weeks to come, they were joined by other detained activists, among them Popo Molefe and Mosiuoa Lekota.

On 25 May, just a few days after we had arrived back home from Johannesburg, the iLingelihle town council drafted a report titled 'Present Situation in iLingelihle Residential Area' for the attention of the Minister of Law and Order, Mr Louis le Grange. After a brief background about its establishment, the council members wrote:

> 'Early during 1984 CRADORA intensified its campaign in iLingelihle. The opposition to the Village Council as a governing body, hereby, took on a new image. The intervention of CRADOYA, resulted in the general boycott of seven (7) schools in iLingelihle. It is a well-known fact that scholars only attended school for ten (10) days during the first quarter of 1984 and on 21 May 1984 only seven (7) pupils from a total of 4500 attended school. Whenever scholars tried to attend classes they were attacked, the parents were intimidated and houses severely damaged.
>
> The following is a summary of the subversive activities at present:
>
> Houses of Village Council members are being damaged by petrol bombs and stones;
>
> Streets are barricaded with rocks, motor wrecks and all kinds of obstructive material;
>
> The lives of Councillors and law-abiding citizens are being threatened and a general spirit of vandalism is present in the township.
>
> Since February 1984 Councillors have been scorned, mocked and intimidated. The Council cannot convene any public meetings for fear of their own lives. The Council is adamant that it intends to promote

the Government policy but, under the present circumstances, Councillors cannot even leave their houses, and those who are employed in Cradock have to be transported in protective vehicles driven by White officials.

The community of iLingelihle is being instigated not to pay any rental with the result that the Council's debts are increasing rapidly.

There is sincere appreciation for the S.A. Police who patrol the streets at regular intervals and for the guards stationed at night in the Councillors' houses.

The barricades in the streets cannot be cleared because the lives of the Council employees and their families are in constant danger.

At the funeral of the Mayor's mother on May 12th 1984 there was absolute chaos in the township. The funeral procession was stoned and various vehicles, including the hearse, were badly damaged. The coffin had to be transferred to a light delivery vehicle which was also damaged en route to the cemetery. Only very brave people attended the funeral and among them were members of the Kayamnandi (Port Elizabeth) and KwaNobuhle (Uitenhage) Town Councils. The Mayor could not attend the ceremony at the grave and had to be rushed to safety.

Since March 1984 four (4) of the ringleaders of CRADORA have been removed from the township and several others have been arrested and are awaiting trial but in spite of this, their subversive activities are still part and parcel of our daily life.'[93]

On 27 May, just two days after the council's report was sent to Minister Le Grange, police and the SADF cordoned off iLingelihle as they launched a large-scale manhunt for those suspected of public violence. Twenty-eight people were arrested and later charged with public violence.

My mother's small shop was well supported by the iLingelihle community, whom she credited with keeping us alive, safe, and well during the months of my father's detention. Sparro Mkonto, a member of the Cradora executive, regularly visited our home, she said, 'to check up on us'.

In early June, Matthew Goniwe, Fort Calata, Mbulelo Goniwe, and Madoda Jacobs were listed as persons of interest in terms of the Inter-

---

93 Henri Fouché. Affidavit. 31 January 1985.

nal Security Act. Lawrence Baxter has written the following about the consequences of being listed in terms of this Act:

> 'The detainee may be held indefinitely, subject only to the require-
> ment that he or she be held in accordance with the general or specific
> directions of the Minister of Law and Order, that a detention of more
> than 30 days be authorised by the minister (every 30 days), and that
> the minister must entertain (though not necessarily follow) the advice
> of an administrative review board if the detention extends beyond six
> months. The Commissioner of Prisons must order the release of the
> detainee when satisfied that the latter has satisfactorily answered all
> questions or if he decides that no further purpose will be served by
> the detention. No one other than the minister or a properly authorised
> state official is entitled to any information concerning the detainee,
> and the only visitors he or she may have without the permission of
> the minister or commissioner of prisons are a magistrate and district.
> surgeon, who must visit every 14 days, and an inspector of detainees,
> who must visit "as frequently as possible". In effect, the detainee lan-
> guishes in solitary confinement and at the mercy of his or her gaolers,
> enjoying only the token protections prescribed by the Act.'[94]

On 15 June 1984, Cradock would see yet another violent standoff between police and residents. A group of youths had gathered peacefully
and begun singing and chanting freedom songs in anticipation of the
next day's planned events to commemorate the eighth anniversary of
the 16 June Soweto Youth Uprising. Police, however, moved in to disperse
the crowd. When the youths disobeyed the order to disperse, police once
again shot teargas and rubber bullets at them. Older residents who had
witnessed the police's assault on the youths were incensed and reported
the matter to Monwabisi Makhawula, who had replaced Matthew as
Cradora chairperson while he was in detention. In response to the
attacks, Cradora, that same evening, called for a one-day consumer boycott of local shops. The next day, on 16 June, residents heeded Cradora's
call and steered clear of shops. That afternoon, police would interrupt
a commemoration meeting under the instruction that any and all

---

94 Baxter, L. 1985. 'Section 29 of the Internal Security Act and the Rule of Law.'
   Reality, vol. 17, no. 6, pp.4–6.

meetings in iLingelihle were banned. This time, they not only fired tear-gas to disperse those gathered, they also sjambokked residents as they ran for shelter away from the community hall. Youths retaliated by stoning police vehicles. More than 200 residents were arrested over the course of the two days and charged with gathering illegally, public violence, and arson.

The on-going police brutality and violence, as well as the community's sustained response to it, was now receiving almost daily coverage in several newspapers. The *Eastern Province Herald* through Jo-Ann Bekker was at the forefront of this reporting. Towards the end of June, Bekker wrote an article under the headline 'Cradock Meeting-Ban Expires Sunday', in which she quoted Law and Order Minister Louis le Grange's responses to questions in parliament. She writes 'that 87 people were arrested [in Cradock] between April 2nd and May 31st 1984. A total of 81 were charged – 64 with public violence, 15 with attempted arson and two with intimidation.' Further on in the same article, she explains: 'Allegations of police harassment raised by Mrs [Molly] Blackburn in the Cape Provincial Council include the sjambokking of a young child and an 86-year-old blind grandmother. "People are scared," a mother of two told the *Herald*. "When it becomes dark, they run into their houses, they fear the police." Concerned residents alleged the police attacks were carried out indiscriminately.'[95]

In another article in the same edition, and under the headline 'Attempt to Settle Cradock Situation', Bekker writes: 'The chief director of the Eastern Cape Development Board, Mr Louis Koch, held a meeting in Cradock this week in an attempt to normalize the situation in the strife-torn African township, iLingelihle.' She ends the article by reporting that 'Mr Andrew Savage and Mrs Helen Suzman, PFP MPs for Walmer and Houghton respectively, will meet with the Minister of Law and Order, Mr Le Grange tomorrow to discuss the situation in Cradock.'[96]

A few days later, on 2 July, Bekker published another article under

---

95 Bekker, J. 28 June 1984. Cradock Meeting-Ban Expires Sunday. *Eastern Province Herald*.
96 Ibid.

the headline 'MPs Meet Minister on Cradock', in which she writes: 'The PFP MP for Walmer, Mr Andrew Savage, and Mrs Helen Suzman, PFP MP for Houghton, met Mr Louis le Grange, Minister of Law and Order and Dr George de V Morrison, Deputy Minister of Co-operation and Development on Friday, to discuss the situation in the strife-torn Cradock African township of iLingelihle. The meeting came a day after Mr Le Grange's visit to the township and his announcement that the three-month ban on meetings was to be renewed for another three months and that the necessary presence of police in the township would be maintained.'[97]

On 23 July, the trial of five youths began, two of whom were just fifteen and the others sixteen years old. They were facing charges of intimidation and alternate charges of malicious damage to property, assault, and public violence. In her report which appeared on 24 July under the headline 'Cradock School Unrest: Five Pupils in Court', Bekker writes: 'The hearings had been transferred from Cradock to the Somerset East Regional Court because of several incidents which had occurred during bail applications in Cradock, including the singing of freedom songs. Mr [H] Van der Walt [for the State] said such behaviour had intimidated State witnesses.'[98]

Two days later, Molly Blackburn and her sister, Judy Chalmers, successfully requested to be admitted to the closed hearings of the Cradock schools boycott trial. The magistrate, Mr AW Meiring, over-ruled an objection by the state prosecutor, Mr H van der Walt.

At the end of July 1984, Cradora, now under the chairmanship of Monwabisi Makhawula, called for a seven-day boycott of white-owned businesses in Cradock. My mother recalled that most residents heeded the call, while those who defied it and spent their money in town were intimidated by some of the youths back in iLingelihle, who would almost always destroy the items bought at shops such as Checkers and OK Bazaars.

---

97 Bekker, J. 2 July 1984. MPs Meet Minister on Cradock. *Eastern Province Herald.*
98 Bekker, J. 24 July 1984. Cradock School Unrest: Five Pupils in Court. *Eastern Province Herald.*

The beginning of August 1984 marked the start of a trial in which my uncle Roy alongside ten others appeared in the Somerset East Regional Court on charges of public violence. In her reporting on the trial, Bekker writes in an article published on 10 August under the headline 'Policeman Threatened to Hit Her': 'Mr Madoda Jacobs (18), Mrs Dinah Malgas (47), Mr Daluxolo Dywili (24), Mr Roy Calata (27), Mr Mpumelelo Faxi (19), Mr Siphiwo Stemele (22), Mr Wekens Zondiwe (25), Miss Thandeka Bholani (32) and three minors have all pleaded not guilty. The State alleges they and a group of 2000 threatened public violence and obstructed police by building barricades in the roads of iLingelihle township at Cradock on March 25. They are also charged with throwing stones which injured a Graaff-Reinet school inspector, Mr Wilson John, his sister Constance Tali, and two police men, and damaged police vehicles and the Church of the Ascension Hall.'[99]

In the same publication, another article about the on-going unrest in Cradock appeared. This time, the by-line was credited to a *Herald* reporter under the headline 'Nine from Cradock Released on R50 Bail'. It reads: 'Nine Cradock residents – some of whom have been in prison since March – were released on bail of R50 by the Regional Court here [Somerset East] yesterday. Mr Thomas Tyulu (18), Mr Sizwe Mgcabusana (20), Mr Mbulelo Puwani (19), Mr Mongezi Matseke, (21), Mr Moppo Mene (19), Mr Zenzile Goniwe (20), Yourone Klaas (25), Mr Makabongwe Gqasana (21) and a minor are facing charges of public violence. Two minors who are being charged with them were previously granted bail.'[100]

One of the officers allegedly injured in the 25 March standoff with Cradoya youths was Warrant Officer Johan Allers. He took the stand as the state's third witness. In her article on Allers's testimony, published the next day under the headline 'Teargas Was Used after Police Were Stoned', Bekker writes: 'The court heard that a stone had hit WO Allers on the shin as the police were retreating to their vehicle. Cross-examined

---

99   Bekker, J. 10 August 1984. Policeman Threatened to Hit Her. *Eastern Province Herald*.

100 Bekker, J. 10 August 1984. Nine from Cradock Released on R50 Bail. *Eastern Province Herald*.

by Mr MTK Moerane and Mr HK Naidu for the defence, WO Allers said he had made a statement about his assault nearly a month after the incident. WO Allers said he had arrived at the church hall with 15 Cradock policemen at about the same time as Lieutenant Henri Fouché of the Security Police. Some policemen in both the Cradock and Port Elizabeth contingents had been armed with teargas pistols and sjamboks. He had not seen teargas fired into the church hall, nor had he noticed pupils being assaulted by police as they were leaving the hall. He described the stone throwing as sporadic. "They used stones and we used gas and people moved back. Then they moved forward again and threw more stones, and we used gas again."'[101]

During this time, Dr Allan Boesak, president of the World Alliance of Reformed Churches and patron of the UDF, paid his second visit to Cradock that year, following an invitation from Cradora. In Bekker's article, published on 10 August under the headline 'Boesak Shocked at Cradock's 'Reign Of Terror'', she writes:

> '[Boesak] was surprised to find about five police vehicles stationed at every entrance to the African township, iLingelihle. He said he and an overseas television crew travelling with him were stopped by the police and told they needed permits before they could enter. "I explained that I did not intend to get a permit," Dr Boesak said. "I said I was a minister and the people of Cradock had asked me to come and visit them."
>
> He said he told them: "I am here to fulfill a need. If you want to stop me please do, but I'm not going to turn back." The police officer then called his superior who treated him "extremely politely" and allowed him to enter.
>
> He said he was deeply shocked by what he saw in Cradock. "I received the impression that at least for a time there was a virtual reign of terror there." In spite of the large-scale imprisonment, and 24-hour police surveillance, the community's spirit and solidarity was astounding, he said.
>
> Dr Boesak expressed concern about the boycott which had disrupted schooling since February. "But the scholars argue they had a legitimate

---

101 Bekker, J. 11 August 1984. Teargas Was Used 'After Police Were Stoned.' *Eastern Province Herald.*

reason: they will not return to school until their people are released." He said until an equal education system was introduced in South Africa, the lives and education of children would be continually disrupted.

"I am amazed that when Mr Louis le Grange (the Minister of Law and Order) came to Cradock he did not speak to the people most deeply concerned – the schoolchildren. Such high-handedness is characteristic of a Government which thinks it can play God. We do not need Mr le Grange to have a change of heart, we need a new Government."

Lieutenant Colonel Gerrie van Rooyen, liaison officer for the police in the Eastern Cape, said last night: "I have no comment to make on allegations made by Dr Boesak."[102]

Growing up in Cradock, I found the name of Allan Boesak was always met with reverence. For the people of my hometown, Dr Boesak is one of us. And for my mother and Sis' Nyami, Dr Boesak continues to hold a special place in their hearts. So, when Abigail called my mother one evening in September 2017 to ask her if she would like to sit in on an interview I was set to conduct with Dr Boesak, my mother couldn't contain her excitement. It had been well over 30 years since they had last seen each other. On the morning of Thursday, 28 September 2017, just before eleven o'clock, Dr Allan Boesak pulled up in front of our home in Milnerton, Cape Town.

The reunion that followed between him and my mother left Martina Della Togna (my producer) and me rather emotional. As my mother welcomed him to our home, he clasped her hands in his and without a word spoken, they fell into each other's arms. Tears streamed from my mother's eyes as they stood there motionless, locked in an embrace in my living room. Martina and I were just as close to tears while witnessing this moment, but we did our best, and stayed strong in order to document the moment.

When we eventually settled down for the interview, I asked Dr Boesak what he remembered about his first visits to Cradock in 1984. In his response (which is reproduced here verbatim), he said:

---

102 Bekker, J. 10 August 1984. Boesak Shocked at Cradock's Reign of Terror. *Eastern Province Herald.*

'I remember the first time I went there. It was quite early on, just after the UDF was launched. It was either [19]83 or '84 that I went there for the first time. They had that organisation Cradora. And from the very beginning, I was told this of course, but it became very clear to me that Cradock is a special kind of place. And it had its young people of course, who were as militant as we needed them to be at the time. But what made Cradock special was that Cradora and Cradock had a history of cultivating leadership, in ways that not all of us had. I came from Somerset West; we didn't have that kind of tradition of cultivating leadership Cradock had. And what that did was that Cradock could fairly early on recognise all of the important issues and targets of the struggle that the UDF had identified and [the leaders in] Cradock could very easily take the national ideals, freedom, democracy, non-sexism, non-racialism, and so forth, and link that to a very local struggle. And they could link that to the international struggle too, so boycott and divestment and sanctions and pressure, both political, economic, and otherwise. And so, when I first went to Cradock and spoke about these things I could see immediately that the connections were made just like that because they were used to doing those things. We [the UDF] had leaders everywhere and they grew as the struggle went on. Cradock was one of those places [where], because of its history, because of Cradora, because of its involvement, because of the people's conscious link to the history and the struggle of our people before that, had come long through the history of the African National Congress. This was all present in Cradock. It was very consciously present. Also, the character of the leaders in Cradock was amazing. It's not just that they were good at talking to the people, it's not that they were good at organising the people – they were good at teaching the people. We [in the Western Cape] always made a point, and I had spent so much time at UWC [the University of the Western Cape] saying to our young people, let's spend some time talking about this, let's analyse this system, so that you can know what you are fighting. So that you can know why we call it evil. So that you can know why we say you have to resist it, so that you can know when we say we want something different, why it has to be different. What are the qualities of a fundamentally different society compared to apartheid, but you've got to understand that. I'd say to them, when you go on the streets tomorrow, you're not going there just to dance or sing – you will, just because that's who we are – but you're going to put your life on the line, and you've got to understand why you are putting your life on the line. And when I got to Cradock, those leaders knew exactly how to do that. So, there was something very special in Cradock.

One of the things that the UDF could do that other organisations could not do before, the ANC was mostly a movement among the urban, black proletariat. What the UDF did was that it succeeded in mobilising the rural areas on a scale that we had never seen before. And that meant all of a sudden that not just those African people who were in the rural areas with a direct connection to the ANC, but also those so-called coloured people who had no connection with the ANC. Who didn't know anything about the history of the ANC (where must they learn it?). We didn't learn it at school, I didn't hear a thing, except that there were some terrorists who had to be dealt with. That's all we knew. But the names of people and so forth, we didn't know that. So, we had to learn that somewhere and then begin to talk to our people and say, this history is also your history. But in Cradock they had that in your great-grandfather, James Calata. I didn't have any grandfather in Somerset West that I could point to [politically]. In Cradock, you had leaders who had all of that understanding. In a book that I wrote in 2005, called *The Tenderness of Conscience*, I quote your great-grandfather – twice. He had a wonderful saying where he says, "I have great, great faith in the future, because the hand that turns the wheel of history is God's hand, and that hand never fails." To a preacher like me, that's gorgeous. That's something I can use, and I did. So, what I'm trying to say is that Cradock had that [history] and I'm sure that kind of story had been told to generations in Cradock. Otherwise you [referring to me and the SABC] would not have made that decision. Your father would not have made that decision, otherwise your mom would not have made that decision. It's in your DNA. I'm sure it's in the DNA of all of us, but we have to work hard at it; you guys just grew up with it. So, for all of those reasons, Cradock was a very exciting place.

When I went there, it was the first march that brought such a large crowd together in the rural areas, that I remember. There must have been 20 000 people that day. It was an immense march. There was a joyfulness and a seriousness all put together. That was the first time that the [Security] Police deployed those huge trucks that they had, where the thing drives along, they open the back, and out fell metres and metres of coiled barbed-wire. It's like some monster vomiting something out. That's where I saw that for the first time. And when you see that, you think, *Whoa!* But when the young people saw that, it riled them up! They got far more excited. They got far more determined. They got angrier. That's when they started to sing something that sounded almost like Afrikaans to me when I heard it. So, I asked somebody, because I could see that some of the policemen were reacting. Some of them got angry, some of them were smiling, mostly the black policemen. So I listened. They were singing, "*Julle moer, la mabhulu, julle moer* [Fuck you, whites, fuck you!]." You know our people. One kilometre, two kilometres, they were still singing the same thing. Every time they would run into new policemen who had to hear their message. I thought, look at these kids, here they are, they've been surrounded by barbed-wire, here are the Casspirs, there are the ratels, there are the policemen, there are the guns and dogs, but listen to what they're singing. It was stunning actually!'

Shortly after Boesak's visit to Cradock, my mother and I once again took the train to Johannesburg to visit my father. By now, he had been in detention for nearly four months. On 21 August, our first or second visit to him that month, my mother recalled the devastating news Fort shared with her. 'He came into the booth where we usually sat and I could tell immediately that there was something wrong. He greeted [me] and the sound of his voice confirmed it. He tried to pretend as if he was okay, though, but I know my husband and I could tell something had changed.' She said she then asked him what the matter was. 'He tried to downplay that there was an issue on several occasions, at least during the first few minutes of our visit. He was more interested in talking to you, who had now learnt not to fall asleep during our visits.' After 20 minutes or so, my father eventually shared with her the news that he too had been dismissed by the Department of Education and Training from his position as a teacher at iLingelihle Secondary School. His letter of dismissal was not much different to that sent to Matthew seven months previously:

'Termination of Service

Due to your continuing absence without leave and failure to assume your duties at the iLingelihle Secondary School, Cradock, within 14 days from the re-opening of schools on 28 March 1984, the Department has approved of the termination of your services as teacher with effect from 1 April 1984 in terms of Art. 21 (2) (a) of the Act on Education and Training, 1979 (Act No 90 of 1979) as amended. According to the said Act, it is regarded that you dismissed yourself by not reporting for duty within 14 days from the date of re-opening of schools.

Kindly furnish this office with the address to which your pension contributions must be forwarded.

Yours faithfully
PA Nortjé
Regional Director: Cape'[103]

The news and the letter of dismissal hit my mother hard. Thousands of questions raced through her mind, chief among them: how would she raise my sister and me? How would she afford the rent? 'I felt all alone – my husband was in detention, and now we were both fired from our state jobs,' she told me. 'I wanted to cry right there and then, but had to hold back my tears. I knew I couldn't show him, or the prison guard [who was in earshot], any vulnerability.' My father tried to encourage her to stay strong, as well as assure her that things would be fine. 'It was hard for me to believe what he was telling me at that moment,' she said. 'From where I was sitting, every day was worse than the day before.' My father's dismissal was a massive financial setback for our family, yet despite this my mom and I continued to visit him every day of the fourteen-day period permitted to us by Lieutenant Henri Fouché.

Back at home, the Security Branch would make our lives a living hell. My mother recalled the diabolical actions of one officer in particular, Henry Wentzel. She said Wentzel (who spoke isiXhosa and referred to himself as *inkom' iyahlaba* [the gorging bull]) was a real bastard, who took it upon himself to visit our home every single day: 'He [often accompanied by at least two younger officers] mostly came at night,

---

103 Goniwe Papers. Cory Library, Rhodes University.

and by the time they left my house it would have been turned inside out.' She said sometimes Wentzel and the younger officers would ransack her little home spaza shop: 'He would tell them to mix the coffee with the washing powder, the sugar with the paraffin, they would break all the eggs, and then they would pull off all the blankets and mattresses from our beds, sometimes while you guys [Dorothy and I] were asleep,' she said. 'The last thing they always did was take whatever money, letters, pictures, postcards, or Cradora/Cradoya T-shirts that they found in the house with them.' Dorothy confirmed that police officers were at our house every day: 'Sometimes they would come in just to walk around our house. For no other reason sometimes other than for us to know that they were watching us.'

Wentzel then found out that my mother was behind with rent. Although no one in iLingelihle paid rent, my mom said, 'Wentzel would harass me endlessly every day about the outstanding rent. He even threatened to carry all our furniture out of the house and lock us out of it.' My mother referred to him as, '*Wentzel, daai fokken vark* [Wentzel, that fucking pig].' The South African Council of Churches often came to our rescue regarding the (increased) R86 to cover the rent. By 1984, the amount was especially steep for her, particularly as our neighbours, the Damoyi family at 28 Siyabulela Street, were only meant to be paying R26 towards their rent, due to the head of the house's employment at the South African Railways. Meanwhile, my mother – a 'single', unemployed, 25-year-old woman, raising two children – was forced to pay an amount almost four times that.

The seven-day consumer boycott of white-owned businesses at the end of July had been a success for Cradora but was disastrous for business owners. It had an adverse knock-on effect for them. Having noted its success, alongside the schools boycott, which was now in its seventh month and with no end in sight, Cradora began to discuss a call for yet another consumer boycott at the end of August. This forced business owners into a panic. In September, they would arrange a meeting with the Deputy Minister of Development and Co-operation to share their angst surrounding the effects of another boycott, which could only be averted by the release of my father, Matthew, Mbulelo, and Madoda from detention.

The first nine months of 1984 had been a torrid time for the residents of iLingelihle, but the first day of October brought with it the first piece of good news for residents. The Minister of Law and Order, Louis le Grange, had decided to lift the ban on public meetings in the location. Bekker once again reported on the minister's decision. In an article published on 2 October under the headline 'Cradock Meetings Ban Is Lifted', she writes: 'After a series of short-term bans on meetings, a three-month order was first imposed on March 31st, the day after four community and youth leaders Mr Matthew Goniwe, Mr Fort Calata, Mr Mbulelo Goniwe, and Mr Madoda Jacobs were detained under the security legislation. When the order's term expired on July 31st, Mr Le Grange and top Government officials visited iLingelihle and announced that the banning order would be renewed for a further three months. Colonel Leon Mellet, liaison officer for Mr Le Grange, yesterday gave no reason for the decision not to renew the most recent order, which expired on Sunday. He said the ban on indoor meetings in 21 magisterial districts (including iLingelihle), which was imposed some weeks ago, had expired on Sunday. The Minister had decided not to renew this ban or the three-month ban of all iLingelihle meetings. Mr Monwabisi (Gladwell) Makhawula, vice-chairperson of the Cradock Residents' Association (CRADORA) said people in the community urgently wanted a meeting. High rents, the high rate of unemployment, and poor wages were the major problems in the community.'[104]

Then, on 2 October, there was more good news at least for some families in iLingelihle. In her 3 October article under the headline '3 To Appeal Against Violence Convictions', Bekker writes: 'The Somerset East Regional Court yesterday found three Cradock residents guilty of public violence – a crime which according to the magistrate, Mr PPJ van der Merwe, struck at the nucleus of a community's peace and order. Two co-accused, Mr Madoda Jacobs (18) and Mr Daluxolo Dywili (24), were acquitted. Mrs Dinah Malgas (47) was sentenced to three years' imprisonment, of which 18 months were conditionally suspended for five years, Siphiwo Stemele (19) to four years of which 18 months were suspended for five years, and Miss Thandeka Bholani (32) received six years'

---

104 Bekker, J. 2 October 1984. Cradock Meetings Ban Is Lifted. *Eastern Province Herald.*

imprisonment of which two years were suspended for five years. Mr MTK Moerane, for the defence, announced his intention to appeal against the convictions.'[105]

Jacobs's acquittal ended a period of six months in prison, the first four of which he had spent detained alongside Matthew Goniwe at Pollsmoor in Cape Town, before he was transferred to Somerset East to stand trial at the end of July.

Another report, credited to a *Herald* reporter this time, and which appeared in the same publication of 3 October, quotes Jacobs saying about Matthew, my father, and Mbulelo's continued detention: '"They can be held until March 30th and I believe the authorities will detain them until then [. . .] Although Jacobs and Goniwe had been in individual cells in Pollsmoor they had exercised together. When I left [Pollsmoor Prison on transfer], Matthew was in good spirits." Jacobs also said "pupils would not return to school until those detained had been freed." His plans are to finish his schooling at the iLingelihle High School if he is accepted back. "I don't want to leave Cradock. If I'm not accepted at school, I will stay and work for the community."'[106]

In another article in the *Herald* under the headline 'Unrest Taking Its Toll on White Business', Bekker investigates the effects of the unrest in iLingelihle: 'Unrest in Cradock's African township, iLingelihle, during the first half of this year has taken its toll on the town's white business sector. The fall-off in commercial activity has taken place against the background of a continuing school boycott and a blanket ban on meetings, a one-day stay-away from work, a boycott of shops in the white town, and an increase in petty crime. Businessmen and municipal officials expressed fears that the adverse publicity arising from the trouble in iLingelihle would harm the town's tourist trade and impede industrial expansion.'[107]

The UDF in the Eastern Cape region, however, wasn't swayed by Le Grange's decision to lift the ban on meetings in iLingelihle. In a statement issued on 5 October, Prince Msutu, the publicity secretary, writes: 'We

---

105 Ibid.
106 Ibid.
107 Ibid.

wish to make it clear that the lifting of the ban on meetings in Cradock will not solve the problems there – if the Government is interested in solving the problems it must release their leaders.' Msutu ends his statement by condemning the government's use of repression in the Vaal Triangle, Cradock, and Soweto, Johannesburg.

On 9 October, my mother, Dorothy and I were in Johannesburg visiting my father. He, Mbulelo, and Matthew had now been in detention for six months.

The next day was a public holiday, Kruger's Day, celebrated on 10 October. Aunt Sisana, whom we stayed with each time we travelled to Johannesburg, had planned to take us on a fun excursion for the day, so my parents agreed we would not visit on the public holiday.

My mother vividly recalled the dream which woke her that morning: 'I dreamt that Tatou had entered my room and said to me, "*Molokozana, vuka uyekhaya. Unyana ubuyile* [Daughter-in-law, you must wake up and head home. My son has returned]." The slam of the door as he shut it behind him woke me up. I immediately went to uSis' Sisana to tell her about the dream.'

About an hour or so after that, the phone rang. It was their aunt, Vuyelwa, whom the family called 'si'Viks'. 'While she and usisi were on the phone, I heard usisi saying, "O si'Viks uFort..." as she started to cry. In that moment, my heart began to race as I didn't know what to expect. I thought my worst fears had come true, that maybe they had killed my husband. I stood there, frozen, just looking at her. Then I heard her say, "Nomonde just told me that she had this dream, where Tatou told her she had to go home because Fort is home. Nomonde is so blessed," she said. Then I realised that maybe Fort must have been released from prison,' my mother told me. It turns out my father, Mbulelo, and Matthew had indeed been released from prison. He had called si'Viks, who also lived in Johannesburg, looking for Sisana's home telephone number.

Minutes later, Sisana's home phone rang again. This time it was my father on the other side, telling my mother to come home. 'I packed our bags immediately. Later that afternoon, we were on the train back to Cradock,' she said. Fort, Matthew, and Mbulelo had been released the night before, without any notification.

Their release, and arrival back home on Wednesday, 10 October 1984, were greeted with much fanfare and excitement in iLingelihle. Among the first reporters to see them was none other than Jo-Ann Bekker, accompanied by photographer Colin Urquhart. The two journalists would set up and capture the now iconic picture of the four recently released detainees walking towards Matthew's home in Qhina Street, iLingelihle.

The train that runs between Johannesburg and Port Elizabeth via Cradock usually pulls into Cradock station at around five o'clock in the morning. When my mother and I arrived the following morning, my father was already there waiting for us. My mother recalled, 'I was happy to see my husband. It had been over six months since I had last held or touched him.'

He explained to my mother that he could not have given her notice of his release, as he himself had not known that he would be released until it happened.

The *Eastern Province Herald* dedicated an entire page to their return. Under the headline, 'Three Cradock Leaders Freed, Returned Home', Bekker writes:

'After more than six months in detention, Cradock community leaders Mr Matthew Goniwe, Mr Fort Calata and Mr Mbulelo Goniwe were released and returned home early yesterday. The men cannot be quoted. Friends said that while the men were extremely happy to be free again, their joy was marred by the knowledge that others were still in detention.

Yesterday, Cradora and pupils boycotting schools in the community welcomed the men's release, but said their demands would not have been met until Mr Goniwe and Mr Calata were reinstated.

Mrs Nyameka Goniwe, Mr Matthew Goniwe's wife, said yesterday her husband had arrived from Pollsmoor Prison and the others from Johannesburg Prison, within minutes of each other at about 3h30 am yesterday. "It came as a surprise to the family and other members of the community. We were prepared for the worst and did not expect them to be released before March [1985]."

The Goniwes' house in Qhina Street, iLingelihle, was flooded by a constant stream of visitors yesterday. Priests, nuns, and Mrs Molly Blackburn of the Black Sash, friends from Port Elizabeth and Cradock came to welcome the men home.

However, the absence of Mr Calata's wife, Liza [Nomonde], placed a dampener on the celebrations.'[108]

Meanwhile, in another article on the same page, under the headline 'No Reason to Celebrate, Says UDF Spokesman', journalist Mandla Tyala writes:

'While spokesmen for several organisations hailed yesterday's release of three Cradock community leaders, the Eastern Cape division of the United Democratic Front said it was "not impressed".

The fact that Mr Matthew Goniwe and the other leaders have been released without being brought to trial shows that there was no reason to detain them in the first place,' UDF Eastern Cape Vice President Mr Fikile Kobese said last night.

He added that there would be no reason to celebrate until Mr Goniwe and Mr Fort Calata had been unconditionally reinstated as teachers. Their services were sorely needed by their communities.

Mrs Di Bishop, MPC (PFP) who campaigned for the release of Mr Goniwe, appealed to the Minister of Law and Order, Mr Louis Le Grange, to lift the ban on the ex-principal to allow him to be quoted publicly. "Our times are desperate and we need to hear the voice of this outstanding community leader," Mrs Bishop said.'[109]

My family quietly celebrated Fort's safe return home. Although happy to be reunited, it wasn't long before discussions turned to how the family would survive. The reality was that life had changed drastically for us during the six months of my father's detention. Both my parents had since been dismissed from their jobs and, as my mother told me, bills – particularly furniture bills – were piling up. 'In those days, the furniture shops still repossessed furniture if you were behind with payments,' she said. 'I was so afraid that they would come and repossess ours.' The small shop was generating an income, but not nearly enough to raise a family of four.

Just four days after their release, Cradora would hold its first meeting

---

108 Bekker, J. 11 October 1984. Three Cradock Leaders Freed, Returned Home. *Eastern Province Herald.*

109 Tyala, M. 11 October 1984. No Reason to Celebrate Says UDF Spokesman. *Eastern Province Herald.*

in six months, following Minister Le Grange's decision to lift the ban on meetings.

Paul Verryn, who had struck up quite a good friendship with my father during his visits at Diepkloof Prison, made an appointment for the two of them to see Beyers Naudé, a critic of apartheid and minister in the Dutch Reformed Church. Just a month prior to this visit, Naudé had had his own seven-year banning order lifted by the government. He had also succeeded Bishop Tutu as the secretary-general of the South African Council of Churches (SACC). My mother remembered that we had all travelled back to Johannesburg for the scheduled meeting between Naudé, Verryn, and my father. The meeting took place at Khotso House, the SACC's headquarters, in the Johannesburg CBD.

Our visit to Johannesburg also allowed Dorothy her reunion with our father. Aunt Sisana had requested that she stay with her for the duration of my father's detention. I suspect this was her way of easing the responsibilities on my mother, who was alone and unemployed during this time. Dorothy, even though she had been in Johannesburg for six months, had always refused to go and visit our father in prison.

Meanwhile, it seems the time in detention had strengthened my father, Matthew, Mbulelo, and Madoda's political resolve and activism. Cradora and Cradoya, under the stewardship of vice-chairperson Monwabisi (Gladwell) Makhawula and Nonyanga Sibanda (known as General), had done extremely well while the four were in detention. Now that they were all back home, it was time to consolidate the gains made: the school boycott had entered its eighth month; iLingelihle had become an increasingly hostile area for the Security Police; residents had maintained strict discipline; and the much-publicised campaign for the four men's release from detention had helped them gain even more prominence and stature, particularly beyond the borders of iLingelihle.

This reputation, however, would prove to be a double-edged sword. According to Lourens du Plessis, a colonel in the South African Defence Force (SADF) in the Eighties, the on-going school boycotts and running battles between iLingelihle residents and the police had become a source of huge embarrassment to the authorities. Senior military generals were also under pressure, especially from politicians, to quell the unrest in iLingelihle[110].

---

110 S Markovits and M Kaplan interview with Col. L du Plessis.

The release of my father, Matthew, Mbulelo, and Madoda that October morning was accompanied, amidst other tensions, by increased surveillance of them. My mother remembered that barely a day after my father's return home, a police van was stationed permanently about 500 m from our home.

Du Plessis said this surveillance of my father and Matthew was critical for the security forces, as it helped them gather the necessary information about their movements, whom they were meeting with, at what time and how long the meeting lasted. At Matthew's house, they'd taken their surveillance operations even further, wire-tapping his telephone line with a device they referred to as the 'tamatie' (tomato).

Disturbingly, Du Plessis said these weren't the only ways of gathering information about my father and Matthew, and the activities of both Cradora and Cradoya. He said, 'First of all, his [Matthew's] telephone was tapped. So, whatever he said to his colleagues was available on tape. Then of course there are paid informers. I think that is one of the reasons why so many people were killed. I think the population started realising there were so many informers, police informers, paid informers – "impimpis" – and they're very effective, because they told us everything.'[111]

Despite both overt and covert surveillance, my father and the rest of the Cradora and Cradoya leadership intensified their political activities once they were back home.

On 24 October, Molly Blackburn and Di Bishop, both members of the Provincial Council representing the Progressive Federal Party, were arrested by the Security Police for being in iLingelihle. They were charged with being in an African township without a permit.

In early November, two justices of the Grahamstown Supreme Court, Judges Eksteen and Zietsman, upheld my mother's appeal against her 10 April conviction for wearing a 'Free Mandela' T-shirt. The judges found that she had not received a fair trial, which had led to her dismissal from her position as a member of the general staff at the Cradock Provincial Hospital. In a statement released by Cradora, the organisa-

---

111 Ibid.

tion wrote: 'As a result of Mrs Calata's successful appeal, we hope to see her reinstated immediatcly.'

Blackburn had attended the hearings in Grahamstown. In an article published on 5 November in the *Eastern Province Herald* under the headline 'Reinstatement of Woman in Mandela T-shirt Trial Is Called For', Blackburn is quoted saying: 'The least that can be done to compensate Mrs Calata for her suffering is to reinstate her immediately as a member of the hospital staff with back pay.' The article further states: 'Mrs Blackburn said that whcn she had asked about the dismissal in the Provincial Council, she was told it had been done on the advice of the Security Police. Mr JMJ van Vuuren, secretary of the Cradock Hospital, said Mrs Calata's position had been filled. Mr Van Vuuren, who is in charge of staff at the Hospital, refused to comment on calls for her reinstatement.'[112]

'Van Vuuren's attitude was heartbreaking for me,' said my mother. 'I mean, I had been wrongfully convicted, then wrongfully dismissed from the hospital and now, even after the Supreme Court had cleared me, he point-blankly refused to give me my job back. It was a very difficult time for me.'

Despite these setbacks, though, my family survived largely through the generous support of Beyers Naudé from the SACC, the Black Sash through Molly Blackburn and her sister, Judy Chalmers, and the residents of iLingelihle, who supported my mother's spaza shop.

With my father now at home (almost) full-time, the harassment and unauthorised 'search and seizures' by Wentzel stopped. Despite being busy and hardly spending an entire day at home, Dorothy has fond memories of this period with our father, also recalling how strict he could be at times. Mene, on the other hand, remembered how generous my father was. He said the Cradoya executive and even some youths who weren't on the executive would visit our house almost every day: 'In the mornings, particularly Saturdays, we would go to uBhut' Matthew's home, but he'd be busy with his yoga or family. Sometimes he wouldn't have

---

112 Herald Reporter. 5 November 1984. Reinstatement of Woman in Mandela T-shirt Trial Is Called For. *Eastern Province Herald.*

time to spend with us, so we'd go down to your home. UBhut' Fort would always sit and chat with us. He'd make sure we had something to eat first and if uBhut' Matthew didn't come to fetch him, we'd spend most of the morning with him. But on Sundays, we knew not to visit because uBhut' Fort would say Sundays are for church and family time.'

My mother confirmed that my father regularly attended church. 'It would not be right if he did not go to church on a Sunday,' she said. 'At times, Matthew would come to our home to look for him and I would tell him that Fort's gone to church, and Matthew would be upset and say, "Hey, this guy knew I am going to come here and he decided to go to church. No man, *mzala*." When Fort came back from his original church, the Anglican Church, he'd sometimes go to the church opposite our home too [the Apostolic Church] for the second time [that day] and sometimes I'd get angry. I'd ask him, "Why would you go two times to church?" For him, it was nice though.'

On 14 November, Cradora and Cradoya unanimously re-elected my father, Matthew Goniwe, and Mbulelo Goniwe to the new extended executives of both organisations. Matthew, however, was no longer chairperson; instead he was elected to the office of general secretary. My father retained his responsibilities as chairperson of the Youth Association and treasurer of the Residents' Association. Mbulelo was also asked to continue for another term as convenor of both organisations. Monwabisi Makhawula, who had served as acting chairperson while Matthew was in detention, was asked to assume the role on a full-time basis.

Matthew's election as general secretary freed him from the responsibilities as chairperson, which meant that he and my father could dedicate themselves to the restructuring and official launch of Cradora.

It was during these first few days and weeks following their release that Matthew first unveiled to the rest of Cradora's leadership a plan which he hoped would revolutionise their organisational structures, in particular its communication channels between the executive and members. The Security Police and government would later come to call it the 'G-Plan'. In its essence, it was an adaptation and modern version of Nelson Mandela's 'M-Plan', first unveiled in the lead-up to the ANC's banning in the Sixties.

In an academic paper by Raymond Suttner, titled 'The African National Congress (ANC) Underground: From M-Plan to Rivonia', he describes the M-Plan as follows:

> 'As with all plans for underground, the M-Plan embraced a hierarchical structure, with very clear "top down" manifestations. Thus, Mandela writes that "[t]he ... organisational machinery ... would allow the ANC to take decisions at the highest level, which could then be swiftly transmitted to the organisation as a whole without calling a meeting" [. . .] "Press statements" and "circulars" would be unnecessary. The same emphasis can be found in the description of the operation of the M-Plan in East London, given by Johnson Malcomess Mgabela:
>
> "Going from house to house we spoke with the people and gave them some orders, trying to bring political understanding of what the ANC were doing. We had to organise small meetings because the government declared any meeting of more than ten people an illegal gathering. So we used the Mandela Plan: going to a house; staying there with ten people; giving them an understanding of what the ANC was doing; giving them orders; going to the next house. We tried to give people a message of what the ANC stood for and what its plans of actions were. You would tell people here, tell people there. You would even go to a public place like a shebeen or stand with a few people on a street corner [. . .] All of this was to be done underground. No name must be written down. Everything must be kept in secret. From the national level the instructions came to us through the leadership of the region. We had to take these instructions to the branches; the branches had to take it to the area committees and the area committees had to take it to the street committees."'[113]

Mbulelo defined the G-Plan to us, saying, 'Every street had at least one street representative. They would then form an area committee, which would then elect an area organiser. These area organisers would report to the chief organiser, who in turn reported to the executive committee of Cradora. This resulted in Cradora's being aware of problems or challenges in literally every street. We wanted to ensure that in each and every mass meeting, there would be at least two or three people from

---

113 Suttner, R. November 2003. 'The African National Congress (ANC) Underground: From the "M-Plan" to Rivonia.' *South African Historical Journal*, 49, pp. 123–146.

each street whose main function would be to go back to their street, call a meeting, and actually report what was decided on an issue such as the school boycott or the rental boycott as an example. So that's how everybody was easily informed.' He added, 'The vision of Cradora was radicalised by the [new] system.'

My mother said that even during this time, Cradora, with the assistance of Blackburn, continued their negotiations and calls for my father and Matthew to be re-instated as teachers, but to no avail.

The new G-Plan would have its trial run in early December 1984, with the boycott of the newly opened beerhall, the first one to operate in iLingelihle in seven years. The beerhall was jointly owned by David Hume, a farmer from Willowmore (a town just over 200 km from Cradock), and his livestock manager, Dial Maseti. The two had amicably split their shareholding 49 and 51 per cent respectively.

My mother recalled that my father was completely opposed to the beerhall operating in iLingelihle from the outset. A joint Cradora and Cradoya meeting was then called and attended by an estimated 1800 residents. Cradora proposed a boycott of the beerhall. Chairperson Makhawula, when addressing the meeting, asked how the council could build a beerhall, 'when there were no crèches, swimming pools, parks or adequate sports facilities in Cradock.' He argued that beerhalls were destructive and were 'scenes of murders, rapes, and hooliganism'. Residents agreed, supporting the call for a boycott. They had previously opposed its rebuilding in any case after it burnt down in 1980. The next day, not a single resident bought sorghum beer from the beerhall, while distributors in iLingelihle stopped supplying it with beer.

The Cradora leadership then set about planning its festive season campaign, dubbed the 'Black Christmas', and its official launch, tentatively pencilled in for 3 February 1985.

After a few days of the strictly implemented beerhall boycott, Hume, one of the owners, pledged to donate one cent of every litre of sorghum beer sold in iLingelihle towards the building of a crèche. Bekker, in an article published in the *Eastern Province Herald* on 11 December 1984 under the headline, 'Owners' Counter Offer to Beerhall Boycott', writes: 'He [Mr Hume] estimated 40 000 litres of sorghum beer would be sold every month, making about R4800 a year available for a crèche. He said there had been a total boycott of the hall and adjacent bottle store since the beginning of the month, although a few cartons were sold yesterday. Mr Hume said he hoped the boycott would blow over.'[114]

A few days later, however, the Eastern Cape Development Board agreed to resume dealings with the distributors, and began to supply the beerhall sorghum beer through its depot in town.

Meanwhile, Cradora chairperson Makhawula rejected the offer by Hume, saying, 'Mr Hume's offer does not impress us. We do not want beerhalls, as they breed crime. Mr Hume's calculations that R400 would go towards the crèche every month from anticipated sorghum beer sales in the township would not compensate for the lives lost in beerhall brawls.' But inside the Cradora and Cradoya executives, Hume's offer was heavily debated.

Mene remembered that Matthew had argued that Cradora allow the beerhall to operate, but that they negotiate for a 50c tax on every litre of beer sold. My father, Mene said, offered a counter argument, insisting that the beerhall not be allowed to operate at all. Mene recalled the intense debate in one executive members' meeting as they interrogated the matter for hours. 'UBhut' Matthew and uBhut' Fort led the opposing arguments,' he said. 'At around eight o'clock that evening, we agreed to hold the matter over until the next day when we would reconvene at noon for a final decision to present before the community at a meeting later that afternoon.' Mene said that Matthew still drove my father home from that meeting, even though they had just had quite an intense intellectual disagreement around the fate of the beerhall. 'The next day, we gathered at Mtutu Ntombela's house [right next door to Tatou's home], to resume the discussion around the beerhall. A few minutes after we had begun the discussion, one of the Cradoya youths came in and said the discussion about the fate of the beerhall was now a moot point as some youths had stoned it and were getting ready to petrol bomb it,' Mene told me. 'All the guys who supported uBhut' Matthew's

---

114 Bekker, J. 11 December 1984. Owners' Counter Offer to Beerhall Boycott. *Eastern Province Herald.*

argument immediately looked at uBhut' Fort with suspicion that he had something to do with the stoning and burning down of the beerhall. As president of Cradoya, nothing like that could've happened without him knowing about it.' Mene said that, although my father tried to deny any knowledge of the destruction of the beerhall, he was delighted that in one way or another its fate was now finally resolved. Matthew, however, was very upset.

The incident led to yet another clash with the Security Police in iLingelihle, who fired teargas to disperse the small crowd.

A day later, Cradora called another community meeting, held at the Methodist Church. 'The people gathered together in the church hall,' my mother said. 'We were all there, singing freedom songs. Matthew addressed us and called for a Black Christmas. This meant that no one in the community was permitted to drink any alcohol on Christmas Day. Street committees were to ensure that no one drank that day.'

Indeed, residents of iLingelihle heeded the call for a Black Christmas. 'I remember there was a nurse who came to our home,' my mother continued. 'She said she wanted to praise Matthew and Fort for what they had done on that Christmas Day. The resident doctor [in Cradock] then was Dr Schoeman. He said to her that he had never had such a peaceful Christmas Day ever since he started working in Cradock. He wanted to know from her what was happening in iLingelihle. She too had never experienced that, as they were used to dealing with alcohol-related violence on "big days" such as Christmas and New Year's Eve. That day, they managed to spend time with their families, as they weren't called out on emergencies to deal with cases of violence such as stabbings, etc.'

The year ended without any further incidents.

Chapter Nine:
'Ambush in the Night'
– Bob Marley

LUKHANYO

The year 1985 had barely started when the entire iLingelihle Town Council announced its resignation on the Friday morning of 4 January.

The announcement came just minutes before Matthew and my father met Danny O'Grady from the United States Embassy. A Security Police surveillance report of that meeting noted that 'due to technical problems, their discussions could not be recorded'[115].

After the meeting with O'Grady, my father and Matthew turned their attention to the resignations of the Town Council. My mother told me that my father was very excited by the news of the council's decision to step down. She said, 'For Fort, the new year could not have started any better.' But she still harboured hopes that things, particularly for our young family, would improve even further. The new year held a new promise, at least for her, that just maybe my father and Matthew could still be re-instated in their positions as teachers in iLingelihle. Personally, she said, 'I had come to terms somewhat [with the fact] that I would not get my old job back.' Her hopes for my father's re-instatement would never come to pass.

Almost as soon as the four-member council had resigned, they were accepted back into the community. In her report of the resignations, published in the *Eastern Province Herald* on 5 January 1985 under the headline, '"Rejected" Cradock iLingelihle Council Resigns En Masse', Bekker writes:

---

115 Declassified National Intelligence Agency Document. Briefing Notes: '"The Cradock Four" – Fort Calata, Matthew Goniwe, Sparro Mkonto, Sicelo Mhlawuli.'

'Cradock's iLingelihle Village Council, one of the first to become a fully fledged council under the Black Local Authorities Act last year, resigned en masse yesterday. Councillors said they had resigned because the community regarded them as civil servants who assisted the Government in implementing Apartheid.

In addition the council had been unable to improve conditions in the township because it had not been given a hearing by the authorities. The decision was taken at a meeting on Thursday and official resignations were tendered yesterday but councillors said they had discussed the action months in advance.

Mr Donald Moni, who was elected Deputy Mayor on the day the council disbanded, said, "We realized that the residents of iLingelihle really did not accept the concept of the Village Council. We were not accepted as the representative body. Since the unrest in iLingelihle last year, residents have seen us as civil servants who help the Government in implementing its Apartheid policy. It was impossible to carry on when we were not wanted and it was useless to sit on a body when it represented nobody."

The regional representative of the director of Local Government, Mr George Reynolds – chief commissioner for the Eastern Cape – said he had no comment on the resignations. He said the iLingelihle Village Council's resignation was unprecedented in the Eastern Cape.'[116]

In a follow-up article published on 8 January, under the headline, 'iLingelihle Resignations Draw Mixed Reactions', Bekker writes:

'The resignation of all iLingelihle Village Council office bearers on Friday was welcomed by the Cradock Residents' Association yesterday, but strongly condemned by the mayors of other Eastern Cape African local authorities. The former Mayor of the iLingelihle council, Mrs Doris Hermans, yesterday endorsed the reasons her fellow councillors gave for tendering their resignations.

Mr Monwabisi [Gladwell] Makhawula, president of CRADORA, a civic body which is affiliated to the United Democratic Front, said the association commended the village council for heeding the commu-

---

116 Bekker, J. 5 January 1985. 'Rejected' Cradock iLingelihle Council Resigns En Masse. Eastern Province Herald.

nity's call to resign and called on all township councils in the Eastern Cape and South Africa to follow this example. The Mayors of Port Elizabeth's Kayamnandi Town Council, Mr Thamsanqa Linda, and Grahamstown's Rhini Town Council, Mr PP Zondani, yesterday told the Eastern Province Herald that they had no intention of resigning.

"As far as I'm concerned we have a mandate from the people," Linda said. "I don't know where CRADORA comes into the picture and I don't think a single member of my council will heed their call." Mr Zondani said, "Cradock was one of the first 29 community councils to be elevated to municipal status on January 16th 1984. If they have called it a day, that is pathetic. It has never happened in our country." Mr Makhawula said the statement by Mr George Reynolds, regional representative of the director of Local Government, that elections would probably be held to elect new members to the village council, "is proof of the Government's ostrich mentality."

"There will be no new community council in Cradock," he said.'[117]

On the same day, 8 January 1985, ANC president Oliver Tambo delivered the liberation movement's birthday address (commonly referred to as the January 8th statement). The theme of that year's address was '1985 – the Year of the Cadre'.

For my father, the January 8th address had always been a momentous occasion. I suspect this was largely due to Tatou's influence. Also, my mother recalled that Radio Freedom was a permanent feature in our home: 'We had those old types of radios, the one with the tube, that first warms up and then becomes brighter and brighter. Fort was very technical – he could fix all old radios, electrical equipment, and things like that. He had found this radio and fixed it. He put it in our room, so every evening we listened to Radio Freedom. Because we were not supposed to have the radio loud, we always sat close to it. Sometimes we could hear how they were chanting in the background, but mostly we listened to the speeches of Oliver Tambo.'

In his 1985 address, Tambo said:

---

117 Bekker, J. 8 January 1984. iLingelihle Resignations Draw Mixed Reactions. *Eastern Province Herald.*

'We have now set out upon this path. We have taken impressive strides towards rendering the country ungovernable. This has not only meant the destruction of the community councils; our rejection of the apartheid constitution was, in its essence, a reaffirmation of our rejection of the illegitimate rule of the Botha regime. Other struggles, including those around the issue of education as well as the stay-at-home, themselves pitted our democratic power against the power of the forces of oppression, racism and counter-revolution, for the defeat of the latter and its replacement with popular power.

In this coming period, we shall need to pursue, with even greater vigour, the task of reducing the capacity of the colonial apartheid regime to continue its illegal rule of our country. The destruction of the organs of government weakens the regime and is a necessary part of our continuing mass offensive.

Furthermore, all the oppressed need to emulate the example of the areas where the democratic movement has emerged as the alternative power. Wherever we are, we must transform our locality into a mass revolutionary base. In such areas, we should also use the democratic power we have accumulated through struggle, to defend and advance the interests of the people. We must use our organised mass strength and, by attacking, consolidate our victorious emergence as the alternative power.

We need cadres of unquestionable loyalty, dedication and understanding of our struggle. In order to achieve such a high standard and spur our nation into a greater onslaught on the enemy and its institutions, we declare this year, 1985, the Year of the Cadre!

Let this year see us take big strides in further strengthening the organised underground structures of the ANC. Let us see greater mass political actions in all the provinces and districts of our country. Let it see us extend people's war to all corners of our land. Let it see the fastest and furthest possible co-ordinated advance on all fronts towards the goal of people's power.

There is no going back.

Forward Always is our battle cry!

The enemy cannot stop us

Our future is in our hands.

Forward with the Year of the Cadre!

Mobilise and March Forward to People's Power!

Amandla Ngawethu!

Power to the People!'[118]

---

118 January 8th Address 1985. http://www.anc.org.za/

My mother told me, 'Fort took these words to heart. Tambo's speech was further encouragement that what he and Matthew and the rest of the Cradora and Cradoya leadership were doing was the right thing, especially after the resignation of the Community Council the previous week.'

Three days later Matthew travelled to Cape Town in the company of Molly Blackburn, among others, where they met with United States Senator Edward Kennedy.

In mid-January, Henri Fouché (the Security Police branch commander in Cradock), in his report addressed to the Joint Management Centre in Port Elizabeth, writes:

'I have obtained information that CRADORA, CRADOYA, CRAWO [Cradock Women Association] and COSAS [Congress of South African Students] plan to host a joint meeting on 1985/02/03 in the Community Hall in Cradock. They have already issued invitations to all regions of the United Democratic Front countrywide to send delegates representing all its affiliates to Cradock. The purpose of the meeting is to gather as many members of the U.D.F. from around the country in Cradock to celebrate the resignations of the iLingelihle black town council on 85/01/03 and to discuss strategy for further actions against the town councils nationwide in order to force them through U.D.F. pressure to resign. They aim also to seek solidarity for the Cradock school boycott which has been in effect since 1984.

The organisers are expecting thousands of people and they have put out a call for funds/sponsorships, hand delivered to all businesses in Cradock. They wrote:

"The Cradock Residents' Association (Cradora) will be officially launched on Sunday, 3rd February. Thousands of visitors from all over South Africa are expected. We, therefore, wish to appeal to all business men for financial assistance or assistance in kind to meet the costs of catering for our visitors.
Thanking you in anticipation
Yours faithfully
Cradock Residents' Association"

Ever since the resignations, of the town council on 1985/01/03, a climate of revolt has existed in the black neighbourhood and meetings of CRADOYA and CRAWO held in recent days have led to the disturbance of public peace, violence and intimidation.

It is my opinion that if indeed the planned meeting on 1985/02/03 takes place, the thousands of people expected to attend from all over the country will most likely be incited to such an extent that they will pose a serious threat to public peace in Cradock.'[119]

What Fouché doesn't say is that the resignations of the members of the town council had effectively rendered iLingelihle a 'liberated zone'. The small location boasting around 24 000 residents was no longer governed in any way by the apartheid government. The people of iLingelihle through Cradora were governing themselves. They, and they alone, were the ones deciding the kind of future they wanted for themselves and their children. The people of my hometown were now the masters of their own destinies.

Towards the end of January, my parents discovered that my mother was pregnant with their third child. 'Although we hadn't planned for the third pregnancy, Fort and I were happy that I was pregnant again,' my mother said. 'Fort, though, started saying [and praying] that this child be a little girl. He could be very foolish sometimes and say, "I don't want anything to come between my son and [me]." Somehow he thought having another boy would come between your and his relationship.'

With the town council now out of the way, the new Cradock government of Cradora and Cradoya set about governing the town. Among the priorities on their list of community programmes was the implementation of a literacy programme for adults and youths, most of whom had boycotted school for a least a year by February 1985. They also opened a community crèche, the first time this amenity had existed in iLingelihle. An advice centre was established, which among its duties supervised the payment of old-age, children's, and disability grants in iLingelihle. Cradoya members were responsible for community safety. My mother recalled that during this time iLingelihle was virtually crime-free: 'At night, you could leave the doors unlocked. In fact, residents were encouraged to leave their back doors open, just in case the youths needed a quick escape route from the Security Police.'

---

119 Henri Fouché. Affidavit. 31 January 1985.

Cradora's version of governance only served to increase its popularity in iLingelihle, with nearly 80 per cent of residents' approval and support[120].

But the situation in this little Karoo town located almost in the middle of nowhere had become a real embarrassment and problem for the government, in particular for Louis le Grange and FW de Klerk, the Minister of Education.

Cradora was eventually denied permission to hold its official launch, much to the frustration and disappointment of the community. A group of outraged youths estimated at around 200 then took to the streets in protest against the government's decision to ban Cradora's official launch. The homes of several suspected police informers were stoned, and at least one was petrol-bombed. The Security Police responded by firing teargas and rubber bullets to disperse the crowd and quell the protest. Similar violent clashes would break out in iLingelihle almost every second or third day as residents stood toe to toe with Security Police. This is evidenced by eleven entries denoting violent clashes in Lt Fouché's report to the JMC between January and February 1985.

On Sunday, 3 February, just after my father, sister, and I had returned from church, Matthew came to inform him that the Security Police had just left his home in a desperate search for Madoda Jacobs. They suspected that he and several other Cradoya members either knew of or were involved in the killing of a police officer, whose body was found on the banks of the Great Fish River that morning. My mother recalled that Matthew was deeply concerned by what could happen to Jacobs if the police were to find him before they did. 'Fort didn't even have time to change into more comfortable clothes,' my mother said. 'He left still wearing his church clothes as they went to find Madoda. Fortunately, they found him before the police could, and they accompanied him to the Sanlam building, where he was arrested on suspicion of murder.'

During their hunt for Jacobs, the Security Police were particularly heavy-handed. Their actions, regarded by residents as agitation, led to

---

120 Declassified National Intelligence Agency Document. Briefing Notes: '"The Cradock Four" – Fort Calata, Matthew Goniwe, Sparro Mkonto, Sicelo Mhlawuli.'

yet another series of violent clashes with the police that afternoon. In the ensuing standoff, a teenager, Thozi Skweyiya, was critically injured by birdshot the Security Police fired at demonstrators. Skweyiya succumbed to his injuries, dying in hospital later that Sunday evening.

'I remember Fort being angry when that little boy was shot by the police,' my mother told me. 'He was really angry. I remember him standing in front of the wardrobe taking out his jacket, because Matthew had asked him to go and pray at that house. He said to me, "You know what, Monde, if ever these policemen will kill me, I promise you today, I will never leave them to rest, I will haunt them each and every day of their lives. I will not be like these innocent little children they are killing." He was saying it in this really angry tone. He was upset because this boy did not do anything wrong. They were just chanting freedom songs and singing in the street, nothing actually wrong, and then the police started shooting at these children. Unfortunately, this boy was his mother's only son and that really hurt the parents. Fort was really very angry at the police.'

While speaking at Skweyiya's funeral a week later, Matthew used his eulogy to criticise the apartheid government's policies on education, labelling the Bantu Education policy as a weapon used by the state to further oppress Africans. He said: 'The subsidy rented by government to white children differs from that of the black child. What I cannot understand is why should they give the white child who already has money, more money and a black child, who has no money, almost nothing. The schools of the whites are like palaces with swimming pools, while we have to teach in shacks.'[121]

Shortly after the funeral, my mother recalled my father telling her that he had to go to Johannesburg for a week or two to see a specialist doctor there who might be able to treat his 'frozen shoulder' problem. This revelation, she remembered, came a day or so after Matthew had told her that he wanted to send my father somewhere. Shortly after that, my father left Cradock in the company of another activist, Obed Bapela.

'I was not aware that he was involved in MK or [ANC] underground structures,' my mother said. 'All I knew was that Fort would disappear

---

121 David Forbes Archive: Henri Fouché Affidavit.

from time to time. In my mind, I thought he had just gone to some conference or something. When Matthew would come and say, 'I want to send Fort somewhere', I thought he was sending him to attend a meeting maybe in Adelaide or somewhere that he, Matthew, could not go to.' My mother added that 'Matthew would come and fetch Fort, and he would be gone for some time. I remember at one stage he disappeared for two weeks, and I was really angry because no one could tell me where my husband was. So, I went to his mother and I said, "*Sis' Ntsiki, if uFort akabuyi, ndizaku thatha impahla, nabantwana bam' ndigoduke* [If Fort does not come back home, then I am going to pack my things and my children, and go to my parents' home]." I was so frustrated because nobody could tell me where he is. Shortly after this, uMzala [Matthew] came and told me that Fort was fine and that he was on his way back home. In that regard, Fort was never open with me. Then one day, I actually overheard him talking to Matthew about taking some of the young comrades away. I realised then that this man is involved [in ANC underground structures], because how does he have connections to take these young men and skip the country into exile?' Matthew is known to have been very influential in the ANC's underground structures, and my mother believed that Fort may have been active too, although he never uttered a word to her about his involvement in these activities.

An opinion piece by an undisclosed author, published in the *Eastern Province Herald* in early February under the title 'Government Must Act on Cradock' speaks to the prevailing public sentiment around the events unfolding in iLingelihle. An excerpt from it, reads: 'The situation in Cradock is crying out for an urgent and thorough investigation at the highest level. What is the Government doing about this Karoo town, where violence and upheaval has become part of everyday life? Has it abandoned the African township of iLingelihle to the ongoing trauma of petrol bombs and rubber bullets, of teargas and murder, of boycotts and bannings? The unrest is now into its second year with no end in sight. Nor is there any sign of attempts to find a solution. Police action in the township can at best be a holding operation, aimed at curbing disturbances while solutions are sought elsewhere. In fact we fear that one of the reasons why the unrest continues has been a dangerous misconception on the part of some people in power that a hardline approach would prove an answer in itself. The folly of such thinking has been demonstrated with shocking regularity in iLingelihle.'[122]

The *Herald*'s continued reportage on the situation in Cradock would draw the ire of the Security Police, who in a clear bid to intimidate the newspaper's reporters and editor began to probe 'six matters in connection with four reports published in paper in the terms of the Police Act and the Internal Security Act'. An article published in the paper under the headline 'Police Probing Four Herald Reports', reads: 'Last week senior police officers visited the Editor of the *Herald*, JC Viviers, seeking statements in connection with the court report. He did not make an affidavit. Today police officers are expected to call at the *Herald* for affidavits from a Port Elizabeth-based reporter [most likely Jo-Ann Bekker], who also worked on one of the November unrest reports and Mr Viviers. Colonel Van Rooyen said last night that two Port Elizabeth reporters were also involved in their investigations.'[123]

Shortly after this article was published, Bekker's editor, JC Viviers, reassigned her, taking her off the 'Cradock beat' and unrest reporting. At the time, Jo-Ann Bekker told me, she was informed that she 'was identifying too closely with the communities who were confronting the police'.

Meanwhile, the school boycotts had spread to schools in other towns including Uitenhage, Somerset East, Fort Beaufort, Port Elizabeth, Port Alfred, and Grahamstown by the end of February.

On 3 March 1985, at the first annual general meeting of the Eastern Cape branch of the UDF, Matthew was elected onto its regional executive committee in the newly created position of rural organiser[124]. His election was received with much joy and optimism back in iLingelihle. Almost immediately, Matthew set about his new role. Accompanied mostly by my father and Sparro Mkonto, they travelled frequently –

---

122 Government Must Act on Cradock. February 1985. *Eastern Province Herald*.

123 Herald Reporter. February 1985. Police Probing Four Herald Reports. *Eastern Province Herald*.

124 Declassified National Intelligence Agency Document. Briefing Notes: '"The Cradock Four" – Fort Calata, Matthew Goniwe, Sparro Mkonto, Sicelo Mhlawuli.'

sometimes every day – to visit surrounding towns which fell under Matthew's 'jurisdiction'. Under the banner of the UDF, they would help establish civic associations, similar to Cradora and Cradoya in Graaff-Reinet, Somerset East, Bedford, Adelaide, Middelburg (Cape), Hanover, Hofmeyr, Pearston, Steynsburg, Steytlerville, Cookhouse, Noupoort, Port Alfred, and Fort Beaufort[125].

News of Matthew's election to the provincial executive of a national organisation such as the UDF wasn't well received by the authorities, who had already branded him and his '*trawante* [gang/posse]' agitators and terrorists. Among those so-called 'terrorists' was my father, Fort Daniel Nqaba Calata.

'Goniwe became a thorn in the flesh of the security forces, there's no doubt about it,' said Colonel Lourens du Plessis. 'The security forces became aware of his activities to such an extent that we could predict afterwards that if they'd been to a place, then we could expect problems there the next day or the day thereafter. His [Matthew's] name featured daily during intelligence meetings. His movements were kept track of day and night. It's a fact, otherwise we would not have known of their activities to the extent that we did know. Everything was tried to neutralise him but to no avail.'[126]

I would find evidence of such intelligence gathering on my father and Matthew in a Security Police surveillance report. It reads:

'1985-03-21: The subject together with Fort CALATA and Sparro MKONTO (fellow CRADORA officials) visited towns surrounding Cradock starting at 10:30. On the same day subject visited Mzukisi MBANZANA from Somerset East in a closed meeting. From 16:00 to 20:00 subject visited Adelaide and conducted interviews with the following persons from Adelaide.
Linda MANGALI alias Bonani
Zola MANGALI
Bhabha TOTYI
Mgcineni Lorence GAZI
    At 22:00 on the same day subject accompanied by two went to

---

125 Classified document. 25 June 1985. 'Uiters Geheim, Suid-Afrikaanse Polisie, Die Kommissaris.'
126 S Markovits and M Kaplan interview with Col. L du Plessis.

Bedford's black residential area. Rumour has it that subject incited children from this area to burn down two black schools, a community and beer hall. Subject also visited Zola MANGALI's house and asked MANGALI to invite some youths, who could serve as leaders, to meet with them there with the view to establish an ADELAIDE YOUTH CONGRESS. This request was acceded to and subject met with nine youths on the same day.

On 85-04-11 a group of some 500 youths marched to the Adelaide community hall to hold the first meeting of the Adelaide Youth Congress. During this march a member of the SA Police's house was pelted with stones.'[127]

In my interview with Dr Boesak, he described Matthew's and my father's work and activities during this time as follows: 'They did not keep whatever they knew just for themselves. Their goal was not to work so that Cradock could have a special place in history. They thought, Cradock is this incredibly privileged place to have all of this history, this business, this leadership, the people. What can we do to make other places like Cradock? Think about what that meant in those days. So all of a sudden there was Middelburg, Graaff-Reinet, Somerset East, Bedford, Hofmeyr, Steynsburg, Adelaide, Steytlerville.'

Colonel du Plessis, in his interview with researchers, seemed to concur with Boesak: 'Things started going wrong from the end of 1984 in the Eastern Cape. That's where it all started in Cradock – where Goniwe [and Calata] originated from. In the military, it was called "*die naaf van die revolusie*" – the axle around which the revolution turned, that was Cradock,' he said. 'The whole Eastern Cape was on fire. People were being killed, necklaced, etc. It was a terrible situation. We had numerous visits from cabinet ministers, generals, and what have you. They were becoming desperate, because we just couldn't handle the situation. It became so bad that the local Military Commander [Christoffel Pierre 'Joffel' van der Westhuizen] was threatened with being fired at one stage by a politician, [by] a cabinet minister. So, people were desperate and I think people then started looking at alternatives to calm down the situation, to sort out matters, and that could have given rise

---

127 David Forbes Archive: Henri Fouché Affidavit.

to murders and that sort of thing.'[128]

Du Plessis's interview is corroborated by a signed affidavit by Briga-dier Joffel van der Westhuizen himself. Due to his rank as military com-mander, he chaired the Eastern Province Joint Management Centre between 1983 and 1987. Van der Westhuizen writes:

> 'The unrest situation in the Eastern Cape considerably worsened as of the middle of 1984. So much so that some parts of it were in complete anarchy. At that stage, the Eastern Province was the hot-bed of the revolutionary onslaught against the State. And because of this the Eastern Province Joint Management Centre was under the political pressure [. . .] Goniwe played a prominent role in the aforementioned revolutionary onslaught in the Eastern Province. He was one of the leaders of the United Democratic Front ('UDF') and to the best of my knowledge, Cradock was the very first town in the Republic of South Africa where they successfully implemented alternative structures [of Government].'[129]

On the evening of 21 March 1985, my father, Matthew, and Sparro re-turned home to bone-chilling news. That's when they first heard about police shooting and killing 20 people in Uitenhage's Langa township earlier that Thursday morning.

Thousands of mourners had defied a court order banning them from attending the funeral of four of six youths killed by the police. The fu-neral would be held at the adjacent KwaNobuhle township. So a large group of them marched from Langa to pay their last respects. But police would instead block their route using two armoured vehicles. They ordered the crowd to disperse. Police had been issued with live ammu-nition ahead of the march. This followed a decision by the government on 14 March for the police to take stronger measures to restore order in a situation of rapidly escalating public unrest. When the crowd of mourners refused to obey the order to disperse, police opened fire. Twenty people were killed, while at least 27 others were injured.

The news of the killings would come as a shock to black people all around the country. And the people of Cradock would be no different.

---

128 S Markovits and M Kaplan interview with Col. L du Plessis.
129 Christoffel Pierre van der Westhuizen. Affidavit. 1992.

Just two days later, on 25 March, Derrick Swartz, the general secretary of the UDF's regional executive council, called an emergency meeting to respond to the deadly shooting. In the letter, he wrote:

> 'Re: Emergency meeting of the Regional General Council: Tuesday
> (26 1985) at 7.00 pm – St. Michael's Church, Schauderville.
> The Secretary
> Cradora
>
> Dear Comrade
> The R.E.C. wishes to convene an urgent R.G.C. meeting to address the
> crisis situation in Uitenhage. With a state of emergency virtually de-
> clared in a community struggling for better living conditions and the
> S.A.D.F. literally militarizing Kwanobuhle and Langa; with more than
> 70 people killed and many missing; with the outcry of the interna-
> tional community, we have the historic responsibility to state our un-
> equivocal support to the democratic voice of the people; to assist them
> in any possible way we can.
>   All affiliated organisations are called upon to show their solidarity
> with the people of Uitenhage and other parts of the country.
>   The meeting will specifically address this issue – the action we deem
> important and delegates are requested to be punctual.
> Yours in Struggle
> D. I. Swartz
> General Secretary'[130]

This meeting would be one of many weekly meetings that my father and Matthew would attend in Port Elizabeth.

Despite his busy schedule, my mother said my father would try as much as he could to make time for family – or at least make the most of it whenever he was home. 'I remember this was around the time I was expecting Tumani,' she said. 'Fort would come home, usually around five o'clock. He'd get here and put on music. Then he'd convince us all to join him, he'd say, "Everyone's got their partner. Lukhanyo, you dance with Dorothy, I dance with Mama," and then we'd dance, you know, all of us right there in the living room. And then all of a sudden he'd just stop, kneel down, and put his head on my tummy, and ask, "What about this one? This one isn't going to have a partner," so he was, you know, fun to be around,' she told me.

---

130 Goniwe Papers. Cory Library, Rhodes University.

Fort, however, would spend less time at home as his political responsibilities required that he and Matthew spend more time on the road. My mother recalled that 'Matthew didn't have a driver's licence. Fort would always be the one to drive his car. He drove everywhere they needed to be. They [the state] would not give Matthew a licence to drive, so he would often only drive his car from his home to ours, and let Fort drive from here. They would be together all day because of this.'

At around the time of Matthew's election onto the UDF's provincial executive committee in early March 1985, Major Eric Winter replaced Lt Henri Fouché as branch commander of the Security Police in Cradock. Fouché had held the position since January 1981. The arrival of the 41-year-old major in Cradock coincided with that of at least three other officers, Sergeants George and Roux, as well as Warrant Officer Hough. All were former members of Koevoet. On its webpage, Koevoet is described as 'One of the most successful police counterinsurgency units during the Border War in Southwest Africa. Koevoet is an Afrikaans word meaning crowbar. Like a crowbar, the Koevoet pried out members of SWAPO's People's Liberation Army of Namibia (PLAN) terrorists out from the midst of Ovamboland better than any other South West African or South African Security Force unit. Koevoet produced eighty percent of the terrorist kills in the operational area. From its inception until the beginning of 1989 the unit killed at least 3000 SWAPO insurgents.'[131]

Major Winter considered being captured and spending time in an Angolan prison among the highlights of his time with Koevoet. He told his juniors, however, that his family had a farm in the Graaff-Reinet area, and that he had applied for the post in Cradock because he wanted to be near them[132].

My mother remembered Major Winter rather well, describing him as being of 'medium build, with greying blond hair; he was clean shaven'. She added that he wore spectacles and had a dark-brown pointer leather jacket that he often wore.

Although my father and Matthew had known about Winter's

---

131 Koevoet homepage. http://koevoet.webs.com/
132 Fred Koni. Affidavit. 1992.

appointment, it would be several weeks before they would come face to face with him.

My mother recalled a conversation between my father and Matthew in which they were discussing the new branch commander: 'Fort was saying that he was worried that the new branch commander was very quiet – that he was keeping his cards close to his chest.' Matthew agreed that his silence made him difficult to read, which meant that if he were planning something, they would not be able to see him coming.

Meanwhile, the police would continue to monitor Matthew and my father at every turn. My mother said that, as unlikely as it was, they'd even grown accustomed to the presence of the police van permanently parked across the open field in front of our home.

In April 1985, the surveillance report included entries such as:

> 'On 1985-04-05, a trip to Johannesburg for the National Executive Committee meeting of the UDF,
>
> On 1985-04-08, The school's boycott was called off. While addressing the audience at a CRADORA meeting in the iLingelihle township, [Goniwe] referred to the boycott as historical as it had been the longest boycott yet in South Africa [15 months]
>
> On 1985-04-10, an invitation by Roland WHITE (NUSAS – Rhodes University) to Port Elizabeth for discussions possibly around the funeral of unrest victims in Uitenhage set down for 1985-04-13
>
> On 1985-04-18, a visit by Jo-Ann Bekker and Mr C B Urquhart.
>
> On 1985-04-28, a visit by Michael Robinson of the BBC. The nature of their discussions are unknown.'[133]

On 8 May, there would be more shocking news coming out of Port Elizabeth. Three community activists, Sipho Hashe, Qaqawuli Godolozi, and Champion Galela, from the Port Elizabeth Black Civic Organisation (PEBCO) went missing. Godolozi was PEBCO president, and Hashe its general secretary.

At the time of the three men's disappearance, Port Elizabeth was in the throes of major unrest similar to Cradock. The declassified 'Final Investigative Report' of the Truth and Reconciliation Commission

---

133   David Forbes Archives: Henri Fouché Affidavit.

depicts the events leading up to the disappearance of Hashe, Godolozi, and Galela as follows:

'Early in 1985, conflict between PEBCO and the iBhayi Council – particularly Thamsanqa Linda, who had been appointed Mayor in December 1984 – intensified. Violence in the townships of PE and Uitenhage, between UDF supporters and black councillors and vigilantes escalated. Godolozi's home was attacked by "Linda's men" and his car was burnt. From March 16 to 18 1985, PEBCO called a "Black Weekend" which involved a stayaway and consumer boycott. Hashe, Godolozi and Galela were instrumental in calling this boycott and distributing pamphlets informing people in the township of the action.

After this action which spread into March 21st (Sharpeville Day) and was successful despite conflict with FOSATU trade unions which opposed the boycott call, the Port Elizabeth Chamber of Commerce made contact with PEBCO. Meetings with a PEBCO delegation led by Godolozi, Hashe and Galela took place.

Shortly thereafter [according to the testimony of Mrs Hashe], on May 8th Henry Fazzie a PEBCO Executive member telephoned Sipho Hashe to request that he meet a visitor from the British Consulate at the H F Verwoerd Airport in Port Elizabeth. Mrs Hashe says her husband left the house at about 8 PM, followed by Fazzie and Edgar Ngoyi travelling in a separate vehicle. The latter two men went to another meeting in Uitenhage leaving Hashe to go to the airport with Godolozi and Galela. They were never seen again. At the time the AZAPO/UDF "feud" was raging in the PE townships. On May 1st, Edgar Ngoyi's home was petrol-bombed, and on May 4th, Henry Fazzie's home was petrol-bombed. Sipho Hashe's home was attacked on May 8th and Qaqawuli's home on June 3rd. The intention of the Security Forces was apparently to make it appear as if the PEBCO 3 were victims of this feud.'[134]

The news of Hashe, Galela, and Godolozi going missing startled my father. My mother remembered that in the days following their disappearance, 'Fort, for the first time ever, expressed fears around his own safety. He was sure that they were kidnapped by the Security Police.' She added, 'He doubted the rumours that they had fled into exile. Their

---

134 David Forbes Archive: Declassified Final Investigative Report of the TRC.

disappearance clearly bothered Fort.' Mene concurred, saying that Godolozi, Hashe, and Galela had often visited Cradock to meet with my father, Matthew, and the Cradora executive. The news of their disappearance shook all of them.

The security concern was valid for the Cradora executive too. Mene remembered that it was around this time when 'a call was made by "Bra Stof" [Makhenkesi Stofile – ANC underground] that Matthew Goniwe and Fort Calata must go into exile, otherwise they will die. We had a meeting up until the early hours of the morning. From six o'clock [the night before] up until two o'clock. They both said they are not going anywhere. When we asked why they were refusing, uBhut' Fort said, "Among the pillars of the movement is mass mobilisation inside the country. Therefore, if we leave, who is going to lead that responsibility?" At the time when they made that statement, in the whole of the [Karoo] Midlands, up until the Northern Cape's Prieska area, they were organising street and area committees, civic associations, youth associations.'

Then, another entry in the on-going surveillance reports, notes that on '1985-05-08 Molly Blackburn gave subject [Matthew] an article titled "Defiance in SA" by Alan Cowell, a journalist for *The New York Times* in Johannesburg. The article reported on what had been happening in iLingelihle in Cradock since February 1984, when the school boycotts in Cradock started as well as subject's involvement in these events. According to report's source, subject together with Fort Calata and Sparro Mkonto visited Molly Blackburn in Port Elizabeth on 1985-05-08.'[135]

PEBCO's modus operandi in the lead-up to the boycott was straight from the Cradora playbook, a fact not missed by government ministers and the state's security forces. This reinforced their views that Cradock or at least iLingelihle had grown particularly problematic. ILingelihle had proved successful in its rebellion against the apartheid system, and the government, besides administering the payout of social grants, had no other input whatsoever in the governance of iLingelihle. The minutes of a report of the Eastern Province Joint Management Centre (EP JMC) on 23 May 1985 read: 'In Cradock the students control the

---

135 David Forbes Archive: Henri Fouché Affidavit.

schools. They are in charge of, among others, the appointments of teachers.'[136]

'Major Winter's arrival in Cradock wasn't by chance either,' my mother says. 'Word in iLingelihle had indeed spread that Lt Henri Fouché had been deemed "too soft" and therefore incapable of handling Fort and Matthew, so they replaced him with someone tough.'

On 22 May 1985, *Eastern Province Herald* reporter Jo-Ann Bekker was given a Stellenbosch Farmers' Winery Award (SFW) for Excellence in Journalism in the category for the 'best reporting under pressure of time or circumstance for her coverage of the black unrest in Cradock'. The awards were first introduced in 1966, and were 'intended to serve as incentives for achieving the highest possible standards of journalism in this country'. Other categories included best investigative reporting, best creative journalism, and best news commentary.

Major Winter would have been properly briefed on the 'enemy', and must've felt rather empowered to be entrusted with such a task as iLingelihle. Matthew's and Fort's names were almost permanent features by then in meetings of the EP JMC, which would forward all its recommendations to the secretariat of the State Security Council.

One such recommendation taken during the EP JMC meeting of 23 May was that a *'seinberig* [signal]' be sent to the secretariat of the State Security Council for the notification of the relevant ministers (FW de Klerk, Minister of Education and Planning) that 'Matthew Goniwe and Fort Calata must never again be employed by the Department as teachers'[137].

This first signal, according to Zenzile Khoisan, a former investigator of the Truth and Reconciliation Commission (TRC), was to him a clear indication that by May 1985, the government had already set its plan in motion for 'security measures' to be taken against my father and Matthew.

In a workshop that Martina Della Togna (my producer), Abigail, and I held with him shortly after we had come across several lever-arch files containing *'Vertroulik* [Confidential]' and *'Uiters Geheim* [Top Secret]'

---

136 Confidential Minutes of EP JMC Meeting 3/85 held at Eastern Province Command Headquarters on 23 May 1985.
137 Ibid.

apartheid-era documents, Khoisan said, 'By the time this first signal was sent, Fort Calata and Matthew Goniwe would've long been identified as "protagonists of the revolutionary onslaught in Cradock". The authorities would've undertaken several in-depth target studies on them in a bid to understand exactly who and what they were dealing with.' He added, 'First they would've wanted to find out what the ideological content of the person is. They would usually do that by analysing the speeches and the public pronouncements of the person. But they would also analyse the nature of how the person operated on the ground. Is this person able to set up street committees with relative ease? Is this person able to mobilise communities with relative ease? Is this a person who can cause a community to go into a state of boycott? They evaluate that. And then they would do what we called "more focused collection". This is a personal target study. This would require a psychological profile of the intended target. This would look out for social aberrations, an example of which is maybe a priest who gets involved in an affair, or somebody who has an inability to work properly with their money. They would want to find out what the structural weaknesses of this person are. Then they would look at what informs this person's fortitude. Why is this person impenetrable?'

When Major Winter eventually announced himself to the people of iLingelihle, including my father and Matthew, a few days later, it was in a manner that they indeed had not seen coming.

At around 4am on Monday, 27 May, my mother said she was awoken by a very bright light shining directly inside our home. It was one of four massive search lights beamed on iLingelihle from a nearby hill. My mother said the lights were so bright they lit up the area as if it were daytime. 'Overhead was a low-flying aeroplane, with the voice of local farmer Mr Copeman booming out of it using a loud hailer. Copeman could speak isiXhosa and he was shouting "*Ze ni ngoyiki. Loo ngumsebenzi wamaPolisa, namaJhoni. Ningabaleki, sizokuni kusela ku Matthew Goniwe. Akakwazi ukunipha amanzi, thina siyakhona. UFort Calata akawazi ukunipha ukhutya, thina siyakhona. Ningoyiki.* [Do not be afraid. This is a raid of the police and military. Do not flee. We are here to protect you from Matthew Goniwe. He doesn't have any water to give to you – we do. Fort Calata doesn't have any food to give to you – we do. Do not be afraid.]"'

This, she remembered, was followed by a knock on our front door. When my half-asleep mother opened the door, Major Winter asked if he could come in. 'He walked in with a number of police officers and soldiers, and headed straight for our bedroom. *Daai vark* [that pig], he was asking, "Where's your husband – where is he?" He sat right on the edge of my bed, nearest to the dressing table, so he could open the [dressing table] drawers and search through them. I don't know what he was looking for, because Fort wasn't in the drawer. He introduced himself as Major Eric Winter and told me that he was now in charge of the Security Police. He kept on asking, "Where's your husband?" I said, "He's in Johannesburg." "When will he be back?" I said, "When he comes back." He looked at me and said, "Oh, you're cheeky," and I said, "And you're in my house." By this time, other officers had begun searching through the house. One of them, Hough, *daai blerrie kort-gat* [that bloody short-asshole], was also in my bedroom. He then removed a suitcase from the wardrobe filled with my unborn baby's new clothes, threw them on the floor, and walked all over them. I don't know why he was looking for Fort in a suitcase,' she said.

'As Winter was leaving, he had to walk past me because I was standing next to the door.' My mother told me he looked at her and said, 'You can hide your husband for now, but tell him, when I find him, he will shit himself.'

She followed him outside, where she was confronted by the sight of all the street's men, each standing in front of his home, with hands raised above their heads. My mother believed this scene was meant largely to humiliate the men, as there was no need for them to have been treated in the manner in which they were.

'Winter,' she said, 'was not like Fouché. *Jy kon sommer op sy gevreet sien hy's 'n moordenaar!* [You could see on face he was a murderer!]'

The raid, which my mother refers to by its Afrikaans name '*klopjag*', had seen members of the Security Police and military completely seal off iLingelihle.

An article published on Tuesday, 28 May 1985, in the *Eastern Province Herald* under the headline 'Cradock Raid: "Some" Arrests', reporter Isabel Koch writes:

'The house-to-house search in which horsemen and a light aircraft assisted for the first time was to round up suspects sought in connection with public violence and was also a show of force said Lieutenant-Colonel Gerrie van Rooyen, the South African Police liaison officer for the Eastern Cape.

In a joint statement, last night the Cradock Residents' Association and the Cradock Youth Association condemned the "unwarranted" raid and "Government intimidation."

The recording secretary of the CRADORA, Mr Victor Puwani, said pamphlets distributed during the operation were an attempt to discredit the two township organisations and unjustifiably linked them to the African National Congress in what was seen as a prelude to their banning.

Unlike other similar operations in the Eastern Cape iLingelihle residents – mostly youths – were reluctant to accept pamphlets and stickers issued by police and members of the SADF.

Defiant youths set fire to pamphlets and stickers outside the home of Mr Matthew Goniwe, the secretary general of CRADORA. Mr Goniwe is a listed person in terms of the Internal Security Act. Some of the 3000 pamphlets scattered by the aircraft were crumpled and torn.

The 24 horsemen on the township's western boundary were members of the Cradock Commando. Four Saracen troop carriers, Casspirs, Buffels, Bedfords Rinkhals vehicles and a helicopter were also used. Four and Five Infantry Battalion, Grahamstown and SA Medical Services members for Eastern Province Command Headquarters in Port Elizabeth were also involved.'[138]

On 5 June 1985, Cradora called a meeting to be addressed by Dr Allan Boesak. He was on a flying visit to the Eastern Cape to raise support for his 16 June campaign to 'pray for the downfall of the apartheid regime'. During the meeting, which took the form of a prayer service and was attended by an estimated 2400 residents, despite only commencing at midnight, Dr Boesak conveyed the greetings of Oliver Tambo to those present.

Afterwards, Boesak slept over at the Goniwe home. The following morning, Matthew accompanied Boesak to Cookhouse and Somerset East, where they held similar prayer services.

---

138 Koch, I. 28 May 1985. Cradock Raid: Some Arrests. *Eastern Province Herald.*

The day prior to Boesak's arrival in Cradock, he had been in Jansenville and Graaff-Reinet for prayer services. Shortly after his departure from Graaff-Reinet, some among those who had attended Boesak's service marched to the home of a black police officer and set his home on fire. The officer unfortunately died during the incident[139].

Meanwhile, the government continued to deliberate on what to do about Matthew. In an official South African police document titled, 'Uiters Geheim – Voorgestelde Optrede teen Matewu Matthew Goniwe, Swartman, Oud-Onderwyser, Cradock [Top Secret – Recommended Action against Matewu Matthew Goniwe, Black man, Ex-Teacher, Cradock]' by Commissioner PJ Coetzee, addressed to the Minister of Law and Order Louis le Grange, the commissioner writes: '10. Die vraag wat nou ontstaan is, wat moet gedoen word om Goniwe se anti-owerheids-optrede aan bande te lê [The question that it raises is, what must be done to foil Goniwe's anti-establishment activities]?' Then, the conclusion to the report states: '23. Ten slotte kan dit ook uitgewys word dat op watter wyse daar ook al teen GONIWE opgetree word, dit in die lig van die bekendheid wat hy reeds verwerf het, buitelands sowel as binnelands, hewige kritiek sal ontlok [To conclude, it must be pointed out that whatever the means taken to act against GONIWE, it must be considered that in view of his popularity both internationally and locally, it will lead to severe criticism].'[140]

The secretariat of the State Security Council had also been debating the situation regarding Matthew for several months. In the minutes of a meeting held on 23 May 1985, the secretariat discussed the following:

'Action against Goniwe Associates
It could be considered to refer Goniwe's associates like his nephew
Mbulelo Goniwe and Fort Calata to the Directorate of State Security
for possible detention or banning. This however must not coincide with
Goniwe's reinstatement as it could yet again provide a possible escape
route for Goniwe. A fitting time and circumstance for such action must
present itself.

139 David Forbes Archive: Henri Fouché Affidavit.
140 Classified document. 25 June 1985. 'Uiters Geheim, Suid-Afrikaanse Polisie, Die Kommissaris.'

<u>Consideration of the Options</u>
The reinstatement of Goniwe in a teaching post does not exclude security action against him eventually. This option is still possible should he not toe the line. Such action must be executed in a well-considered way such that it holds up in a court of law.'[141]

I have read this section of the minutes over and over again. And every time I read it, it becomes clearer to me that the secretariat of the State Security Council had by May 1985 resolved that Matthew Goniwe, and possibly Fort Calata and Mbulelo Goniwe, must be killed. My understanding of this is further reinforced by a statement by Colonel Lourens du Plessis, who said, 'Very seldom was it actually said that someone had to be killed, but the implications were there. And people did get killed.'[142]

On 5 June, Adriaan Vlok, Deputy Minister of Law and Order, visited iLingelihle as a passenger in a military Casspir. He was shown Matthew Goniwe's home at 44 Qhina Street, before the Casspir took the five-minute drive down Ntenetyana Street, turned right onto iKwezi Street, and then left onto Siyabulela Street, coming to a stop in front of our home. My mother recalled watching them from inside the house as Vlok and one of his escorts peered from the Casspir's open-roof section, their hands gesticulating – probably from Vlok's asking the officer several questions.

The next day, Vlok would chair a meeting of the EP JMC in Port Elizabeth attended by 31 SAP and SADF generals, brigadiers, lieutenants, colonels, and one Lieutenant Colonel GM Smit from the secretariat of the State Security Council. The meeting would resolve that a committee under the guidance of the State Security Council would deliberate on the Goniwe matter and make recommendations to the chairperson (Vlok) by 12 June[143].

But on 7 June 1985, Colonel Du Plessis said he was called into Brigadier Joffel van der Westhuizen's office:

---

141 Ibid.

142 S Markovits and M Kaplan interview with Col. L du Plessis.

143 Classified document. 25 June 1985. 'Uiters Geheim, Suid-Afrikaanse Polisie, Die Kommissaris.'

'He was chairman of the [Eastern Province] Joint Management Centre at the time – he instructed me to send a signal to the secretariat of the State Security Council. He explained to me that he had held a telephone conversation with General Van Rensburg at the Secretariat of the State Security Council and his words to me were – "Ek het met Hekkel gepraat en hy sê hy kan ons help om van Goniwe ontslae raak." [I spoke to Hekkel and he said he can help us get rid of Goniwe]. He instructed me what to say in this signal message. The signal read:

"Voorrang uitvoering: Prioriteit
Datum tyd groep: 07 14 30 B
Hanteringsinstruksies: 0
Van: OP GBS
Aan: S SVR PTA
Sekerheidsklas: UITERS GEHEIM
Opstellersnommer: OP GBS/ 191/ 7 Junie
Persoonlik vir Genl van Rensburg
1 Telegesprek Genl van Rensburg/Brig vd Westhuizen op 7 Junie '85 verwys
2 Name as volg
   Matthew Goniwe
   Mbulelo Goniwe (Broer of neef van BG)
   Fort Calata
   Dit word voorgestel dat bg persone permanent uit die samelewing, as saak van dringendheid, verwyder word
4 Wye reaksie kan plaaslik sowel as nasionaal verwag word agv belangrikheid van hierdie persone, veral eersgenoemde, vir die vyand bv
A. Interdikte soos onlangs met verdwyning van Godolozi, Hashe and Galela (PEBCO ampsdraers)
B. Reaksie van linkse politici soos Molly Blackburn
C. Protes soos geval Oscar MPETHA in simpatie
Bladsy: 1 of 1
Verwys in geklassifieërde berig: Nee
Berigskrywer se naam: L du Plessis

Precedence action: Priority
Date Time Group: 07 14 30 B
Handling Instructions: 0
From: EP JMC
To: S SSC PTA

Security Classification: Top Secret
Originator's number: EP JMC /191/ 7 June
Personal for Genl van Rensburg
1 Teleconversation Genl van Rensburg/Brig vd Westhuizen
2 Names as follow
  Matthew Goniwe
  Mbulelo Goniwe (brother or cousin of abovementioned)
  Fort Calata
3 It is recommended the abovementioned persons be permanently removed from society, as a matter of urgency.
4 Widespread reaction should be expected both locally and nationally due to the importance of these persons, especially the first mentioned, for the enemy eg
A. Interdicts such as in the recent disappearance of Godolozi, Hashe and Galela (PEBCO Executives)
B. Reaction of Leftist politicians such as Molly Blackburn
C. Protests similar to instance of Oscar MPETHA in sympathy
Page: 1 of 1
Refers to a classified message: No
Drafter's name L du Plessis]"'[144]

Du Plessis added that 'Everybody [who] has read that signal message can be assured that I wrote what I understood him to have told me. I sent it off. I've said on many occasions that it didn't really penetrate me at the time what I was writing.'

The *Weekly Mail* newspaper published an article on 14 June under the headline 'Focus on Township Unrest – Missing: The List Grows Longer', stating: 'The mysterious disappearance of three Port Elizabeth civic leaders who vanished while travelling to collect a person from the airport on May 8th is the latest and most dramatic addition to the growing list of missing persons in the Eastern Cape. Prominence has been given to the more than 20 people who were unaccounted for after the police shot dead 20 people in Langa, Uitenhage, on the anniversary of Sharpeville in March. But hundreds of people have been reported missing since the beginning of the year.'[145]

---

144 S Markovits and M Kaplan interview with Col. L du Plessis.
145 Missing: The List Grows Longer. 14 June 1985. *Weekly Mail*.

My father had remained in Johannesburg for most of the month of June. My mother recalled that he returned home only on Saturday, 22 June 1985. 'While Fort was out of town, his younger brother Roy had accompanied Matthew to his weekly UDF executive meetings in Port Elizabeth. The week before, Roy had come back from PE a bit shaken. He told me that he and Matthew were followed by a kombi, and that they suspected it was a police vehicle,' she told me. 'Fortunately, Roy was fast, so he managed to escape them. We didn't make much of that incident, you know; we really took it lightly. Anyway, Fort was back that weekend, so he went with Matthew to PE the following week.'

The decision not to make much of the incident with the kombi might have been born out of naivety, especially since the kombi in question was most likely one belonging to the Hammer Unit. The Hammer Unit was the personal task force of Brigadier Joffel van der Westhuizen, established in 1983. In an exposé by investigative reporter Sam Sole, first published in the *Sunday Tribune* on 31 May 1992 under the headline 'Wraps Come off General's "Personal Task Force" as Ex Members Spill the Beans', he writes: 'It [the Hammer Unit] was conceived as a covert reaction force which could neutralise anti-apartheid activists and generally disrupt the "enemy" in urban counter insurgency operations. "We had to be ready 24 hours a day," said one member. "I would sometimes be phoned at 2 am." He said members of the unit used their own private weapons and almost always operated in civilian clothing. He also said there was "quite frequent" involvement or co-operation with the Civil Co-operation Bureau (CCB) and other special forces units'. Sole then expands on the modus operandi of the unit. His source said, '"We went in [into the townships] at night in a "war wagon". This was a Toyota Hiace [kombi] with false number plates equipped with a "trommel" [chest] containing weapons, ammunition etc. We were dressed as kaffirs with our faces and heads blackened."'[146]

On Monday, 24 June, Matthew called Derrick Swartz (general secretary of the UDF in Eastern Cape based in Port Elizabeth) to tell him that he would not be able to make the weekly executive meeting scheduled

---

146 Sole, S. 31 May 1992. Wraps Come off General's 'Personal Task Force' as Ex Members Spill the Beans. *Sunday Tribune*.

for Wednesday, 26 June, but that he would travel to Port Elizabeth the day after.

My mother remembered that week quite vividly, recalling that on the Wednesday before they left for PE, I was sick with the mumps and that my father had taken me to our family GP, Dr Peter Scholtz. She remembered that we had returned home with a parcel of fish and chips. 'Fort used to like hake,' she said. Later that evening, my mother remembered my father had knelt in front of me while I sat on their bed. 'He was trying to get you to eat something before he left to attend a community meeting. When he returned home, he reminded me of the Baptist priest [attending a conference in iLingelihle] who would come and stay with us for the duration of the three-day conference.'

On the morning of Thursday, 27 June, Swartz telephoned Matthew to confirm that he would travel. Police officer Fred Koni, whose job it was to monitor Matthew's telephone calls, confirmed that, although 'they spoke in codes, we knew what they meant because we understood these codes and the person who telephoned was a coloured man, Derrick Swartz'.

The priest (whose name my mother has forgotten) arrived just as Matthew pulled up in front of our home. Fort greeted him on his way out to the car. He was wearing his blue Adidas tekkies, blue jeans, a brown T-shirt under his short-sleeved checked shirt, with a brown V-neck pullover. And of course, his sunglasses. 'Fort hardly left the house without putting on his sunglasses,' my mother said with a smile.

It was very cold that morning, and just before he got into the car, my father ran back inside the house to fetch a jacket. He chose a tweed-like lumber jacket and went back out. Matthew, Fort, Sparro Mkonto, and a friend of Matthew's, Sicelo Mhlawuli, then left Cradock at about ten o'clock that morning headed for Port Elizabeth some 243 km southwest of Cradock. Sicelo, a teacher and political activist in his own right, was visiting Cradock from Oudtshoorn for the school holidays. He had asked Matthew for a lift to PE so he could spend the day with his wife, Nombuyiselo, who was back at her parents' home, mourning the death of their newborn baby.

My mother, now seven months pregnant, had a doctor's appointment that afternoon. When she returned home, she began to prepare supper. At around five thirty, Dorothy – as she had done every Thursday – recorded *Pop Shop*, her and my father's favourite television show. She recalled the episode well, as it debuted the song 'When I need you' by Latin crooner Julio Iglesias. 'I remember watching the video and thinking, *Tata is going to like this song*,' she said.

Earlier that afternoon, Major Winter, Warrant Officer Hough, and Sergeant Labuschagne signed out a car and left Cradock for PE.

My mother served supper at around six thirty and set aside a plate of food for my father. She then got Dorothy and me ready for bed. She went to bed around nine or ten pm, but she had trouble falling asleep. 'Fort and Matthew would usually be back around ten o'clock whenever they travelled to PE,' she told me. 'At around midnight, I went to wake the priest. I told him I was worried that Fort wasn't back yet. He answered, "No, ma'am. I'm sure they will be back. Maybe they decided to sleep over in PE." I said, "But Fort would let me know if he was going to sleep over."' My parents didn't have a phone in the house, so my father would've called the Methodist Church to ask them to relay the message if he wanted to contact my mother. The priest, sensing my mother's unease, again tried to reassure her: 'Don't worry, ma'am, I'm sure they are safe,' he said. My mother returned to her bed, where Dorothy and I were fast asleep, still deeply troubled.

A few minutes later, she was up again. This time, she went to the front door, unlocked it, and stepped into the cold, dark night. She looked up and down the street, hoping that at any minute she would see the friendly headlights of Matthew's Honda Ballade coming towards her. 'The street was very quiet as I stood on the stoep. I wondered, *Why was it so quiet?* Normally, the police Casspirs would be driving up and down the street, and the van usually parked opposite the veld was also not there. It was very strange.' My mother eventually consoled herself with the thought that maybe my father, Matthew, and Sparro had slept over at Molly Blackburn's house. She returned to her restless sleep.

Meanwhile, my father, Matthew, Sparro, and Sicelo had left the home of Michael Coetzee in Gelvandale, Port Elizabeth (where they had held their meeting), at around nine o'clock that evening. Just before they left, Matthew assured Derrick that they would stop for no one other than the police on their way home.

215

But the four men in the Honda Ballade – Fort Calata, Matthew Goniwe, Sparro Mkonto, and Sicelo Mhlawuli – would never make it back home to Cradock.

Despite the 32 years which have elapsed, the exact details of what happened that night remain largely unknown. So, what follows is my personal summation of the sequence of events which led to their murders. This is based on my own investigation and conversations with individuals, some of whom had first-hand knowledge and experience of the Security Police and the Hammer Unit. This is what I believe happened that night.

Before my father and his three comrades departed from Port Elizabeth in the beige Honda Ballade that evening, members of the South African Security Police, among them Eric Taylor, Gerhard Lotz, Harold Snyman, Johan 'Sakkie' van Zyl, Herman du Plessis, Nic van Rensburg, Glen Mgoduka, AT Faku, and DD Mapipa, got into position for the 'operation' along the Olifantskop Pass en route to Cradock. Alongside them were members of the Hammer Unit. The unit, however, was still in its infancy and on that specific night, would only have been responsible for the 'set up and break down' of the 'roadblock'. According to Brett Viviers, who had trained the Hammer Unit between 1984 and '85, it would have taken a four-member crew minutes to set up a 'roadblock' and even less time than that to break it all down. Viviers would know; he helped get them that efficient. He described the Hammer Unit as 'not a special reaction unit at all. Hammer was a special tactical unit used for extracting individuals from the townships. They were used for obtaining intel[ligence] and for strategic purposes under the direct command of Brigadier Joffel van der Westhuizen of the Eastern Province Command.'

The murderers would've had a 'spotter team' positioned at least three kilometres ahead of the 'roadblock' location to look out for the Honda Ballade as it drove towards Cradock.

In 1985, legislation did not allow for the military or any special reaction unit such as 'Hammer' to act without the involvement of the Security Police. I believe Major Eric Winter, from Cradock, would also have been among those co-ordinating the 'operation' that night.

216

Once the Honda with the four 'terrorists' was identified, the 'spotter team' radioed their position to their colleagues who were lying in wait. After being stopped, I believe that Sparro and Sicelo would then have been separated from my father and Matthew and driven back towards Port Elizabeth in separate vehicles, most likely two Toyota Hiace kombis belonging to the Hammer Unit. The responsibility to dispose of the Honda would have been assigned to the junior members of the Hammer Unit. My father and his comrades would have been transported to the then municipal police training college called uMtombolwazi (the fountain of knowledge).

Knowledge and information (or at least the flow thereof) was key to the functioning of the apartheid state. So, I believe that the kidnappers' first task would have been to prise as much information out of their captives as possible, while they detained, interrogated, and tortured them. This most likely happened in the massive steel hangar on the grounds of the training college, lasting several hours.

The group of around eleven black and white officers had split their 'responsibilities' among them. The one team comprising three officers left with Sparro, another team of three took Sicelo (although they still had no idea who he was), and headed towards Kwazakhele, a suburb of Port Elizabeth just north of the Swartkops River. They turned off the highway, onto a dirt road. It was here that they would kill Sparro Mkonto by shooting him once through the head and then stabbing him multiple times. They would stab Sicelo Mhlawuli too – multiple times.

They then returned to the hangar, where the remaining five members would use one of the kombis. They drove with my father and Matthew Goniwe in the opposite direction towards the beach of Bluewater Bay. It was here in a bushy clearing near the beach where the two would meet their violent deaths. Both were stabbed multiple times. A number of those blows penetrated my father's heart. On the night my father was killed, I was three years and eight months old. Dorothy was just weeks away from her tenth birthday, while my 26-year-old mother was seven months pregnant with my younger sister, Tumani.

The next morning, Friday, 28 June 1985, there still was no word from or about my father. Dorothy, who used to deliver the *Eastern Province*

Herald in the neighbourhood in a bid to make extra money, kept our father's usual copy aside for him. Other than my mother's sense of unease, there was nothing much out of the ordinary that morning. At least, not until a very brief but strange exchange that she had with a white man, who came to replace the cooking gas canister at our home that morning. While she was busy paying him for the gas, he asked her in Afrikaans:

'*Waar is die pa van die huis?* [Where's the father of this house?]'

'*Hoekom? Wat pla dit vir jou, waar die pa van die huis is?* [Why? Why are you worried about where the father of this house is?]' she retorted.

'*Nee, dit moet vir jou pla – nie vir my nie* [No, you're supposed to be worried. Not me],' he said before getting into his bakkie and leaving.

By midmorning, Sis' Nyami had already called Derrick in Port Elizabeth to ask him if he knew where her husband was. His response to her that 'Matthew and the other comrades had left for Cradock the previous night already' sent shivers down her spine[147].

The family and Cradora then began to organise transport and a small delegation to travel towards Port Elizabeth in search of the men. Roy (Fort's younger brother) came to tell my mother that a group with Sis' Nyami among them would go looking for the four men. Although worried by now, my mother continued to hope that maybe they had just been detained and that my father would soon be home.

The delegation set off for Cookhouse, Bedford, and Paterson near Port Elizabeth, making enquiries as they went along at police and fuel stations about Matthew and my father's possible whereabouts. They would come back empty-handed. Then, Thembani Goniwe (Matthew's fourteen-year-old nephew) told Sis' Nyami that while she was gone, a police officer named Els had called from Port Elizabeth and told him that they had found Matthew's car near the Scribante Race Circuit just outside the city. It had been burnt out.

My mother – who was still waiting on news or any developments late that afternoon – would dish up a second plate of food for my father. A youth dance social planned for that Friday evening turned into a meeting, where the iLingelihle community called for an immediate consumer

---

147 David Forbes Archive: Declassified Final Investigative Report of the TRC.

boycott. They vowed to lift it only when there was news of their leaders. Mene remembered that 'In our anger, we made it a point that no [police] van, nothing would come into iLingelihle. We barricaded the township; we opened big holes in the road. No Casspirs, no nothing that moves around. It was just a night of our worst nightmare. We were just fighting with the police that particular night. It was very bad.'

The next morning of 29 June, the *Eastern Province Herald* published an article by Lloyd Coutts on its front page, under the headline 'Goniwe Missing with Others: Car Found Burnt Out'. Coutts writes: 'The gutted shell of a car belonging to Mr Matthew Goniwe, Cradock community leader and an Eastern Cape executive member of the United Democratic Front, was found on the outskirts of Port Elizabeth last night. There was no sign of its owner and three other occupants. Lieutenant-Colonel Gerrie van Rooyen, the SA Police Liaison officer for the Eastern Cape, said last night the car had been found at 3.30 pm yesterday. Registration number checks revealed that it belonged to Mr Goniwe. However, a second number plate belonged to another car registered in Port Elizabeth.'[148]

When the Saturday edition of the *Herald* arrived on our doorstep that morning, Dorothy was anxious to draw our mother's attention to the front-page picture, to no avail. When Dorothy eventually returned from her delivery run, she sat our mother down and forced her to look at the picture of the burnt-out car on the front page. 'Look!' she said. 'That is Bhut' Matthew's car.' My mother looked at the picture in disbelief and shock. It is only then that she allowed the hope to which she'd been hanging on so tenuously to start cracking. 'Then I started to become miserable,' she said.

Later in the day, a friend of both my father and Matthew, John Balie, who lived in Michausdal (the coloured neighbourhood across the N10 main road), came to fetch us from our home and drove us to the Goniwe home. As my mother and I walked in, she saw Sis' Nyami crying and then began to cry herself. 'When I saw *umzala* crying there, I just knew

---

148 Coutts, L. 29 June 1985. Goniwe Missing with Others: Car Found Burnt Out. *Eastern Province Herald.*

something was wrong. I just knew,' she told me. It was then that we were informed that Sparro and Sicelo's bodies had been found. 'I didn't want to believe that Fort and Matthew were also dead. You know, I had that hope that maybe they'd escaped or something.' Sis' Nyami, it seemed, had clung to the same hope too.

By Monday, 1 July 1985, four days after they had first gone missing, there was still no news of my father and Matthew. My mother, Dorothy, and I had by now moved to my father's family home – Tatou's home – at 26 Mongo Street.

That morning, the *Eastern Province Herald* published a follow-up article by Coutts under the headline 'Burnt-Out Car: Two Bodies Are Found'. Coutts writes:

> 'The bodies of two of four missing African community leaders, whose car was found burnt out near Port Elizabeth on Thursday night, have been found near the car. The other two men are still missing.
>
> Those found were Mr Sparro Mkonto, a member of the Cradock Residents' Association (CRADORA), and Mr Sicelo Mhlawuli, an Oudtshoorn teacher. Mr Mhlawuli's body was found after an unidentified caller informed the police of a body in the bush between Bluewater Bay and the sea. He had been stabbed and set alight: his right hand was severed.
>
> Mr Mkonto's body was found on Friday night, one kilometre away from the car. He too had been stabbed and burnt [. . .]
>
> A distraught Mrs Nyameka Goniwe, Mr Goniwe's wife, said yesterday that the news of the two deaths had come as a great shock. "We've heard nothing of Matthew and Fort yet and I am very worried about my husband," she said.
>
> SAPA [South African Press Association] reports that Dr G Blackburn, the husband of Mrs Molly Blackburn, the MPC for Walmer, said his wife had gone out to the burnt-out car which was found off the Grahamstown road just outside Port Elizabeth.
>
> "One must assume at this stage that the other two have also been killed." He said Mr Fort Calata was the grandson of the first [sic] secretary-general of the ANC Canon Calata.
>
> The mystery surrounding the Cradock and Oudtshoorn men comes in the wake of the disappearance on May 8th of three prominent Port Elizabeth activists.'[149]

---

149 Coutts, L. 1 July 1985. Burnt-out Car: Two Bodies Are Found. *Eastern Province Herald*.

That Monday evening, a young lawyer named Lee Bozalek from the Legal Resources Centre (LRC) in Cape Town drove into Cradock. He had been assigned to the case following a request by Sis' Nyami to the LRC for legal assistance. When Abigail and I met Bozalek (now a sitting judge in the Cape High Court) in March 2017 at his home in Cape Town, he recalled two distinct impressions Cradock had made on him that afternoon. 'It was bitterly cold,' he remembered, and then he said, 'You could almost touch the repression in Cradock. There were police and soldiers everywhere, particularly at the entrance to the iLingelihle, the township on your left as you drive in from Port Elizabeth.'

My mother remembered that while she and Sis' Nyami were meeting with Bozalek on the afternoon of 2 July, he interrupted their meeting at the request of Gillie Skweyiya: 'He stepped outside and when he came back into the room where we were meeting, he asked that we should stop the conversation because there were people that wanted to see us at home. They took me to my mother-in-law's home. When we got there, Rev Christopher Dano [the local Anglican priest] and other priests were sitting there. They asked me to sit down. Then they told me that Fort and Matthew had been found and unfortunately they were also late.' My mother then said to me, 'When you heard that, you started to vomit, you started feeling ill and you cried. Dorothy, who was also at home, she started to sing very loudly. She sang this one hymn. She just sang. I too started to cry. My life changed there and then. I just couldn't see myself living. It was so terrible and you were so sad. So very, very sad. You didn't want to be far from me. When I would go to wash, you would sit there. You would sit by me all the time.'

On the same day that my father and Matthew's bodies were found, the state declared a prohibition order, effectively banning 64 civic and youth organisations in 30 magisterial districts of the Eastern Cape. Cradora and Cradoya were among those banned.

My uncle Patutu 'Duva' (Fort's elder brother) and a friend of his from Dimbaza, Mzwandile Gxuluwa, made the trip to Port Elizabeth to identify my father's body. My mother recalled that at the time my father had been wearing her wedding band; her fingers were swollen due to the pregnancy, so she had taken it off and put it on his left ring finger. On his return, Patutu reported to the family that the fingers on my father's left hand were severed, and had been placed next to his body on the mortuary tray. That day, Patutu brought the fingers back to Cradock, and they were buried together with my father's remains three weeks later. My mother's wedding band with the engraving 'CALATA' on the inside was nowhere to be found.

In the days leading up to the funeral, my mother descended into a deep depression, caused largely by her inability to give full expression to her grief. She, like the other three widows, was expected and encouraged to 'stay strong'. They couldn't publicly grieve or show any sign of weakness to the state and its main operatives, the Security Police. 'Sometimes,' she told me, 'it was difficult for me to just get up and wash myself. My mom had to come over to my in-laws' home every day to encourage me to wake up and wash. To sit in front of those people.'

Mene said the residents of iLingelihle, in particular the executive of Cradoya, were devastated by the news of the murders. He remembered sitting in a kombi (bought by Beyers Naudé for the community of Cradock) and their asking, '"Who's going to lead us now?" We were all so young at the time. All of us were just crying. We thought of asking Bhut' Charles [Nqakula] to come back or Mr Solo [my uncle Bangilizwe] to come and provide leadership. We all knew that now we would be leaderless.'

On Wednesday, 3 July 1985, the *Eastern Province Herald* would lead with the discovery of my father and Matthew's bodies on its front page. Under the headline 'Goniwe and Calata Are Found Dead', reporter Anne Rogers writes:

> 'The badly burnt bodies of two Cradock community leaders, Mr Matthew Goniwe and Mr Fort Calata, were found in a clearing near St George's Strand outside Port Elizabeth yesterday afternoon – five days after they went missing after attending a United Democratic Front meeting in the city.
>
> Mr Goniwe – a listed person – and Mr Calata, both teachers, were central figures in the 15 month Cradock schools boycott which ended in April this year, and were also executive members of the Cradock Residents' Association.
>
> Their bodies were found at about 3.15 pm – an hour after members

of the Eastern Cape Murder and Robbery Squad, assisted by about 35 South African Defence Force personnel, accompanied by local reporters and photographers launched a search for the men who had been missing since Thursday.

They were lying in a small clearing, metres from the dirt road between Bluewater Bay and St George's Strand and about 1.7 kilometres from the spot where the body of Mr Sicelo Mhlawuli, an Oudtshoorn primary school principal, was discovered by a fisherman at the weekend.

Police did not initially launch a search for Mr Goniwe and Mr Calata because, according to Lieutenant-Colonel Gerrie van Rooyen, SA Police liaison officer for the Eastern Cape, no-one had officially reported them missing.

Mr Goniwe and Mr Calata were lying about three metres apart on their backs, their burnt arms outstretched. Between them lay a sports shoe, the only article of their clothing which was not burnt. The bodies were so charred that it was difficult to see whether they had been stabbed or mutilated, although some of Mr Calata's fingers appeared either to have been burnt or amputated. There were no apparent signs of a struggle.

Later when the bodies were removed, the only remaining evidence of their presence were two charred patches in the short grass where they had been lying.'[150]

The news of the discovery of my father and Matthew's burnt bodies sent shockwaves throughout the country. The UDF in the Eastern Cape, including their former colleagues and friends, were outraged.

In an article published soon thereafter in the *Eastern Province Herald* under the headline 'Grieving Cradock Widow Says: "I Am Just Empty"', Jeremy Maggs writes: 'Mrs Molly Blackburn, Progressive Federal Party MPC for Walmer and a friend of Mr Goniwe and Mr Calata, said that when one looked at motives behind the deaths one arrived at a frightening conclusion. She said all four men were people South Africa could be proud of. Their deaths were shattering, and the manner in which they died appalling. Mrs Judy Chalmers of the Eastern Cape Branch of the Black Sash said: "We mourn the deaths of these four men. Matthew Goniwe was an associate member of our organization and a man of

---

150 Rogers, A. 3 July 1985. Goniwe and Calata Are Found Dead. *Eastern Province Herald*.

the highest integrity and ability. All four men stood for what was right in life." Mr Derrick Swartz, Regional General Secretary of the UDF, to which CRADORA is affiliated, said the deaths of the four men could only be attributed to the social system in South Africa.'[151]

In the editorial comments printed in the same publication, an article under the headline 'Find These Killers', states: 'The foul spate of political kidnappings and murders – which now apparently has also claimed the Cradock activists Matthew Goniwe and Fort Calata as victims along with their two companions whose bodies were found earlier – will aid only the forces of evil in this country. Whatever ideological attachments these young men may have had, their brutal deaths should be mourned by all decent people. Thugs and assassins are seeking to impose their own choice of future on us through killing off leaders who are needed to help shape our society. Every such murder diminishes the chances of South Africa steering a course away from conflict and violence. Only cowards will accept that. We hope the perpetrators of these acts are tracked down, brought to justice and punished with the outrage their deeds demand.'[152]

Despite the government's best efforts to portray the killing of my father and his comrades as 'black-on-black violence' – attempting to link the murders to the on-going feud between the UDF and AZAPO in the Eastern Cape (more specifically, Port Elizabeth) – all fingers pointed straight back to the murderous state.

The Deputy Minister of Foreign Affairs, Louis Nel, would try his utmost to deny that the state was involved. In one article published in the *Eastern Province Herald* on Friday, 5 July 1985, under the headline 'Nel Denounces "Insinuations" about Killings', a group of the paper's reporters writes:

'The Deputy Minister of Foreign Affairs, Mr Louis Nel, yesterday strongly denounced "callous insinuations" about the recent murder of three Cradock civic leaders and an Oudtshoorn teacher.
    Mr Nel said he wished to express his condolences to the family of

---

151 Maggs, J. 3 July 1985. Grieving Cradock Widow Says: 'I Am Just Empty.' *Eastern Province Herald.*
152 'Find These Killers'. 3 July 1985. *Eastern Province Herald.*

the deceased "and assure them that legal procedures will continue, in order to bring the perpetrators of these deeds to justice."

In London, three lawyers associated with the UDF to which CRADORA was affiliated called a press conference and said they wanted to "alert the international community to the widespread disappearance of leading activists of the democratic movement against apartheid."

They said in a statement that the Government had been "unable to contain the people's anger" and added "This has, we believe, given rise to a new phase of terror against the people. A number of activists from the UDF and its affiliates have been abducted, and some have been killed. These people have not been selected at random. They are key leadership figures in their regions."'[153]

In my interview with Dr Boesak, he would concur that he and most of the UDF's national leadership were in no doubt about the state's role in the killings in the Eastern Cape, particularly those of my father and his comrades. Dr Boesak believed that the apartheid government had not expected the revolution to come from a rural town such as Cradock and that it would spread as it had to other '*platteland dorpies* [rural towns]'. 'It was a total shock,' he said. 'Politically, they were not prepared for that. Just as they were not prepared for the non-racialism, just as they were not prepared for the militant non-violence. So, they had to do everything they could and their first response, of course, was to be as brutal as they possibly can, because it was always their way of thinking.'

He added: 'To the apartheid government, it didn't matter how small or big a march was, all they knew was they had to nip it in the bud. Because they were so lulled into their positions of power, they were so arrogant, they were ready for what might happen in the cities, but they were never ready for what might happen in the rural areas, and Cradock was one such a shock. And then the reaction is much harsher, because they then had to understand that this thing is not as easily controllable as they thought. So they were very harsh.

'What they did with your father and Matthew, Mhlawuli and Sparro [here he paused for a long time] . . . I mean, to deceive them with a

---

153 Herald Reporters. 5 July 1985. Nel Denounces 'Insinuations' about Killings. *Eastern Province Herald.*

roadblock, that's nothing I can understand that [*sic*]. They did the same to me, but to then abduct them and for us to find out, not only that they were tortured, but, the pathologist's report said, that they were tortured with a blow-torch, that was not just torture. That was a demonstration, a lesson that the people had to learn. They had to learn that this is what happens to you when you challenge us. This is where the power lies, this is what our power can do, not only do, but that we can get away with it. That was the lesson.

'Remember,' Boesak said, 'they were not just killing a person here – they were killing in a way that does the most damage. That it intimidates more than you can imagine. It is a lesson in terrorist tactics from the side of the state. And so, it's not just a human being here, this is an activist, so other activists must now see that this is what happens to you: "They must see the extent of our power." It's not just an activist, but here is a leader, if we can break him and do with him what we're doing with him, other leaders will be so afraid to step into his shoes. This is a leader with integrity, with honesty, with a quality that if we take him out, and if we take the others out, what are the chances that those left behind will find somebody else with the same qualities.'

Boesak continued: 'I tried never to underestimate, not only the power of the white regime or the things that they will do, but the reasons behind it. So that's what they were trying to destroy – so that, for us of course, we had to mourn a colleague, a brother, a comrade, a leader. We had to mourn a father. Of course, you can replace a leader, because if that leader was wise, he would've begun to put in place a second generation of leaders which your father and Matthew had tried to do as well. But you cannot replace a father. Your father is gone. So, the lessons they wanted to teach us, for me as a father, they wanted me to ask a question, *Am I ready for that? Is it worth it? What if this happens to me? Can my family take it?* We look at your mother and she's been extraordinary in her courage and her strength – but not everybody is like that. So they were not just killing persons that night; they were looking at the maximum damage that they could do, to you, to the family, to the community, to Cradock, to the struggle as a whole, to the hopes of a whole generation. I say this because they were hoping that just as Cradock was setting an example for other places that we have talked about, so this lesson in "terrorist destruction" will become a lesson in intimidation for those other communities.'

Finally, Boesak said, '[Nelson] Mandela said a long time ago, when he was testifying in the Rivonia Trial, "There comes a moment where you really have only two options, you submit or you fight." What the deaths of the Cradock Four did was for us to raise the question, "Is this a moment to submit, or to fight on?" We decided we will never submit. We will fight on. And that [violence] was a pattern that they had repeated just about everywhere. It was of a brutality that was in many ways unique, and that is why apartheid was officially declared a crime against humanity. But we need to remember it was not a crime against humanity in general. It was a crime against *our* people. It was a crime against *our* leaders; it was a crime against *our* children – that is how we need to remember it.'

Boesak's understanding of the apartheid apparatus was confirmed by Colonel Lourens du Plessis, who said of his former colleagues, 'People became in my opinion obsessed with their power. You know, when a person becomes obsessed with power, then they become nasty people. They lose their decency, I think, to such an extent that you don't even normally get them to utter a decent word. They almost become barbaric.'[154]

Like everyone else, my grandmother (Fort's mother) was deeply traumatised by her son's murder. My mother said, 'You could see she was hurt, you know, but Sis' Ntsiki was one of those people who didn't show much emotion. She was terribly hurt because she loved Fort. She trusted him. Actually, Sis' Ntsiki always thought that Fort was one of her best children, she would, however, never show or even say it. Although she did say to me once [while he was still alive] that she trusted him.'

Dr Scholtz, our family GP at the time, was very worried about the child my mother was carrying. She recalled his telephoning every day to tell her that she was welcome to come to see him at any time. But she would only go to see him for her monthly check-ups. 'One afternoon, I had to go and see Dr Scholtz for a check-up. Roy took me. Before I left the house, I had lectures from the comrades: "If you want to cry, cry now in the

---

154 S Markovits and M Kaplan interview with Col. L du Plessis.

house and wipe your tears. When you go to the doctor you must be all right, you cannot show weakness,"' she told me.

On her arrival at the doctor's office, she noticed all the policemen at his surgery. 'When I got there, it was full of [members of] the Special Branch. And, mind you, we had our own side. We had medical [aid], so we had our own side and then the people who didn't have medical [aid] had their side. When I arrived there, there were police officers in both waiting rooms.'

The doctor confirmed that all was well with the baby and personally sympathised with my mother for her loss. He then asked her who she thought had killed my father. Without hesitation, she told him, 'The police killed Fort.'

Dr Scholtz retorted, 'No, Mrs Calata, it can't be the police. It's AZAPO.'

'I said, "No, doctor, my husband had nothing against AZAPO."

'He then responded, "No, you know in PE AZAPO is fighting against the UDF, and your husband was UDF." I was getting frustrated with him and I said, "I'm still saying it's the police."

'He said, "No. You can be arrested for saying that. You can't say it's the police when they are not allowed to kill people."

'I said, "I don't care if they arrest me. They killed my husband." Then I left. When I got home, I was so angry, I started to cry again. But, ja, I survived that.'

There was a time when my mother herself was concerned for her unborn child's health: 'I was worried a bit about Tumani because at one stage she was not kicking or moving. After a few days, she started to move and kick around again. She moved a lot when you [Lukhanyo] were very close to me.'

Chapter Ten
State of Emergency

LUKHANYO

The state had expected a reaction to and even condemnation of the murders, but they did not anticipate just how widespread that criticism would be.

Almost three weeks would pass from the day my father and Matthew's bodies were found to the day of the funeral. The delay was caused largely by the families' inability to find an independent pathologist to conduct a post-mortem. Molly Blackburn would eventually acquire the services of renowned pathologist Dr David Klatzow.

According to Mene, the executive members of Cradora and Cradoya spent every one of those days working tirelessly to help organise the funeral. They had also established the Cradock Burial Action Committee, which Mene recalled received hundreds of phone calls from the UDF's national leadership and other UDF-affiliated organisations from all around the country, offering their assistance or notifying them of their intention to travel to Cradock for the funeral.

The iLingelihle Town Council, under the acting town clerk, Mr Ettienne van Rooyen, had offered its assistance. Even Jo-Ann Bekker, who had been taken off her 'Cradock beat' in February that year, was asked to resume her reporting on Cradock. In an article published on 11 July 1985 (my sister Dorothy's tenth birthday) under the headline 'Council Assistance for Cradock Funeral', Bekker writes: 'The acting Town Clerk, Mr Ettienne van Rooyen, said the sports stadium, where the funeral service would be held, was being cleaned. A rostrum, seating, electricity and microphone equipment would be laid on. Arrangements had been made for extra water and toilet facilities while parking and camping areas had been marked out. Mr Monwabisi [Gladwell] Makhawula, the chairman of the Burial Action Committee, said the largest funeral in Cradock had been that of the first secretary-general of the African National Congress, Canon [James] Calata in June 1983. He expected the funeral on July 20th, at which Canon Calata's grandson, Mr Fort Calata, the founding chairman of the Cradock Residents' Association, Mr Matthew Goniwe, CRADORA's chairman Mr Sparro Mkonto and an Oudtshoorn teacher, Mr Sicelo Mhlawuli, will be buried to be even larger.'[155]

The next day, the newspaper reported that the 'Black Sash and other groups had approached the Anglican Cathedral in Grahamstown to allow those who wished to pray for the situation in Cradock after the recent murders of four community leaders to do so. Prayers will be offered from 1 to 1.30pm today.'

By Wednesday, 17 July, thousands of South Africans from all walks of life and every corner of the country had begun to arrive in iLingelihle for the funeral.

Bekker would report in an article published the next day (18 July) under the headline 'Scores Converge on Cradock for Funeral', that: 'Scores of people started converging yesterday on Cradock's African township where four community leaders will be buried this Saturday. People streamed into the homes of the bereaved families to pay tribute to the four murdered men – Mr Matthew Goniwe, Mr Fort Calata, Mr Sparro Mkonto and Mr Sicelo Mhlawuli – as crowds of youths chanted freedom songs and danced in iLingelihle's dusty streets. Policemen and soldiers in armoured vehicles were seen to maintain a strong presence on the outskirts of the town and at entrances to the township. But security forces patrolling the township took no action against the spontaneous open-air demonstrations. The Rev Arnold [Makhenkesi] Stofile of the UDF's Border region, who returned recently from New Zealand, will be the master of ceremonies at the funeral. Makhawula said Dr Allan Boesak, senior vice-chairman of the South African Council of Churches, has been invited as the main speaker.'[156]

---

155 Bekker, J. 11 July 1985. Council Assistance for Cradock Funeral. *Eastern Province Herald*.

156 Bekker, J. 20 July 1985. Scores Converge on Cradock for Funeral. *Eastern Province Herald*.

One of those thousands of people who arrived in Cradock to attend the funeral was Jan van Eck, a young politician from Cape Town who had been invited by Molly Blackburn. In his book *Eyewitness to 'Unrest'*, Van Eck recounts their arrival in Cradock the night before the funeral as follows:

> 'iLingelihle that evening was a beehive of activity. Thousands of people were pouring in by bus, kombi, motor car and other forms of transport from all four corners of South Africa. It soon became obvious that an event of major importance to the black community country-wide was taking place right here in this isolated corner of the Karoo.
>
> At the tiny homes of the widows and family of the slain men we joined hundreds of people taking part in the all-night vigil. There are moments in everyone's life which remain unforgettable, events that make a deep and indelible impression. Such a moment for me was the vigils at the home of Matthew Goniwe. I did not need any knowledge of the Xhosa language to understand what was being said. Although I have already forgotten his name, I will never forget the booming, but gentle voice of the minister expressing all the anger and grief of the people sitting with bowed heads around me. Had someone told me a few months earlier that a black minister of religion praying in Xhosa would bring a lump to my throat and tears to my eyes, I would have shaken my head.'[157]

That same night, Mene remembered how he and fellow activists – among them Mbulelo Goniwe, Obed Bapela, Alex (Stanza) Bopape, Zenzile Blou, Mamagase Nchabeleng – 'bought material at Zenzele [a general dealer] in iLingelihle. We then went to the Methodist Church, where we re-arranged all the chairs, so we could lay out all that material. Sis' Nowise Dywili [a local seamstress] was the person who helped us sew all those flags together. It was very huge flags, eh? When we finished there, we had an ANC flag, Communist Party flag, it was a Russian flag, we had an uMkhonto weSizwe flag, and we had a SADTU flag. We finished those flags late in the evening; the funeral was the following day.'

On the Saturday morning of 20 July 1985, the *Eastern Province*

---

157 Van Eck, J. 1989. *Eyewitness to 'Unrest'*. Taurus: Pretoria.

Herald's lead story was an article credited to *Herald* reporters under the headline, 'Appeals for Calm at Cradock Funeral', stating: 'The regional vice-president of the United Democratic Front, Mr Henry Fazzie, said he had received reports that funeral-goers were being stopped at roadblocks and turned back yesterday. The duty liaison officer for the SA Police in the Eastern Cape, Lieutenant-Colonel Louis Paulsen, said roadblocks had been mounted by police on the Port Elizabeth–Cradock road.'[158]

On page two of the same publication, an officer from the SAP public relations division in Pretoria is quoted as saying: 'Outdoor meetings are banned and the police have a duty to perform.'[159]

About 20 years later, when I first started working in the eNews newsroom, one of my colleagues at the time, Ayesha Ismail, would tell me the story of when she and a group of student activists had boarded a bus in Cape Town headed to my father's funeral. She said they had just passed Worcester on the N1 when they were stopped by the police who wanted to know where they were going. 'When the police heard Cradock, they told the bus driver to turn right back around and go back to Cape Town. I was heartbroken that I didn't make it to your father's funeral,' she told me.

My mother remembered a heavy fatigue descending on her as day broke on 20 July. 'On the day of the funeral, I was tired,' she said. 'I was so very tired. And I was not myself. I was just surrounded by darkness.' That morning, she would defiantly wear a dress in the black, green, and gold colours of the ANC.

The remains arrived in Cradock quite early that Saturday morning. My father's coffin was brought and placed on the stoep of Tatou's home, almost on the exact spot where his grandfather's coffin had stood just two years previously. The remains of the other three men were taken to their respective homes.

Paul Verryn would insist that the coffin with my father's remains not be opened, in a bid to shield my mother from the trauma of seeing her husband's badly mutilated body. On my father's death certificate, the

---

158 Herald Reporters. 20 July 1985. Appeals for Calm at Cradock Funeral. *Eastern Province Herald*.

159 Ibid.

cause of death is ascribed to 'stab wounds to the heart and the consequences thereof'. What it neglects to mention is the number of times he
was stabbed – at least 25 times. It also doesn't mention that his tongue
and several fingers on his left hand were cut off. His body, and in particular his face, was then doused with petrol and set alight – to make
identification difficult.

Despite this, one of my mother's biggest regrets was that she never
got to see my father's body. Over the years, she always wondered if it
would've helped her gain closure on his death if she had insisted on seeing his lifeless body one last time before he was buried.

On the day of the funeral, my mother said that I was still struggling
to come to terms with my father's death. She told the story of how I had
come to call her after I had just seen 'my father' get onto one of the many
buses parked outside the house in Mongo Street. She said I wanted the
two of us to slip out the back and join 'Tata' on the bus. She answered,
'Tata is not there. He is in that red thing, there on the stoep.'

'You said, "No! He is not there. I saw him, believe me."'

I actually remember this incident and how I had begun to pull her
towards the back of the house, which was closest to the bus I had 'seen'
my father get onto.

My uncle Patutu had to explain to me again that my father had passed
away, and therefore could not be on one of the buses outside. My mother
recalled that I pinched her to express my displeasure with her telling on
me like that. Paul Verryn would then insist that the bus be moved from
where it was parked.

After the home service was concluded, the four families then accompanied the coffins to the stadium, where thousands of mourners were
braving the bitterly cold winter morning. My mother remembered the
guard of honour lining the streets from Tatou's home to the stadium.
'There were people everywhere, in the streets, even on the rooftops of
houses. Everywhere you looked, you just saw people,' she said.

Mene recalled that as the funeral got under way, they had to go back
to the church (a distance of approximately four kilometres) to transfer
the flags to the stadium. 'The police are all over at the stadium, in
Isikhulu Street, eLuxolweni Street, going all the way around. It's all
closed off by the police. Those flags were huge, but Mbulelo had a bakkie.

We feared that they'd be taken by the police if they saw us transport them to the stadium. There were about four guys including Nchabeleng and Stanza Bopape, who were MK cadres at the time, who then drew their AK47s and said, "We will go with those flags." We put them into the bakkie and then we drove towards the stadium. Luckily, there were no issues. It was like a miracle, you know. Police and soldiers opened up just like that and we passed through. When we were around six houses to the stadium, we started looking for guys who are huge to carry the flags. I could not carry the flags myself. It had to be huge guys who could carry those flags. When they carried those flags and they got into the stadium, it was a miracle. The whole stadium just went up and said, "ANC, ANC, ANC!" And those flags were coming in, you know. It was very nice. The journalists . . . the photos they took there, were so beautiful photos.'

On the funeral programme was the quote: 'The blood of our martyrs will nourish the tree that will bear the fruits of our liberation.'

Unfortunately – but understandably – my mother also didn't remember much of the speeches or anything else of that day. She did remember crying through most of it and being seated next to Ma Leah, the wife of Desmond Tutu, then Bishop of Johannesburg, upon our arrival at the stadium. Pictures show that my maternal grandmother Nothobile stayed close to her.

'I can't remember what was said,' my mother told me. 'I saw Stone Sizani and them talking, the bishop [Bruce Evans] and everybody else. I really can't remember. Sometimes I so wish the [video] recordings were not confiscated by the police, so that we could play it back and listen to what was said.'

Unlike my mother, Dr Boesak recalled the funeral as if it were just yesterday. He started his account by remembering that he had first visited all the families and personally spoke to all four widows that morning. Then he said, 'Beyers Naudé of the Christian Institute asked me whether he could come with me, so I met him in Port Elizabeth and we drove through to Cradock together. Most of the township's kids did not know him. He was just this old white guy who came with me. But at the gate of the stadium, where we got out, they picked me up and put me on their shoulders, and they picked Beyers Naudé up and they put

him on their shoulders. He is "family" so to speak of those white security policemen who kidnapped, tortured, and killed their leaders. They
did not say, "We do not want this white man here"; they did not look at
him strangely; they did not whisper in my ear and say, "Doc, don't
bring him." They saw him with me and they lifted him on their shoulders. I still find it hard to find words for that kind of action. You cannot
for the life of anyone say, "Oh, it's because Cradock had such respect
for white people" – that was not true, we know that. It was something
that said, even in this brutality, this murder, even in everything that's
happened, we refuse to let that undermine or take away or cloak our
own humanity. And even as they [the white apartheid government] took
away the humanity of our leaders by killing them in the way they did,
we will envelop you [Beyers Naudé] with a humanity that you have
never seen before. He had never forgotten that moment and neither will
I,' Boesak told me.

In archival video material of that moment, both Boesak and Naudé
can be seen clearly on the shoulders of the crowd as they chanted,
'Boesak, Boesak, Boesak!' It's a scene and chant that still rings vividly in
Dorothy's memory today.

Dr Boesak then remembered, smiling wryly, that 'it was the first day
that the Communist flag was put up at the back of the stage. Youths
sitting on the vibracrete were holding it up.

'I said three things that day, that all had consequences. That was the
day that I said the South African government and the white people of
South Africa who support them are the "spiritual children of Adolf
Hitler". They went crazy about that. The second thing that I said to white
people was please stop telling us that my heart is with you. We don't
want your heart in the struggle, we want your body in the struggle,
right there next to us. And it's remarkable how many young white people, especially, responded to that. How many heard me and said, you're
right. And the third thing was we called for a boycott. And the boycott
took off that day. I was very angry, and I had to speak out of that anger
so that the people can know that I am with them. And they felt that,
but then how to express this anger without becoming reckless so that
the lives of the people are further endangered . . .' He added, 'How do
we channel this anger into something creative. And that's what we did

in Cradock. We launched that boycott, which began in Cradock and once again spread across the country.'

Other speakers at the funeral included Steve Tshwete, chairman of the UDF's Border region. In his address, he would speak about the potential declaration of a State of Emergency, saying, 'The declaration is a clear indication that the National Government is "a government in exit".'

Also among the speakers that afternoon was Victoria Mxenge, the wife of slain KwaZulu-Natal attorney, Griffiths Mxenge. Victoria had spoken at Tatou's funeral two years earlier.

In the book *Oliver Tambo: Beyond the Engeli Mountains*, author Luli Callinicos writes: 'At the funeral of the Cradock Four, attended by many thousands, ANC and SACP banners were unfurled in the open for the first time. Victoria Mxenge, widow of the murdered Griffiths Mxenge and human rights lawyer who had defended many young people, students and scholars, spoke passionately at the funeral, referring to the deaths of the four comrades as "a dastardly cowardice". The dead, she said, had gone to deliver messages to the ancestors. "Go well, peacemakers. Tell your great-grandfathers, we are coming because we are prepared to die for Africa."'[160]

Van Eck recounts the proceedings in his book as follows: 'Although the speeches, sermons and prayers coming from the platform were powerful and emotional, reflecting the feelings and often the anger of the communities, it was the crowd, which to me, was the most impressive of the whole ceremony: their completely disciplined behaviour, yet their frequent outbursts of anger and hatred: their shouts of laughter, but most of all their passionate singing and dancing. How can I ever forget the clear voice of a six year old boy, standing right next to me on a trestle table, singing the verses of "Nkosi Sikelel' iAfrika" and "We Are the Soldiers of Mandela [Singama soja kaMandela]" with dedication and passion that sent a shiver of hope and fear up my spine.'[161]

The unfurling of the Communist or 'Soviet' flag alongside that of the

160 Callinicos, L. 2004. *Oliver Tambo: Beyond the Engeli Mountains*. David Philip: Cape Town.

161 Van Eck, J. 1989. *Eyewitness to 'Unrest'*. Taurus: Pretoria.

ANC at the funeral had drawn a huge response from the crowd and the security forces who had maintained a strong monitoring presence on the *koppies* surrounding iLingelihle.

After several hours at the stadium, the large funeral procession wound its way peacefully through iLingelihle. I remember being in the back of a blue Mitsubishi kombi (called a Star Wagon). The rear sliding door was open as it drove slowly through thousands and thousands of people next to us walking and singing freedom songs. I sat next to my mother, while my sister Dorothy, aunt Sisana, and grandmother Nothobile were in the row of seats behind us.

Once at the gravesite, I remember holding onto my mother's dress, too afraid of letting go. The up-and-down stamping by toyi-toyiing mourners shook the ground under my feet. I had never felt anything like that before, and I remember being so afraid of the ground collapsing underneath me. Every time the people's feet hit the ground, they would kick up small puffs of dust, which would be blown up by the wind. At some point, the crowd went very quiet. Then I saw the coffins, one of them with my father inside it, begin to lower slowly into the ground. My mother started crying even louder. Although I didn't understand what was going on, I knew that whatever was happening, it wasn't good. I remember being very, very afraid. I was still clutching my mother's dress so tightly. Then people started throwing handfuls of sand on the coffins, and my mother couldn't stop crying.

We were then taken back to the kombi. This time, though, someone closed the door. As we drove back to my great-grandfather's home, I saw many, many people who were still making their way to the graves.

Van Eck writes about the funeral:

'As I – a lone but not the only white – made my way through the thousands of mourners thronging the streets of iLingelihle after the funeral service, I knew that the proclamation of the threatened State of Emergency by the Government (about which rumours were running high) would merely drive these South Africans, united in their desire for total freedom, further along the road to confrontation and violence. The funeral vividly illustrated that the oppressed people of South Africa were developing a unity of purpose which no state would be able to stop.

Even if the revolution were not upon us yet and even if their liberation were still a long way off, nothing could prevent that liberation from coming about. Even if the state were able to slow down the process of liberation by using all the legislative and military powers at its disposal, it would never stop it permanently [. . .] I left Cradock a different person. The "struggle" was no longer an event of academic interest only, being waged by people unknown to me. The struggle had been personalised for me.'[162]

My father, Fort Calata, and his comrades, Matthew Goniwe, Sparro Mkonto, and Sicelo Mhlawuli became known as the Cradock Four.

The state, having monitored events of the day, including the unfurling of both the Soviet and ANC flags in iLingelihle, would give credence to the rumours of a pending State of Emergency. Just hours after the funeral, State President PW Botha went on SABC television and radio to declare a partial State of Emergency starting at midnight in 36 magisterial districts across the country, including Cradock and surrounding towns in the Eastern Cape.

At midnight, Mene was fast asleep though. He said, 'We had not had a good night's rest for about fourteen days. We'd sleep maybe an hour or so as we prepared for that funeral. The T-shirts, the food, the flags, everything else that had to be there. You know, we had meeting after meeting after meeting to make sure that everything was prepared and ready. After the funeral, iLingelihle was full of people from throughout the country. Cradock was a playground for guns during those few days. Anyway, the evening after the funeral there was shooting in Cradock. It was as if iLingelihle was a battleground, between the police, the soldiers, and the people that had arrived in Cradock. Unfortunately, we took a decision to go and sleep. I got arrested the following day.' Here, he laughed, before continuing, 'So, on the 21st we [Madoda Jacobs, Zenzile Blou and others] went to prison. We were detained there from 1985, the 21st of July, just after the funeral, up until 1989. I was never charged with anything.'

On 24 July, the other daily newspaper in the Eastern Cape, the *Daily Dispatch*, published an article under the headline 'East Cape Emergency:

---

162 Ibid.

The Terms'. Attributed to a *Dispatch* reporter, the article defines the measures imposed by the State of Emergency declaration:

'The State of Emergency announced by the State President Mr P W Botha, with effect from midnight last Saturday will affect 17 magisterial districts in the Eastern Cape.

They are: Adelaide, Albany, Alexandria, Bathurst, Bedford, Cradock, Fort Beaufort, Graaff-Reinet, Port Elizabeth, Humansdorp, Uitenhage, Hankey, Jansenville, Steytlerville, Somerset East, Kirkwood and Pearston.

The emergency measures announced fall into two categories – some which came into effect immediately and others which will be announced from time to time.

The following emergency measures came into effect immediately.

Any commissioned, warrant or non-commissioned officer of the various law enforcement agencies may – when he considers someone to be endangering life, property or public order – order the person to move and warn that force may be used if the order is disobeyed.

Any member of the security forces may without warrant, arrest any person when he deems it necessary for the maintenance of law and order.

Such a person can be detained for up to 14 days (or longer if the Minister of Justice so decrees) under a written order signed by any member of the force.

A member of the force may interrogate a detained person.

The minister may impose any conditions he deems necessary upon people who are released from detention.

No person will have access to detained people without the consent of the Minister or Commissioner of Police.

No person will be entitled to any information about, or received from detainees.

It is an offence to threaten anyone, verbally or in any way, with harm, hurt or loss.

Any member of the force may at any time search or order the search of any person, premises, place, vehicle, vessel or aircraft. He may also seize any article he deems to be intended for an offence.

Members of the public are obliged to re-arrest people who escape detention.

Orders which extend to the police, Defence Force, prison service and Railway Police – and which could be issued by the commissioner from time to time include:

The demarcation of areas.

The control of all movements in such areas.

The control of all traffic.

The closing of any public or private place, business or industry.

The removal of any person out of or to any area.

The control of essential services and the security of any installation.

The imposition of curfews.

Complete control over the gathering and distribution of news about these regulations.

Any other action deemed necessary by the Commissioner.

It becomes an offence to disclose, without authorization, the identity of arrested people or to deface any notice issued under the emergency regulations.

The maximum penalty for offences under the emergency regulations is a fine of R20 000 or imprisonment for 10 years without the option of a fine.

Complete indemnity against any criminal or civil proceedings is granted to the State, the State President, his Cabinet, any member of a law enforcement force, any public servant or anyone acting under his or her instructions.'[163]

For those detained under the State of Emergency, such as Moppo Mene, prison was akin to hell on earth. He said:

> 'It was a very bad situation because it started in fact at the police station in Cradock. The police wanted the people who had designed those flags and they wanted to know where those flags are. I must say, I have respect for Zenzile Blou, he knew where those flags were, he knew where and how those flags were prepared, he knew every step of those particular flags. He was beaten. His whole body, his back was full of scars. He was beaten, tortured, put into deep waters and everything else, and he said he knows nothing. They would take him from his cell at six o'clock in the morning and only bring him back at seven o'clock at night. He would be beaten all day by the police. He would come back and just sleep. Fortunately, I had some tablets for pain and I had to give [them to] him almost every night because of the way he was beaten. But he stood firm and said, "I know nothing about it." People that were arrested were those people who carried the flags and

163 Dispatch Reporter. 24 July 1985. East Cape Emergency: The Terms. *Daily Dispatch*.

fortunately not a single one of those were part of the preparation of those flags and they could not tell where these flags were from. We were beaten every day until we were transferred to St Albans Prison in Port Elizabeth. When we were in PE we were tortured like anything. It was so bad, until it got to a point where there was a doctor who challenged the beating of the detainees in court.'

That doctor was Wendy Orr. In his book, *No One to Blame? In Pursuit of Justice in South Africa*, George Bizos writes:

'In 1985 Wendy Orr was a young doctor working in the Port Elizabeth district surgeon's office. Her duties included the examination of all new prisoners who complained of assault by the police and had injuries to confirm their stories. Her immediate superior was Dr Ivor Lang, who was concerned about the number of alleged assaults Dr Orr was recording, and the subsequent police investigations which might follow. The prisons department, more concerned about protecting itself from any claims than the welfare of the detainees, instructed Orr to stop recording prisoners' complaints of assault. All the detainees examined by Dr Orr complained of assaults and had the wounds to prove it. Driven by desperation at her helplessness, Orr decided to go public. On the strength of Orr's affidavit and those of selected detainees, an application was launched to interdict the police from assaulting detainees. The application was successful. For her trouble, Wendy Orr was suspended from her work with prisoners by Dr Lang. Later that year, she resigned her position after an anonymous donor paid off her government bursary.'[164]

On 1 August 1985, barely twelve days after delivering a rousing speech at my father's funeral, Victoria Mxenge was attacked and killed by a group of four men in the driveway of her home in Umlazi, Durban. She was stabbed and shot while her children looked on through the window.

Exactly a week later, on 7 August, just a day before Ma Victoria's memorial service, my mother decided it was time for us to go back to the house we used to share with my father. She remembered it being a Tuesday when she and I made our way home to Siyabulela Street.

---

164 Bizos, G. 1998. *No One to Blame? In Pursuit of Justice in South Africa.* David Philip & Mayibuye Books: Cape Town.

Dorothy decided against going, preferring instead to accompany our grandmother Sis' Ntsiki to church. 'You and I went to the house and stayed there the afternoon. You know, trying to get used to the house without Fort. I sat there trying to pull myself together, but both you and I were crying the whole time. I decided, no, it was getting late. I was pregnant, so I said let's go. And we went back to Mongo [Street],' my mother told me.

On the way there, she said I then demanded that she carry me on her back. She reluctantly obliged, but after a while I got too heavy for her. Fortunately, a young Anglican priest, Luyanda Tuku, who lived in the same street as my grandmother, was driving by. He saw what was happening and came to our rescue. He offered my mother and me a lift. 'Shortly after Luyanda dropped us off, my contractions started. Roy took me to the hospital,' my mother said. After a few hours in labour, the doctors decided that it would be safer for the baby to be born by caesarean section. Nurses then prepped my mother and wheeled her into the operating room for the procedure. At four o'clock the following morning, exactly nineteen days after our father's funeral, my sister Tumani was born.

Her arrival sent my mother's emotions in a whirlwind. 'For me, the heartache started all over again,' she said. 'This was the baby girl Fort was so looking forward to seeing. She was here – he was not. But,' she said, shrugging her shoulders, 'what could I do, I had to accept it. I stayed with my in-laws for about a month, then I took my three children and decided to go home [to Siyabulela Street].'

Molly Blackburn, who had regularly travelled to Cradock to visit my family after Tumani's birth, would die in a tragic car accident on 28 December 1985. She and her friends Di and Brian Bishop were travelling from Oudtshoorn to Port Elizabeth when a suspected drunk driver smashed into their car. Molly and Brian lost their lives in what is believed to have been a deliberate attempt on her life.

Chapter Eleven

A Life Betrayed

LUKHANYO

It would be another four years before there was any news or movement with regards to the killings of my father and his comrades. It came in the form of a judicial inquest presided over by Magistrate Eric de Beer, starting in February 1989.

Arthur Chaskalson (the then national director of the Legal Resources Centre) represented our families. His instructing attorney was Fikile Bam, the director of the Port Elizabeth office of the LRC. George Bizos writes that, in the lead-up to the inquest, Chaskalson asked him to represent our families, but 'I was not available. He did it himself.'[165]

Chaskalson, working with very little in terms of evidence, would do his best to try to convince the court that the deaths of the Cradock Four were at the hands of the state, and were not a result of the UDF/AZAPO feud which had played itself out in Port Elizabeth at the time.

In his closing arguments, Chaskalson said: '"Your worship, I believe on the evidence [the court] is unable to make a finding as to who is responsible for the killings but Your Worship can, and indeed will, make a finding that they were murdered and that the circumstances of their deaths are as I have described them to Your Worship today."'

Bizos adds:

> 'At the time of the first inquest even a suggestion of the existence of hit squads within the security forces would have been denied as "communist and ANC propaganda" and could have exposed whoever suggested it to serious danger. Arthur Chaskalson had to tread a fine line.

---

165 Ibid.

Magistrate de Beer did not take long to deliver his finding. After referring briefly to the "war" between UDF and AZAPO, he sketched the events on the evening of 27 June 1985, the post-mortem results and the evidence led. His conclusion was:

"Finally, I find that it has been clearly proven who the deceased were, when they had died and what their cause of death was. As I have already said, the only real issue before me is to determine the identity of the actual killer or killers, and from what I have already said, this is not possible. The only finding I can make in this regard, which is also a finding to which all parties have agreed, is that their deaths were brought about by a person or persons or group of persons unknown." '[166]

My mother remembered how all four widows, Sis' Nyameka Goniwe, Sis' Nonkosi Mkonto, Sis' Nombuyiselo Mhlawuli and she were devastated by the magistrate's ruling. They had hoped, she told me, that the inquest would help heal their wounds. But it turned out to be the first in a series of disappointments in our efforts to obtain justice for my father's life.

In December that same year, three black police officers from Port Elizabeth and an informer were killed when the car they were travelling in was bombed. A report on the incident was published in the *Evening Post* on 15 December under the headline 'PE Blast Kills 4', stating: 'The vehicle was torn apart by the explosion, and a crater was left in the road. Today police examined the wreckage before loading the fragments on to a bakkie and cleaning up the area along a lonely stretch of country road. The dead policemen were Detective Warrant Officer Glen Mgoduka, Detective Sergeant AT Faku, and Detective Constable DD Mapipa. The name of the informer would not be released.'[167] These three police officers are believed to have been part of the hit squad responsible for the murders of my father and his comrades.

Then, in 1992, right in the midst of the Convention for a Democratic South Africa (CODESA) negotiations, President FW de Klerk was forced to establish a second inquest into the murders of the Cradock Four. This occurred after the *New Nation* newspaper, edited at the time by the

---

166 Ibid.
167 Post Reporters. 15 December 1989. PE Blast Kills 4. *Evening Post*.

late Zwelakhe Sisulu, published on its front page a copy of the signal sent by Colonel Lourens du Plessis to the Secretariat of the State Security Council. The signal had ordered the permanent removal from society of Matthew Goniwe, Mbulelo Goniwe, and Fort Calata as a matter of urgency.

Bizos, who represented our families in the second inquest, writes: 'The publication of the signal took the country by storm, as it seemed to contradict what Judge [Louis] Harms had found a year and a half earlier and showed that everything that President PW Botha and the security forces had been accused of was true. The authenticity of the signal was not denied.'[168]

Colonel Lourens du Plessis said of this period: 'When the Goniwe bubble burst, when that signal was published in the *New Nation*, from then on my life changed considerably. I was called to Pretoria, I met with the state attorneys. I got the impression that they wanted me to say what I didn't think was the truth. Although I did make a sworn statement at the time, it wasn't quite what I wanted to say.'[169]

George Bizos adds: 'The publication of the signal and [the subsequent] reopening of the inquest also reopened old wounds for the four widows and other family members of the murdered men. The prospect of reliving the events was painful but was outweighed by the possibility of finally finding the killers.'[170]

The newspaper reports were greeted with much optimism in Cradock. For my mother, it represented a step forward in the case. She hoped that the talks around a second inquest would finally reveal the truth around my father's murder. I was around ten or eleven years old at the time and one of my school teachers, Felicity Meyer, would quiz me in class about the Cradock Four matter whenever there was a story broadcast on SABC News the night before. Out of fear of being unable to answer her questions, I watched the news religiously, often asking

---

168 Bizos, G. 1998. *No One to Blame? In Pursuit of Justice in South Africa*. David Philip & Mayibuye Books: Cape Town.

169 S Markovits and M Kaplan interview with Col. L du Plessis.

170 Bizos, G. 1998. *No One to Blame? In Pursuit of Justice in South Africa*. David Philip & Mayibuye Books: Cape Town.

my mother for 'exclusive details' to report back to my teacher and class.

To the ANC and other liberation movements around the CODESA table, the signal was evidence of the state's dastardly deeds in which death squads were allowed to kill 'the enemy', which included the likes of the Cradock Four, the PEBCO Three, and Victoria Mxenge.

The second inquest, which only started about a year later in 1993, was presided over by Judge Neville Zietsman, the then Judge-President of the Eastern Cape Division of the Supreme Court.

Bizos writes: 'We arrived in Port Elizabeth on March 1, 1993 to begin the Goniwe inquest. There was great excitement within and outside the courtroom. The large crowd that had come to see justice done sang freedom songs and toyi-toyied outside and packed the gallery.'[171]

On 28 May 1994, a month after South Africa's first democratic election was held on 27 April, my mother and the other three widows were back in court for the judgment. It had been over a year since the start of the inquest in which the defence force generals, among them Hekkel van Rensburg, Joffel van der Westhuizen, Lourens du Plessis, as well as Security Police Colonels Eric Winter and Harold Snyman, all suffered from a collective case of amnesia. Judge Zietsman ruled that the murderers of my father and his colleagues were indeed members of the security forces.

Zietsman stated: "'A case of suspicion had been made out against certain members of the police force, among them Colonels Snyman and Winter, as well as against Generals Van der Westhuizen, Van Rensburg and Du Plessis. But suspicion does not constitute prima facie proof. This would require some link between the deaths and acts committed by the persons under suspicion, which the evidence led did not establish."

Judge Zietsman then concluded his judgement by saying: "'I am not able, on the evidence placed before me, to identify the murderer or murderers.'"[172]

Judge Zietsman's judgement was yet another blow to our families' hopes of finding justice for the murders of my father and his comrades.

---

171 Ibid.
172 Ibid.

In June 1995, President Nelson Mandela visited iLingelihle to commemorate the tenth anniversary of the deaths of the Cradock Four. In his address to my family and the community at the graves, where he laid wreaths, he said: 'Cradock was the first to render the apartheid organs of government unworkable. The only crime of the Cradock Four was their unbending commitment to the struggle for the liberation of the motherland. The deaths of these gallant freedom fighters marked a turning point in the history of our struggle. They were the true heroes of the struggle.' Madiba added: 'Despite the revelations that have been made, the full story has not been told. There can be no reconciliation without truth. All those responsible, irrespective of their political affiliation, must own up. Their motives must be known. Only then can we prevent the repetition of such crimes.'[173]

On 19 July 1995, just over a month after his visit to Cradock, President Mandela signed the Truth Commission Bill into law.

My mother was among the first people to testify at the Truth and Reconciliation Commission (TRC) hearings chaired by Archbishop Desmond Tutu in the East London City Hall in 1996. Author Antjie Krog, who at the time served as a radio reporter for the SABC, would describe the moment my mother was overcome by her emotions during testimony as 'an indefinable wail that would become the signature tune' of the TRC hearings[174].

Alex Boraine, Tutu's deputy chairperson, recalls the moment as a 'primeval and spontaneous wail that caught up in a single howl all the darkness and horror of the apartheid years'[175].

Six police officers, Eric Taylor, Gerhard Lotz, Harold Snyman, Johan 'Sakkie' van Zyl, Herman du Plessis, and Nic van Rensburg applied to the Amnesty Committee of the TRC for amnesty for the murders of my father, Fort Calata, and his comrades, Matthew Goniwe, Sparro Mkonto, and Sicelo Mhlawuli. Their applications, however, were all denied as

---

173 Nicholson, C. 2004. *Permanent Removal: Who Killed the Cradock Four?* Wits UP: Johannesburg.

174 Hartle, R. 20 April 2016. On a Tortured Path to Incomplete Accounting. *Daily Dispatch*.

175 Ibid.

the Commission felt they had failed to disclose the truth about the murders. But even the TRC, it seems, would fail to bring our families much-needed justice and closure on the murders.

In September 2017, over 32 years after the murders of the Cradock Four, I sat down for an interview with Deputy Minister of Justice John Jeffery. I wanted to hear his explanation for why the ANC-led government had failed to prosecute those responsible for the deaths of my father and his colleagues. He began by saying, 'Part of the problem is the nature of our transition [from apartheid to democracy] – the negotiated settlement. That was the price that had to be paid.' I then asked the deputy minister if he was implying that the murders of my father and his comrades, as well as those of many other South Africans, including the likes of Victoria Mxenge, the PEBCO Three, and even that of Bantu Stephen Biko in 1977, were used as pawns or tools during the negotiations for a democratic South Africa. His response astounded me when he said, 'That's part of the price that had to be paid.'

The deputy minister, who himself had lost a close friend and comrade in Reggie Nkabinde in the political violence which enveloped KwaZulu-Natal from the late Eighties to the early Nineties, astounded me even further when he said, 'We [the ANC-led government] don't have the resources to re-open all these investigations. We don't have the resources to have inquests into all these murders. Some can be done, as has happened with Ahmed Timol, as has been done with Nokuthula Simelane.

'The problem is that there are so many. That raid into Mthatha in the Transkei, that killed two young boys and I mean literally boys, was openly admitted as an operation. It was the army I think that went in, and they claimed they were raiding some or other PAC or MK person's house and they killed two young boys. I mean, there's so many. The whole of KZN, nobody knows what happened to most of the cases. It's unfortunately the result, I think, of our transition.'

I wasn't satisfied with these almost callous responses, so I pushed him a little harder. I asked him if this meant that I would now have explain to my mother that, according to the Deputy Minister of Justice, she and the rest of my family – in particular, my younger sister, Tumani, who had never seen our father except in pictures – would never see justice for the life of Fort Calata. He answered, 'The problem we've got is, yes, you want to know what happened, but what happens if we can't do it all one time, as it were? I appreciate that what I am saying must sound terrible, but for me the pressure is the issue of getting a functioning justice system now that can deal with present-day crimes and ensure that perpetrators get brought to book.'

In my interview with Dr Allan Boesak, he told me that the murders of the Cradock Four were probably part of, if not central to, the secret negotiations between the ANC and apartheid leaders way before they ever set foot in the World Trade Centre in Kempton Park, Johannesburg, for CODESA in December 1991.

Indeed, our families had spoken of that very same fact. We as a collective had always suspected that the generals and architects of apartheid had negotiated themselves out of murder, making the ANC – in whose name Fort Calata, Matthew Goniwe, Sparro Mkonto, and Sicelo Mhlawuli were killed – complicit, at least in our opinion, in their murders.

Deputy Minister Jeffery's statement that the government has no resources to prosecute these crimes rings hollow. How dare he cite a lack of state resources as explanation for what is clearly a lack of political will? I find this most insulting. Especially when I consider that in the two weeks prior to my sitting down to pen this chapter, the Office of the Auditor-General of South Africa reported to parliament that state-owned entities Eskom and Transnet had in the previous financial year (2016/2017) squandered a total of R5,7 billion through irregular, fruitless, and wasteful expenditure. Just this week, on 9 October 2017, the CFO and COO of the SABC, which is once again mired in controversy and is currently without a Board of Directors or permanently appointed executives, reported to parliament that it had lost R4,4 billion in the previous financial year through irregular and wasteful expenditure. I'm certain that in the weeks to come more government departments and entities, including the very same Department of Justice and Correctional Services, will report large amounts of public monies lost through government wastage. I find it an outright insult to the thousands of South African families who lost loved ones at the hands of the apartheid state. Why would Jeffery cite a lack of resources as an excuse for why the ANC-led government would not help our families by investigating and prosecuting those responsible for the deaths of our loved ones? This is shameful considered in light of the R250 million of tax-payers' money illegally spent on former president Jacob Zuma's Nkandla compound.

As I write this, it's barely 24 hours after Judge Billy Mothle of the North Gauteng High Court ruled anti-apartheid activist Ahmed Timol, who died in police custody in 1972, was pushed and fell to his death from the tenth floor of the notorious John Vorster Police headquarters in Johannesburg. Although I celebrate the judgment and this moment with the Timol family, I have very little hope that the government will in fact adhere to the judge's ruling and investigate one João Rodrigues as 'an accessory to Timol's murder'.

There's very little to suggest that the governing party will honour this court ruling, which, in essence, vindicates the family's long-held quest for justice. But I draw inspiration from their quest, as it will surely blaze a trail for many families, including mine, to continue to pursue justice for our loved ones. In the 23 years of ANC rule, the once-glorious liberation movement of Tatou and my father has not honoured the pain of our people in its politics, in the seeking of justice, and in securing the future of our children. That, to me and my family – and I'm sure to the families of Matthew Goniwe, Sparro Mkonto and Sicelo Mhlawuli – is the greatest betrayal which we could have imagined.

The ANC, in my opinion, has lost its revolutionary and moral moorings. Many in the party, chief among them its former president, Jacob Zuma, have their eyes so firmly fixed on self-interest and the power that they have taken – 'unredeemed from the hands of the apartheid government,' according to Dr Boesak – that they have lost sight of the sacrifices made by so many South Africans and, in doing so, greatly dishonour and disrespect these sacrifices for our freedom.

I feel that at no point did the ANC look at the power it was inheriting from the National Party in 1994 and say we must use our power differently. We must use our power to serve our people; we must use our power to bring justice to our people. Instead, many have looked at it as a power to enrich themselves.

My opinion on the ANC and how it has treated the people is shared and perfectly articulated by Dr Allan Boesak. In our interview, he said,

'I don't know how any leader in the ANC can look your mother in the eye, without feeling that they must be damned to hell for what they did and continue to do. If I think of what we have gone through and the price that has been paid, how can people walk through this country, how can we walk our streets, how can we walk through our townships and not see the blood still on the soil?'

He then asked me, 'How can I look you in the eye, Lukhanyo, and not think about what happened when you were three? Your father did not die of some illness, that [his death] was a deliberate act of murder and terrorism. So how can they look you in the eye, yet steal the money that's meant for our children and elderly? How can they look you in the eye and sit in their ministers' chair and yet they don't care what happens to our people? How can they fight about the size and the price and the colour of their ministerial automobiles like two ministers from the SACP *nogal* have been fighting? And those are the things that they worry about? And think that is okay?

'How can they talk about a National Democratic Revolution that has changed nothing for our people? Instead, it has reconfirmed the old inequalities, the old injustices. It has made this vast abyss between the rich and the poor in South Africa wider than it was in the days of apartheid. How can they do that?'

And, almost as if to challenge me, Dr Boesak made eye contact, a smile spreading across his face, and said, 'We must ask the question that I think your father and his three comrades would've asked. In a situation like this, what does integrity do? What does honesty do? What does decency do? And if you can answer those questions, then we might still save this place.'

Dr Boesak's questions would ring in my mind repeatedly over the next few days. They were still swirling around one Monday afternoon when I received a telephone call from Krivani Pillay (one of the SABC 8). She wanted to know if we as a group of journalists should issue yet another statement about the latest shenanigans at the SABC. Without stopping even once to consider the possible implications that yet another statement with my name on it (pertaining to the nonsense at the SABC) might entail, I agreed and began to give my input. It read:

'9 October 2017

To all News Editors

OPEN LETTER RE: SABC8 IMPLORES PARLIAMENT TO ACT ON BROADCASTER'S GOVERNANCE CRISIS

At the start, we the SABC8, want to affirm the good work done in 2016 by parliament's portfolio committee on communications, the ad hoc committee on the SABC and the interim board of the SABC. However, it is with deep regret that we write to you to register our alarm and deepest disappointment at the reckless abandon to which the public broadcaster has descended. We are extremely concerned at the governance crisis at the SABC. We believe that a recapture project of the public broadcaster is afoot and would like to endorse the open letter written to you by our fellow colleagues under the banner of BEMAWU (Broadcasting, Electronic, Media & Allied Workers Union). We wish to reiterate their statement that we are prepared to strike over the issues underlined. We will not allow our short-lived, recently gained freedom of expression to be rolled back.

It has been nine days since the term of the Interim Board has expired. However, there has been no political will to remedy the governance crisis at the broadcaster. The President has delayed the ratification of the permanent board members duly advised by Parliament. In terms of the Broadcasting Act, Section 14 (1), concerning the executive committee, "the affairs of the corporation are administered by an executive committee consisting of the group chief executive and six other members appointed by the board." In other words the Act makes absolutely no provision for the ministerial appointment of executive members; in fact the Act frowns on such. We have been told today, by acting GCEO Nomsa Philiso, that the Minister is currently preparing herself to extend the contracts of the current acting executives. If the Minister proceeds with such plans she would be usurping the powers of parliament or a board that should have been appointed by parliament. We wish to inform the executive arm of the state that we do not belong to them but to the people of South Africa via their public representatives – the Parliament of the Republic of South Africa.

In terms of the Companies Act, the current state of affairs amounts to reckless trading as no one is accountable for the major decisions and transactions of the insolvent entity that we work for. It is clear that the SABC is unable to pay its debts as they become due in the normal course of business. The attendant risks and implications are dire and grave. It would be reckless of us not to responsibly raise these concerns with Parliament as we do now by this correspondence.

Regarding the reversed merger between the News Resources Department and Henley; while on the surface it may seem resolved, we still call for a forensic investigation into how this merger came about in the first place and a full account of the moneys transferred and spent, particularly the millions transferred from the news division to the bankrupt Henley technical department. The Combating and Prevention of Corrupt Activities Act stipulates that we have an obligation to report such matters. Further, we have seen how when corruption is allowed to run rampant, the quality of news and governance decline.

We note, with concern, a reported meeting held at Luthuli House, wherein we believe it was said that the SABC news division is "the only propaganda tool left to the African National Congress"; and that the loss of this "tool" would be resisted by the governing party. In addition, we find that the meeting held by our Acting-GE of news with the head of the president's private office and spokesperson, Dr Bongani Ngqulunga, to be injudicious and we call on our head to exercise more circumspection in the future and to protect the newsroom from perceptions of bias. We also call on him to make the minutes of that meeting public. Editorial independence must not only be practised, like justice, it must be seen to be done.

We also raise concern that the editorial review process has been halted by the absence of the appropriate governance structures. ICASA has ruled that the SABC revert to the editorial policy of 2004. In this editorial policy the official mandated person to preside over the editorial process is the Group Chief Executive. We note with concern that the acting Chief Operating Officer has installed herself at the apex of this process, thus continuing with the practices of Hlaudi Motsoeneng under whom she gladly served. This is why we call on the presidency to ratify the board members so that we can institute the measures to ensure editorial independence, such as the Editorial Forum, as envisaged in the Broadcasting Act, clause 13 (b) which calls on board members to be committed to fairness and freedom of expression and the right of the public to be informed.

It has been eight months since the release of the final report of the SABC inquiry's ad hoc committee which recommended, among others, that the enforcers of unlawful instructions by Hlaudi Motsoeneng and his regime be held accountable. Instead, there appears to be efforts to launder their conduct and reinstate them as credible journalists. This is just a cosmetic exercise designed to ensure that they remain long enough to cover up the corrupt excesses and decisions of the past. Given the acting head of news' reluctance to correct the wrongs of the past, our faith in his leadership is gravely shaken.

We call upon parliament to hold the executive to account and bring the corporation in line with the governance principles outlined in the Broadcasting Act. We cannot proceed in this fashion for much longer. Yours sincerely
Thandeka Gqubule-Mbeki
Busisiwe Ntuli
Krivani Pillay
Foeta Krige
Lukhanyo Calata
Vuyo Mvoko
Jacques Steenkamp
Nonkululeko Zonke Smith (convenor of SABC 101 – News Technical Staff)'

It's been a week since that statement and, so far, I'm happy to report there's been no comeback – besides the small matter of a response from the Office of the President. The fact that the highest office in the land would concern itself with a statement from a bunch of journalists at the SABC has once again made me realise how important it is for me either to speak up or act when I am confronted by injustice. It matters not in which form the injustice may present itself, what matters is that I (and to a large extent all well-meaning people) confront those behind the injustice. This is, after all, the legacy of my family through my great-grandparents, James and Miltha, their daughter (my grandmother) Nontsikelelo Calata, and my father, Fort Calata. It is also the legacy of my community of iLingelihle, through Matthew Goniwe, Sparro Mkonto, Sicelo Mhlawuli, Jamani Goniwe, Gangathumlungu 'Gandhi' Hlekani, Ben Ngalo and Lennox Melani, General Nonyanga, Madoda Jacobs, Mbulelo Goniwe, Daisy and Vulindlela Bontsi, Charles Nqakula, Moppo Mene, and the thousands of other activists who risked their lives every day for me to live in a South Africa that is free of the oppression and injustice of apartheid. I hold dear their sacrifices and honour their lives. I hope to also tell their stories. In my father's case, however (and of course that of Matthew, Sparro, and Sicelo), it means a continued pursuit of justice for his life. I'm certain it is what he and his comrades would want. *A luta!*

Acknowledgements

It would be remiss of us to take credit for this book and not to acknowledge the contributions of the many cheerleaders who helped bring it to light.

Firstly, we would like to give thanks to our God, the Redeemer, for without Him nothing, particularly this book, would have been possible.

Secondly, we would like to acknowledge our mother, Nomonde Calata, for her steadfast love and dedication to her late husband, Fort, throughout the decades. It is that undying love that kept alive the memories, which allowed us to tell his story. Ma, we honour your strength, your passion and absolute faith in us as we embarked on this project. You helped in so many ways. Not only were you available to answer our questions at the drop of a hat, you also put us in contact with the necessary and relevant people, personally at times set up interviews, and generally paved the way for this book. *Siyak'bulela mam' Tshonyane.* The loss of your husband when you were just 26 years old had threatened to break you, but you took that heartache and channelled it into us, your children, and into preserving Fort's legacy. We honour your heart and stand amazed at the strength you so consistently display. We love you, Ma.

We also owe a big debt of gratitude to David Forbes, who so generously made his document and video archive available to us. Your journey, David, to tell the story of the Cradock Four has been littered with obstacles and difficulty, including your battle with cancer. Yet you kept on fighting – at times with your life depending on the outcome. By fighting these battles with the authorities, you have spared us the same agony and troubles, and for that we are deeply grateful to both you and your wife, Nadine.

Another chronicler of the story of Cradock and the Cradock Four is

Jo-Ann Thesen [née Bekker], a former reporter of the *Eastern Cape Herald*. Your work in the township of iLingelihle in the Eighties has been exemplary for young(er) journalists such as us. It was your first drafts of our history between 1984 and 1985 that allowed us to tell this story today. Also, by keeping meticulous records of your articles and then generously handing them over to us, you saved us so much time, which we could use writing this book. We hope that, above all else, we have done you proud. Thank you!

We also wish to extend our gratitude to the Valley Trust administered by Anton Harber from Wits University's Department of Journalism for the research grant from the Taco Kuiper Fund for Investigative Journalism. The grant enabled our research and investigation, which resulted not only in our accurate account of the Calata family history, and the historical understanding of Cradock's contribution to the dismantling of apartheid, but also facilitated our knowledge of the hit squads which operated in the Eastern Cape in the early to mid-Eighties.

Finally, we are grateful to our families and friends, who were unrelenting with their encouragement. Your love and interest kept us buoyant and motivated to produce this tribute to Fort Calata and the other brave, selfless individuals, who, despite mortal danger, never wavered in their pursuit of freedom – an idea the apartheid government of PW Botha despised so much, it was prepared and, indeed, killed to prevent that freedom from being realised.

We salute your brave and gallant struggle. We promise never to forget. *A luta!*

Lukhanyo and Abigail Calata

Bibliography

Books

Bizos, G. 1998. *No One to Blame? In Pursuit of Justice in South Africa.* David Philip & Mayibuye Books: Cape Town.

Callinicos, L. 2004. *Oliver Tambo: Beyond the Engeli Mountains.* David Philip: Cape Town.

Cupido, AB. 1991. *Matthew Goniwe, 'n Biografie* (unpublished).

Duka, Dr MM. 2011. *Canon James Arthur Calata: A Biography of One of the Greatest Sons of Africa.* Khoi Publishers: Queenstown.

Gumede, WM. 2005. *Thabo Mbeki and the Battle for the Soul of the ANC.* Zebra Press: Cape Town.

Luthuli, A. 2006. *Let My People Go: The Autobiography of Albert Luthuli.* Tafelberg: Cape Town.

Manong, S. 2015. *If We Must Die.* Nkululeko Publishers: Johannesburg.

Nicholson, C. 2004. *Permanent Removal: Who Killed the Cradock Four?* Wits UP: Johannesburg.

Tetelman, M. 2012. *We Can! Black Politics in Cradock, South Africa, 1948–85.* Rhodes University: Grahamstown.

Van Eck, J. 1989. *Eyewitness to 'Unrest'.* Pretoria: Taurus.

Verwey, EJ (ed.). 1995. *New Dictionary of South African Biography, Volume 1.* HSRC Publishers: Pretoria.

Journal Articles

Baxter, L. 1985. 'Section 29 of the Internal Security Act and the Rule of Law.' *Reality*, vol. 17, no. 6, pp. 4–6.

Suttner, R. November 2003. 'The African National Congress (ANC) Underground: From the "M-Plan" to Rivonia.' *South African Historical Journal*, 49, pp. 123–146.

Newspaper Articles

Eastern Province Herald

    Bekker, J. 2 April 1984. *Cradock Meetings Banned.* 28 June 1984. *Cradock Meeting-Ban Expires Sunday.*

2 July 1984. *MPs Meet Minister on Cradock.*

24 July 1984. *Cradock School Unrest: Five Pupils in Court.*

8 August 1984. *Teargas Was Fired 'While Pupils Were Leaving Hall'.*

10 August 1984. *Policeman Threatened to Hit Her.*

10 August 1984. *Nine from Cradock Released on R50 Bail.*

10 August 1984. *Boesak Shocked at Cradock's Reign of Terror.*

11 August 1984. *Teargas Was Used 'After Police Were Stoned.'*

2 October 1984. *Cradock Meetings Ban Is Lifted.*

11 October 1984. *Three Cradock Leaders Freed, Returned Home.*

11 December 1984. *Owners' Counter Offer to Beerhall Boycott.*

5 January 1985. *'Rejected' Cradock iLingelihle Council Resigns en Masse.*

8 January 1984. *iLingelihle Resignations Draw Mixed Reactions.*

11 July 1985. *Council Assistance for Cradock Funeral.*

20 July 1985. *Scores Converge on Cradock for Funeral.*

Coutts, L. 29 June 1985. *Goniwe Missing with Others: Car Found Burnt Out.*

1 July 1985. *Burnt-out Car: Two Bodies Are Found.*

Herald Reporter. 5 November 1984. *Reinstatement of Woman in Mandela T-shirt Trial Is Called For.*

February 1985. *Police Probing Four Herald Reports.*

5 July 1985. *Nel Denounces 'Insinuations' about Killings.*

20 July 1985. *Appeals for Calm at Cradock Funeral.*

Koch, I. 28 May 1985. *Cradock Raid: Some Arrests.*

Maggs, J. 3 July 1985. *Grieving Cradock Widow Says: 'I Am Just Empty.'*

Rogers, A. 3 July 1985. *Goniwe and Calata Are Found Dead.*

Tyala, M. 11 October 1984. *No Reason to Celebrate Says UDF Spokesman.*

February 1985. *Government Must Act on Cradock.*

3 July 1985. *Find These Killers.*

Daily Dispatch

Dispatch Reporter. 24 July 1985. *East Cape Emergency: The Terms.*

Hartle, R. 20 April 2016. *On a Tortured Path to Incomplete Accounting.*

Evening Post

Post Reporters. 15 December 1989. *PE Blast Kills 4.*

Sunday Tribune

Sole, S. 31 May 1992. *Wraps Come Off General's 'Personal Task Force' as Ex Members Spill the Beans.*

Weekly Mail

Missing: The List Grows Longer. 14 June 1985.

Webpages

Who Was Ntsikana? www.historicschools.org.za

Strikes in the Schools. http://www.sahistory.org.za/archive/strikes-schools

Pass Laws. https://en.wikipedia.org/wiki/Pass_laws

Padraig O'Malley Archives. https://www.nelsonmandela.org/omalley/index.php/site/ q/03lv01508.htm

January 8th Address 1985. http://www.anc.org.za/

Koevoet homepage. http://koevoet.webs.com/

Archives

Jo-Ann Bekker Archives.

David Forbes Archives.

Rev James Arthur CALATA Papers 1909–1974. University of the Witwatersrand.

Calata Papers. Cory Library, Rhodes University.

Goniwe Papers. Cory Library, Rhodes University.

Affidavits: Henri Fouché. 31 January 1985; Fred Koni. 1992; Christoffel Pierre van der Westhuizen. 1992.

Classified document. 25 June 1985. 'Uiters Geheim, Suid-Afrikaanse Polisie, Die Kommissaris.'

Confidential Minutes of EP JMC Meeting 3/85 held at Eastern Province Command Headquarters on 23 May 1985.

Declassified National Intelligence Agency Document. Briefing Notes: '"The Cradock Four" – Fort Calata, Matthew Goniwe, Sparro Mkonto, Sicelo Mhlawuli.'

S Markovits and M Kaplan interview with Col. L du Plessis.

Index

South African Broadcasting Corporation (SABC) 8, 18, 26, 30, 40, 52, 251

South African Coloured People's Organisation (SACPO) 92, 96

South African Communist Party 45

South African Congress of Democrats (COD) 92, 96

South African Congress of Trade Unions (SACTU) 92, 96

South African Council of Churches 9, 159, 173, 179, 250

South African Defence Force (SADF)151, 179, 223

South African Indian Congress (SAIC) 92, 96

South African National Editors' Forum 26

South African Police 56, 137, 159, 208-209

South African Railways 133, 173

Southwest Africa 201

Soweto 111, 113, 125, 160, 163, 176

Soweto Youth Uprising 111, 163

SPG, *see* Society for the Propagation of the Gospel in Foreign Parts

SRCs, *see* Student Representative Councils

SSC, *see* State Security Council

St Albans Prison 241

St Barnabas Primary School 58

St Cyprian's Church 61

St Cyprian's Cricket Club 61

St Cyprian's Higher Mission School 60

St Dennis missionary school 67

St George's Strand 11, 222-223

St James Higher Primary School 71

St James Lawn Tennis Club 84

St James Mothers' Union, 1960 Report of 76

St James Street (Number 81) 101

St John's Catholic Church 116

St Matthew's High School 58

St Matthew's Practising School 59

St Michael Cathedral Church 63

St Ninian's 64

St Ntsikana Memorial Association 79

St Peter's Church 68

St Peter's Parish 79

St Philip's 81-82

St Stephen's Mission 61

State of Emergency 13, 17, 45-46, 200, 236-240

State of the Nation Address 34, 43

State Security Council 151, 205, 209-211, 245

Steenkamp, Jacques 25, 27, 38, 40-41, 254

Stellenbosch Farmers' Winery Award 205

Stemele, Siphiwo 151, 166, 174

Steynsburg 197-198

Steytlerville 46, 197-198, 239

Stranger 69

Student Representative Councils (SRCs) 143

Students for Christian Action 144

SUCA, *see* Students for Christian Action

Sun City 9

Sunday Tribune 213

Sunday World 26

Suppression of Communism Act 121, 126

Supreme Court of Appeal 41

Suttner, Raymond 182

Suzman, Helen 158, 164-165

SWAPO 201

Swartkops River 217

Swartz, Derrick 200, 213-214, 224

Sweden 44

Tambo, Oliver 45, 48, 87, 90-91, 189, 208, 236

Tarkastad 46, 67

Taylor, Eric 216, 247

Tetelman, Michael 69

Thabo Mbeki and the Battle for the Soul of the ANC 82

The New York Times 204

The Other Face of China 124

The Star 26

The World 111

Third Class Senior Teachers Course 60

Timol, Ahmed 248, 250

Togna, Martina Della 168, 205

Tosh, Peter 153

Transkei 87, 107, 116, 124-125, 136, 248

Transnet 249

TRC, *see* Truth and Reconciliation Commission

About the authors

Lukhanyo Calata is an award-winning journalist, who has worked for eNews – now eNCA – among others before joining the SABC's parliamentary bureau in 2011. He became part of the 'SABC 8' in July 2016 when he challenged Hlaudi Motsoeneng's reign of censorship at the public broadcaster. He is the son of Fort Calata, one of four anti-apartheid activists from Cradock, assassinated by the government in 1985.

Abigail Calata is a former journalist who currently works for the Shoprite Group as publicity manager: CSI and Africa. She has worked in the communication departments of the University of Cape Town and the Cape Peninsula University of Technology. Before joining the realm of corporate communications she was parliamentary reporter for *Beeld* and worked in production and the newsroom of *Die Burger*.